ELL 1985/6 x

(.270

30130 127428620

Piers L. Chance
from his Mother
Jany 28
1902

The Shrine of St Alban

*From " The Abbey Church of St. Alban."   Illustrated
by James Neale, F.S.A.   (By permission.)*

SKETCHES OF CHURCH LIFE

IN THE COUNTIES OF

ESSEX AND HERTFORDSHIRE

FORMING

THE DIOCESE OF ST. ALBANS

BY

D. W. BARRETT, M.A.

RECTOR OF CHIPPING BARNET, AND RURAL DEAN ;
COMPILER OF CHARTS FOR THE DIOCESE OF PETERBOROUGH, ST. ALBANS, ETC.

WITH MAP

" Ave Proto-martyr Anglorum,
Miles Regis Angelorum ;
O Albane, flos Martyrum :"

BREVIAR. SARISBURG IN OFFICIO S. ALBANI

LONDON

SKEFFINGTON & SON, 163 PICCADILLY, W.

Publishers to His Majesty The King

1902

PRINTED BY
WILLIAM CLOWES AND SONS, LIMITED,
LONDON AND BECCLES.

THESE SKETCHES

ARE

RESPECTFULLY DEDICATED TO THE

RIGHT REVEREND FATHER IN GOD

JOHN WOGAN FESTING, D.D.

AS A HUMBLE AND IMPERFECT ATTEMPT

TO INDICATE THE WITNESS OF

THE BUILDING UP OF

THE LIFE OF THE CHURCH IN THE TWO COUNTIES

OVER WHICH HE RULES

AND IN GRATEFUL APPRECIATION

OF THE

WISDOM, SYMPATHY, AND JUSTNESS

WITH WHICH HE PRESIDES

OVER

THE SEE OF SAINT ALBANS

PREFACE

THE idea of undertaking to write these Sketches of the Diocesan History of St. Albans suggested itself to me during the compilation of a Chart, showing the various changes by which the diocese has been built up. Finding so many notes of interest in the lives of the Bishops, it occurred to me that the great movements with which they were identified might be illustrated by incidents of local Church life. It is hoped that a narration of some of the leading features of the parts which the two counties now constituting the diocese took in the building up of the story of the Church, may induce a more thorough study of Church History in general, together with its development in our shires. It has been asserted that St. Albans, as a diocese, is too young to have a history, but it has attained its majority, and the story of twenty-five years of vigorous life would in itself entitle it to claim a place in the library of diocesan literature. My purpose, however, has a wider scope, and I have tried to give glimpses of the Church History of the two counties as members of older dioceses, and of the various steps by which their completed diocesan unity was brought into existence. It has, moreover, been objected that, as these counties were constituent parts of older dioceses, any attempt to record the story of their Church life would necessitate some encroachment on other histories, and so the tale would be twice told. This objection, at first sight, seems plausible ; but we must look at facts.

The two old dioceses mainly concerned were Lincoln and London. Both were wide in area, and one so important in its dominating central population and life, being the focus of the leading events of the Church in the nation, that it would have been well-nigh impossible to present the history of the outlying members of the dioceses in anything like a compendious form.

The Diocesan History of Lincoln has been written, and it is full of the deepest interest ; but as the late Canon Venables, the reverend Precentor of Lincoln, from whom I received so much encouragement and assistance, informed me, it could only touch the fringe of the Hertfordshire portion of the diocese. In the work, as edited and completed by Archdeacon Perry, the fact is evident, and though I am deeply indebted to the joint authors for considerable information and illustrations, they have been obliged to content themselves with scanty notice of Hertfordshire, which was so small a member of the diocese which, at one time, extended from the Humber to the Thames, and included within its area the counties of Lincoln, Leicester, Northampton, Rutland, Huntingdon, Cambridge, Bedford, Buckingham, Oxford, as well as a part of Hertfordshire.

The modern diocese even now, bereft of nine out of its ten counties, exceeds in size all the other dioceses, except St. Davids and Norwich, and has an area of 1,767,879 acres. It has, therefore, been a necessity that the outlying members should receive only a comparatively small share of illustration at their hands.

The Diocesan History of London has yet to be written. From the earliest times the fortunes of the counties seemed to have been linked. The origin of their Christianity is Celtic, for without injustice to the Roman Mission of Mellitus, we assert it was a failure in Essex, while the disciples of the Celtic Finan of Lindisfarne succeeded in laying the foundations and building up the faith, both among the East Saxons of Essex and the Mercians of Hertfordshire.

From the time of Cedd (who was consecrated " Bishop of the East Saxons "), Essex, and no inconsiderable part of modern Hertfordshire (the Deanery of Braughing) was under the episcopal rule of London, leaving only a portion of the ancient Archdeaconry of Huntingdon to the care of the see of Lincoln.

This early witness to the unity of the two counties

received new emphasis when the jurisdiction of the Abbey was constituted an Archdeaconry, and placed under the see of London, in 1550. In 1846, the bond of union was further strengthened when the counties were placed (with the exception of the deanery of Barking) under Rochester.

It will be seen, therefore, that the two counties have been more or less united in a common diocesan life. The erection of the new see of St. Albans, in 1877, completed and sealed the union.

As to the historical treatment, I have adopted the plan of giving a general view of the great movements, illustrating them, when possible, from local sources. Thus it is hoped that local readers may be attracted to view Church history as possessing a living interest, and to understand how its wide-reaching issues have engraved themselves, not only in the hidden archives of their parish chests, and on the very stones of their parish church, but in the expressions of worship, and in the customs which have come down to them, tempered by the changes of many a bygone generation. I trust it may inspire, at least, a few readers to study the history of the Church in the nation by the light of its record in the place where they dwell.

The associations which cluster round every ancient parish church are instinct with the story not only of the Church to-day, but of generations past.

The length of the period from the dawn of

Christianity in our own counties covers fifteen hundred years and more; it has been, therefore, impossible in these mere sketches to do more than glance rapidly at some of the chief events and leaders of English Church life, and to give a few indications of the way in which the counties, and the Bishops who ruled over them, have illustrated the story of each successive period. A great mass of material has been at my command, and I have had to exercise stern repression, not finding it very easy to discriminate between the relevant and the irrelevant. Sometimes it may appear that the illustrations are trivial, but straws show which way the wind blows. The undertaking has been a labour of love extending over some few years. From the necessity of taking up the work at intervals, as time could be afforded, the thread of the narrative may, I fear, be here and there tangled, if not indeed broken. Books and manuscripts at the public libraries and elsewhere have afforded me some delightful hours of recreation and information. The scattered state of the diocesan records is much to be regretted, and has added a great obstacle to complete research.

No claim is laid to literary merit. My desire has been to illustrate a complex story in as simple a way as possible, and in many instances to adopt the *ipsissima verba* of various authors to whom, in most cases, I have in the notes made open reference. It would be impossible, when so many authorities have been consulted, to do more than to record here my most grateful acknowledgment of their labours, and to express my apologies to any, of whose researches I may have taken advantage without such acknowledgment.

I ought, however, in addition to the mention of the late Precentor Venables, specially to express my gratitude to the authorities of the British Museum, and of other public libraries, for their ready assistance in my reference to books and manuscripts ; to the diocesan authorities and clergy for much kind help in various ways. My thanks are also due to the Rev. J. B. Lee, Head Master of Barnet Grammar School, for valuable hints in respect to the matter of one or two chapters ; to the family of the late Bishop Claughton ; to Mr. A. De Bock-Porter, C.B., the courteous secretary of the Ecclesiastical Commission, for much information respecting the foundation of the see of St. Albans ; to Mr. James Bailey of the *Guardian;* to Canon Procter for statistics and other matters connected with the work of the Church in " London over the Border ; " to the late Mr. E. Durrant, of Chelmsford, and to Miss E. Fell Smith, one of the editors of the *Essex Review,* for several useful suggestions ; to Mr. James Neale, F.S.A., for the privilege of reproducing the sketch of the Shrine of St. Alban, from his invaluable work on the Abbey Church ; to Mr. J. C. Traylen, of Stamford, for the design of the book cover, chiefly from his drawings of the famous Delamere brass, with its mediæval figure of the proto-martyr of England ; to the editors of the *Diocesan Kalendar* for permission to insert the map of the Diocese ; to Canon Owen Davys for notes on the restoration of the Abbey, which, to my regret, I found could not be included more fully in the space at my disposal. I am also under grateful obligation to several kind friends whose willing services in transcriptions, reading proofs, etc., have greatly lightened my task.

My acknowledgments are due also to Messrs. Wm. Clowes & Sons, who have bestowed much care and pains in printing, and have rendered me every assistance in passing the book through the press.

I am also sensible of the kindness of the subscribers to this edition for their generous readiness to help me in this humble attempt to promote a deeper interest in the history, work, and unity of the Church in the two counties under review.

The very nature of a diocesan history renders it more or less a compilation, and this present effort pretends to be but little else. Doubtless each parish could contribute abundant evidence of some share in the great movements which are here touched upon.

Imperfect as is my effort in conception, design, and execution, I must ask my readers to accept it for what it is worth, to correct me where I am wrong, to supply me with new facts and illustrations from parochial records, in order that I may give a still stronger local colouring to the "Sketches," should it be found necessary to supplement it by a new edition.

I further beg a lenient judgment on the result of a somewhat difficult and complicated story. I hope that those who may honour me by reading this book will mercifully remember the couplet—

> " In every work regard the author's end,
> Since none can compass more than they intend."

May we all strive to make history by doing our share, according to our opportunity, in contributing to the glory of God by loyal adherence to the doctrine and discipline of our Church, which is at once the bulwark of the nation's liberty and the salt of the nation's life.

D. W. BARRETT.

CHIPPING BARNET,
1st *January*, 1902.

Errata : p. 102, *lines* 15, 16, *vide appendix K.*

CONTENTS

Contents

SKETCHES OF CHURCH LIFE

DIOCESE OF ST. ALBANS

CHAPTER I

*DAWN OF CHRISTIANITY IN THE TWO
COUNTIES*

"*'Tis first the night,—stern night of storm and war,—
Long night of heavy clouds and veilèd skies;
Then the fair sparkle of the morning star,
That bids the saints awake, and dawn arise.*"

BONAR.

" *The blood of the martyrs is the seed of the Church.*"

THE area covered by the diocese of St. Albans
consists of the two counties of Essex and
Hertfordshire, together with North Woolwich, which, though actually within the geographical
borders of Kent, is practically in Essex. To get
a complete view of the foundation and development
of the Church in the two counties, it will be
necessary to trace the beginnings of the secular
history of each. Let us take first what is definitely
known of Essex, without attempting speculation
as to its state in the misty times before tradition

B

can be trusted. The county formed a portion of the lands of the *Trinobantes*, a tribe which probably extended over the county of Middlesex. Evidences of the habitations of British tribes are believed to have survived in the so-called *Dane pits*, near East Tilbury, and at Lexden. Doubtless, Colchester itself occupied the site of a British town.

It is difficult to say to what extent Christianity had permeated British Essex as distinguished from the rest of the country. The dominance of London as a British settlement cannot have been without its influence, and the known existence of a line of British Bishops of London is at least some presumptive evidence of the very early existence of the faith in the county.

We must now deal with the Roman occupation of Essex which dates from about 44 A.D. Sixteen years later, the seat of government was fixed at Colchester; this was the first Roman Colony founded in Britain, and, in spite of a few attempts at revolt on the part of the conquered race, it sealed the subjugation of the county. Abundant evidences of the conquest are found in various places, notably, of course, at Colchester itself; others have been unearthed at Barking, also in the neighbourhood of Maldon, at East Ham, Chesterford; near to Romford, Bartlow Hills, Billericay, Bradwell, Hazeleigh, North Ockenden, Witham, Chelmsford, and at Bishops Stortford. Of the evidences of the survival of Christianity in the county during the occupation, it is impossible to speak with certainty, though it is asserted that Adelphius, one of the British Bishops present at the Council of Arles (314 A.D.), had his see at *Camulodunum*. It has been argued that the existence of the cross on Roman pottery found in the neighbourhood points to some Christian influence, but this opens a wide field of discussion, and is of little value. If, as was undoubtedly the case, Christianity existed in other parts of the country during the Roman tenure, why not also in Essex?

Let us now turn to Hertfordshire. The mists of history which hang over the flats and marshes of Essex, are no less dense when we look back to the early times of Hertfordshire. It would be easy to speculate in probabilities, and to draw fancy pictures of the native Christians in the wooded seclusion of this inland county, but it would serve no useful purpose. We come, therefore at once, to known facts. The British inhabitants of Hertfordshire, at the earliest date of which we can speak with certainty, were known as *Catuvellauni*, and were under the great chief *Catuvellaunus*, whose successor, *Tasciovanus*, appears to have fixed his seat at or near the site of modern St. Albans. After various struggles, the Catuvellauni, like their allies, the Trinobantes of Essex, fell before the Roman power which became ascendant in Hertfordshire, as it did throughout the island, and

Verulamium became its capital. In A.D. 61, Boadicea reconquered *Verulamium*, but it was soon restored to Roman rule. Traces of the early British tribes have been found at Ickelford, Stevenage, Knebworth, Welwyn, in the valley of the Lea near Hertford, Ware, Cheshunt, near Wigginton, Kings and Abbots Langley. The evidences of Roman rule are scattered all over the county, though the chief centre of interest lies at St. Albans. Remains of the Roman occupation have been discovered at Braughing, Cheshunt, Boxmoor, Abbots Langley. Coins, pottery, glass, etc., have been found at Hoddesdon, Pirton, Ashwell, and Caldecote. Three great Roman roads run through the county. The testimony of Christian influence on the Romans is more marked by the witness of Herts than of Essex, and though we must make allowance for legendary accretions of detail, we cannot but admit the story of St. Alban, as told by the Venerable Bede, coupled with the known existence of a British hierarchy, as evidences of the widespread work of a more or less organized Missionary Church. How the teacher of St. Alban came to a knowledge of the gospel, no man can say with certainty; it will suffice to record the story of the saint's martyrdom. We cannot do better than relate it in the words of a well-known Church writer.[1]

" During the Diocletian persecution, Alban, a citizen of

1 Cutts, " Turning-points of Church History," p. 13, *et seq.*

Verulamium, sheltered in his house a priest who was fleeing from his persecutors. The sight of the good man's life, his watchings and prayers, impressed his entertainer's mind, and he became a convert. After some days, it became known where the priest was concealed, and soldiers were sent to seize him ; but Alban put on the priest's dress, and allowed himself to be taken, while the priest made his escape. On being brought before the judge, he was ordered to sacrifice to the gods, but, refusing, and declaring himself to be a Christian, he was ordered to execution. The place of execution was a grassy hill at some little distance outside the city walls, and divided from it by a river. The people of the city rushed out in such numbers to witness the martyrdom that the bridge over the river was crowded and made impassable ; whereupon Alban, impatient for the crown of martyrdom, walked to the river bank, and the waters opened, like those of Jordan, and made a dry road for the party to pass over. The executioner, seeing this, threw down his sword and declared himself converted to the Christian faith. Arrived at the summit of the hill, Alban prayed for water to quench his thirst, and immediately a fountain burst forth from the earth. One of the soldiers at length struck off the martyr's head, and his own eyes fell upon the ground with the victim's head. The converted executioner was beheaded also at the same time. Then the judge, astonished at these miracles, ordered the persecution to cease. When the Church had peace under Constantine, a church was built on the spot, which existed in Bede's time. Then, in 793, King Offa founded a monastery. The noble Abbey Church, founded on the site of its predecessor, is still one of the most interesting churches in England. The mediæval town of St. Albans gradually grew up about the monastery, and the ruined walls of deserted Verulam are still seen half a mile off across the little river."

There is yet another fact which has a special interest to Hertfordshire Churchmen, and proves the existence of the long organized system of Christianity in the country, whatever doubts there may be about the details of its introduction. As the Bishop of Stepney points out, "the Pelagian question is the most important fact in the history of the British Church."[1] It affected the Church to no small extent in the beginning of the fifth century. It was to settle this question that the two Gallican bishops, Germanus of Auxerre, and Lupus of Troyes, were sent to Britain, in 429. In their journeyings through the island, among other places, they visited this county, and held a disputation at or near St. Albans.[2] The Pelagians, who appeared "conspicuous for riches, glittering in apparel, and supported by the flatteries of many," were worsted in the debate. The chronicler goes on to relate that the bishops hastened to the shrine of St. Alban. At the request of Germanus, it was opened, that he might deposit there some relics which he had brought with him. The chapel in which this shrine existed was afterwards called the Chapel of St. Germanus. He took away in exchange some earth from the actual spot of martyrdom. It may be mentioned that the churches of Bobbingworth and Faulkbourne, in Essex, are dedicated to St. Germanus.

The story of the general state of Christianity

---

[1] "The Christian Church in this Island, before the Coming of St. Augustine," p. 83.

[2] *Vide* Haddan and Stubbs, "Church Councils," vol. i. p. 16.

throughout the island, prior to the revival of the faith, is foreign to our present purpose. Enough has been said to show that the British Church existed in this county before the Saxon hordes laid it waste, and drove its adherents to the fastnesses of the mountains of Wales and the north-west, and to the hills of Cornwall and Devon. How the life of the Church was restored in each county of the modern Diocese of St. Albans remains to be told. The lamp of the British Church was flickering in its socket, but God gave new supplies of oil to revive the flame.

CHAPTER II

FIRST MISSION TO ESSEX

" First the rough seed, sown in the rougher soil."

BONAR.

" Some fell on a rock, where it had not much earth."

" True wonders still by Him are wrought,
Who setteth up, and brings to nought."

G. NEWMARCH, 1653.

HAVING pointed out the indications of British Christianity in the two counties during the Roman occupation, the outlines of the new conversion must now be sketched. The Romans had not left the island more than forty years when Hengist and his Saxon warriors landed at Ebbsfleet, in the Isle of Thanet, in 449. The British were driven westward, and such Christians as were left were hunted down, the churches destroyed, the priests slain, and heathenism reigned again supreme. For the sake of clearness, the story must be told as it concerns each county. It must not be forgotten that, in describing the conversion of Essex during the Saxon period, our thoughts should not be limited to its present area. Saxon

Essex extended into the present county of Hertford, *i.e.* further westward than it does now. Roughly speaking, it then included so much of the modern shire of Hertford as is comprised in the ancient deanery of Braughing, which contains 34 parishes[1] and which from the first constituted a part of the see of London remaining under that Bishop till its inclusion in the see of Rochester. How and when it was included in Hertfordshire is a matter of some uncertainty. A line drawn nearly paralle with the Roman Ermine Street, from Cheshunt to Ware, and from thence to Braughing, Buckland, and Royston, will fairly indicate the ancient boundary.

The first recorded attempt to evangelize the county of Essex is due to the Mission of St. Augustine, who landed at Thanet in the spring of A.D. 597. The story of his reception and progress is well known, and we need not re-state its details. His advance to the episcopate, which took place in the same year, gave new force to the mission, and his consecration at Arles, by Roman Bishops, marks the distinct character of his succession. No British or Celtic Bishop took part in it. It was meant to emphasize the purpose of Gregory, "Britain for Rome." That the attempt was only a partial success, we know now. The monastery and Church of Canterbury arose, and here Ethelbert "gave his teachers a settled place in Canterbury,

---

[1] *Vide* Ecton's "Thesaurus Rerum Eccm.," p. 259.

with such possessions of different kinds as were
necessary for their subsistence."[1] Augustine then
established a residence for himself and his successors.
The purpose of extension gained strength. London
and York were fixed on as centres for the whole
country. In 601 the *Pallium* was sent to Augustine, and he was not slow in considering it as a
mark of special distinction and authority. This
may be regarded as the turning-point towards the
encroachments of Rome on the liberty of British
Christianity. Armed with its authority, he pushed
his mission and its papal claims. Rochester was
the first objective in his advance, and a see was
founded there. Justus, its first Bishop, was consecrated in 604. Rochester thus became the half-
way house to London, where a British see had been
already established, Restitutus having been its first
recorded Bishop.

The next advance at the same date, as Professor
Hole reminds us, should be thought of in connection
with the exhortation of Gregory to Ethelbert, King
of Kent and *Bretwalda* of Essex: "Let your glory
hasten to infuse into the Kings and people that are
subject to you, the knowledge of one God, Father,
Son, and Holy Ghost."

It must always be remembered that the early
mission work of the Church was tribal in character;
but the personal as well as the tribal element
had a very direct bearing on the beginnings

[1] Bede, Bk. I. chap. 26, 33.

of the mission in Essex as well as elsewhere.
Ethelbert of Kent, besides being over-lord of
Essex, was allied by marriage to its King
Sabert. Thus the way was paved for the revival
of the British see of London. Mellitus, one of
the additional supply of priests sent by Gregory,
four years after the landing of Augustine, was consecrated to the see in 604. "This year," runs
the Anglo-Saxon Chronicle, "the East Saxons
received the Faith and Baptism under Sæbright,
King, and Mellitus, Bishop." Bede states the
fact thus :--

"Augustine, Archbishop of Canterbury, ordained two
Bishops, viz., Mellitus and Justus. Mellitus to preach to
the province of the East Saxons, who are divided from
Kent by the river Thames, and border on the Eastern
Sea. Their metropolis is the city (*civitas*) of London."[1]

Thus Augustine secured his first two Suffragans,
and we may be sure that such a man, with such a
purpose, allowed but little independence of diocesan
action, nor was the time indeed ripe for it. Augustine took care not to invite any British Bishops to
take part in the consecration, thus showing the dis-
tinctive character of the mission.

Mellitus was the bearer of a remarkable series
of letters on ecclesiastical subjects from Gregory to
Ethelbert, Bertha, and Augustine. One was also
addressed to himself in which he (Gregory) "re-
tracts the advice given to Ethelbert to destroy the

---

[1] Bede, Bk. II. chap. 3.

heathen temples, and desires Augustine to convert them into churches."[1]   He was also himself the joint author of a letter to the Irish Bishops urging compliance with the Roman customs, especially as to the observance of Easter.

From these letters it is possible to gather some hints as to the method and mind of Mellitus.   He would utilize, for Christian service, such Roman temples as might still be remaining, and his teaching would undoubtedly have been such as his Roman allegiance prompted.

It is impossible, with certainty, to connect his work with any special locality in the county, though his name is associated with Tillingham in a Charter of Ethelbert, to which Dr. Stubbs attaches some measure of importance, granting land *ad monasterium sui solatium*.   The fact of the patronage of Tillingham and its manor being still in the hands of the Dean and Chapter of St. Paul's, seems to confirm the assertion.

Sabert, the nephew of Ethelbert, was the first fruits of the mission of Mellitus.   Thus, with the Court and Augustine at his back, his work received its first great impetus.   Augustine died 26th May, 605.   The two succeeding Archbishops were not of the same calibre as Augustine, and Mellitus seems to have represented the strength of the mission when Augustine was gone.   We find him ranked next to the Archbishop Laurentius in a letter

[1] Haddan and Stubbs' "Councils," vol. iii. p. 37.

which he addressed to the Scottish and British Church on the subject of keeping Easter. The next we read of Mellitus is as to his interview on the affairs of the Church, in 610, with Boniface at Rome, when a Synod of Bishops was assembled, with Mellitus amongst them. He brought back letters from the Synod—

"to the end that he, also, by his authority, might comprise such things as should be regularly decreed, and at his return into Britain might carry the same to the Churches of the English to be prescribed and observed ; together with letters which the same Pope sent to the beloved of God, Archbishop Laurentius, and to all the clergy, as likewise to King Ethelbert and the English nation." [1]

In 616, the mission of Mellitus staggered under a heavy blow in the death of Ethelbert, " who having gloriously governed his temporal kingdom fifty-six years, entered into the eternal joys of the kingdom which is heavenly." He was succeeded by Eadbald, who not only refused to embrace the faith, but set all morality at defiance. With the *Bretwalda* a heathen, though Sabert, King of Essex, was a professed Christian, work in the county must have been rendered more difficult. The confusion came to a climax on the death of Sabert. His three sons, Sered, Seward, Sigebert, never very favourably inclined towards the mission, on their father's death granted liberty to their people to serve idols, and they themselves openly profaned the rites of the

[1] Bede, Bk. II. chap. 4.

Church.   Here, again, we are indebted to the
graphic pen of the Venerable Bede—

"When they saw the Bishop give the Eucharist to the
people, they, puffed up with barbarous folly, were wont (*ut
vulgo fertur*) to say to him, 'Why do you not give us also
that white bread, which you used to give to our father
Saba, and which you still continue to give to the people in
the Church?' Mellitus replied, 'If you will be washed
in that laver of salvation in which your father was washed,
you may also partake of the holy bread of which he par-
took; but if you despise the laver of life, you may not eat
the bread of life.' They replied, 'We shall not enter into
that laver, because we do not know that we stand in need
of it, nor yet will we eat of that bread.' Being often
admonished by him, at last they said in anger, 'If you
will not comply with us in so small a matter as that is
which we require, you shall not stay in our province.'" [1]

They carried out their threat, and Mellitus and
his followers were expelled, or, if not expelled,
beat a retreat.   The revolt from the faith was
complete.   The Bishop, together with Justus of
Rochester, on the advice of the Archbishop, with-
drew to France to mourn the lapse, and await the
turn of events.   The Archbishop was about to
follow their example, but on the eve of his
departure, the influence of a dream (as it is
alleged) led him to change his mind.   Eadbald,
who was still on the throne of Kent, moved by
the relation of this dream, and by the sight of
the wounds which had been inflicted on him in
the course of the dream, abjured heathenism, and

[1] Bede, Bk. ii. chap. 4.

determined to embrace the faith. At his instance Mellitus and Justus were recalled. Justus returned to Rochester, but the Londoners (*Londonienses*) refused to receive Mellitus, "choosing rather to be under their idolatrous high-priests." However, he found some consolation in his promotion, on the death of Laurentius (619), to the see of Canterbury, as its third Archbishop. Bede tells the story of his quenching a fire in his Cathedral city by prayer. He is said to have been a martyr to the gout; but, in spite of it, he was a man of action. He passed away on the 24th April, 624, and was buried, like his predecessor, in the church of his monastery. He left behind him no permanent mark of his work, at least on the original sphere of his mission.

So ended the first Roman mission to Essex, and for well-nigh half a century heathen darkness reigned once more over the county.

CHAPTER III

CELTIC MISSIONS TO ESSEX

" Hark, hark, my soul! angelic songs are swelling
O'er earth's green fields, and ocean's wave-beat shore ;
How sweet the truth those blessèd strains are telling
Of that new life when sin shall be no more ! "

FABER.

WE have dealt with the fact of the existence of the Church in the two counties during the Roman occupation, and with the part that the Roman Church took in the evangelization of Essex after the Saxon invasion. The effort of Mellitus, though in some measure successful, was, in the end, a practical failure. It is certain, at any rate, that it failed in the purpose of establishing an organized and continuous mission. We have, therefore, now to attempt to elucidate the steps by which the heathen invaders of the two counties, after they had driven the terrified Britons westward, and had lapsed from their new faith, as taught by Mellitus, became again the children of the Church ; how, in fact, the lamp of the ancient Church of the land was re-lighted in this county.

To effect this, a new, and second, mission was necessary, the story of which is most interesting. The Saxons, by about A.D. 520, had become the dominant power in the country, and had established more or less settled forms of government. Mellitus died on April 24th, 624, about twenty years after his consecration, and thirty years had elapsed before the Celtic Cedd had his thoughts turned to the Saxon shore, and the new dawn arose. He was from Northumbria, and was one of a remarkable band of four brothers, another being, as is well known, the great Chad, Bishop of the Mercians. The daughter of the powerful Penda, King of Mercia, married Ælfric, son of Oswy, King of Northumbria. Her brother Peada, paid a visit which will be described later on, to the northern court, and was converted to the faith. On his return from this visit (653), he took with him four priests, Adda, Betti, Cedd, Diuma of the Celtic Church, which then had established a powerful centre at Lindisfarne, of which Aidan was the first Bishop, to preach the faith in his own kingdom of Mercia.

Shortly after this, Sigebert the Good, King of the East Saxons, paid a similar visit to Oswy's court, which led to Sigebert's conversion, and ultimately to his baptism by Finan, Bishop of Lindisfarne. Sigebert having requested teachers for his people, Oswy recalled Cedd from Mercia, and sent him, with a companion, to Essex.

So successful was this mission (*perambulantes*

multam domino ecclesiam congregassent) that it was
deemed expedient to raise Cedd to the rank of the
episcopate. Accordingly, in 654, he was consecrated,
as *Bishop of the East Saxons*, by St. Finan and two
other Bishops. The event is thus recorded by the
venerable Bede:—

"fecit eum in episcopum in gentem Orientalium Saxonum,
vocatis ad se in ministerium ordinationis aliis duobus
episcopis." [1]

In support of the fact of Cedd's Celtic succession,[2]
we may interpolate a few remarks on St. Aidan.
Aidan was a priest in the monastery at Iona, which
was founded by St. Columba of Clonard in Ireland,
and when Colman returned dispirited from a mission
in Northumbria, Aidan suggested that the failure
was due to want of gentleness and patience, and it
was owing to this circumstance that he was consecrated Bishop, and was sent to Northumbria.
Obtaining a grant of land from the Northumbrian
King, he created his see at Lindisfarne, which
became the centre from which so large a portion of
England was evangelized, and at which Cedd received
his training and consecration. This is enough to
identify Cedd with Northumbria. The Bishop of
Bristol makes a strong point of the appointment
of Cedd, when there was a Roman Bishop at
Rochester, as showing the trend of opinion against

[1] Bede, Bk. III. chap. 22.
[2] Dr. Stubbs, in his " Episcopal Succession in England," places
Cedd amongst the Bishops of London.

foreign influences. We now return to his mission in Essex. He found that he had to begin the work *de novo*. Bede tells us that he established two missionary centres, one at *Ithanacester* (*Othona* of the Romans), now Bradwell-on-Sea, another at *Tilaberg* (West Tilbury).

The original passage is worth quoting :—

"Fecit per loca ecclesias, presbyteros et diaconos ordinavit, qui se in verbo fidei et ministerio baptizandi adjuvarent, maxime in civitate quæ lingua Saxonum Ythanacester appellatur ; sed et in illaquæ Tilaburg cognominatus ; quorum prior locus est in ripa Pentæamnis (Blackwater) secundus in ripa Tamensis ; in quibus collecto examine famulorum Christi, disciplinam vitæ regularis, in quantum rudes adhuc capere poterunt custodiæ docuit.[1]

Let us take these two centres in turn. First, as to *Ythanacester*, probably Bradwell-on-Sea. The absence of any certain mark of identification may be due to the encroachments of the sea. That the Roman *Othona* and the Saxon *Ythanacester*, are one and the same is by no means improbable. *Ythan* is not unlikely a Saxonized form of *Othona*, and *cester* is certainly the survival of Latin *castrum*. In 1864, during the reclamation of some waste land on the flats near Bradwell, the wall of the *castrum*, enclosing three or four acres, was laid bare. Of the importance of the place there is no doubt, from its being dignified with the title *civitas*. It was quite a natural proceeding for the mission to attack one

[1] Bede, "Hist. Eccl.," Bk. III. chap. 2.

of the great centres, more especially with the countenance of the King.

With regard to Tilbury, the balance of probability seems to be that West Tilbury was the *Tilaburg* mentioned by Bede. In confirmation of this, there still exists, near West Tilbury, the village of Chadwell. The name is said to have been derived from Cedd's well at the foot of the hill, on the edge of the marsh, and here the Saint is reputed to have administered the rite of baptism. There is also a Cedd's well at Lastingham, with which place, as we shall see, he was also connected. Chadwell church is one of the ancient churches of the county, and this is presumptive evidence at least of the early establishment of Christianity, though I am not aware whether any Saxon remains exist in the church itself. These facts are sufficient to locate the earliest centres of the second, and Celtic mission to the rude tribe of the East Saxons. If Cedd had a " stool," it was probably at Tilbury.

Now let us refer to the method of Cedd's mission. He came first as a priest, and baptized and did such acts as fell to the lot of a missionary. He appears to have acted under the direction of St. Finan, the head of the famous monastery at Lindisfarne, whither we find him returning— *redire domum*, being the significant expression of the chronicler,—there to tell the story of the Cross, and to confer with his chief as to the progress of the work. This visit led, as we have seen, to his advancement to the episcopate. Thus he returned to Essex with greater authority, ordained priests and deacons to assist him, built churches in various places, probably of timber rough hewn from the forests, and doubtless served them from the two great centres of *Ythanacester* and *Tilaburg*. In each of these places the churches were most likely of a larger and more substantial character than the rest, and may well have been adaptations of the remaining Roman buildings, according to the plan Mellitus had adopted. At all events, it is clear that they were centres of some sort of religious rule. We can hardly suppose, however, that the rule was of a rigid character in view of the record of Bede, who says : " When gathering a flock of the servants of Christ, he [Cedd] taught them to observe the discipline of regular life, *as far as those rude people were then capable.*"

The character of Cedd comes out in various ways. He was a disciplinarian, as the following story shows. One of the nobles who had contracted an unlawful marriage, and had refused the correction of the Bishop, was excommunicated by him. In spite of the bann, Sigebert the King determined to pay a visit to the proscribed Earl. On his way, the Bishop met him. The King beholding him, dismounted from his horse trembling, and fell down at his feet. The Bishop, who was likewise on horseback, had also alighted. Being much incensed, he touched the King, lying in

that humble posture, with the rod he held in his
hand and using his pontifical authority, he spoke
thus : " I say to you, for as much as you would
not refrain from the house of that wicked and
condemned person, you shall die in that very
house." Thus it happened to him, and he there
fell a victim to the violent hands of his kindred
(A.D. 660), and was succeeded in his kingdom by
Swithhelm.

Cedd does not appear to have confined his
ministration to Essex, for it is recorded that he
went into the neighbouring kingdom of East Anglia,
and there at Rendlesham, in Suffolk, baptized
Swithhelm, who was not allowed to ascend the
throne till this rite had been administered, Ethelwold,
the East Anglian King, standing as sponsor. The
position and opinion of Cedd respecting the observance of Easter (and of the tonsure), ought to be
noticed as giving some clue to his attitude towards
these controversies. It will be remembered that
the Roman and the Celtic rule differed. The
Romans, and with them, of course, the successors of
St. Augustine of Canterbury, held that the Latin
view should be observed in Britain. It was manifestly an inconvenience that members of the same
family should be at variance, for it sometimes
happened at Oswy's Court, as Cutts points out, that
the Northumbrian King, who had been converted
under Celtic influence, was keeping Easter, whilst his
Queen, a convert of the Roman Mission, was still

observing Lent. This variance resulted in the Council of Whitby (664). It is not our purpose to relate the details of that Synod further than they are connected with Cedd. His own rule was that of Lindisfarne, but he attended the Synod, and acted as interpreter. King Oswy opened the discussion by declaring " that it behove those who served one God to observe the same rule of life, and as they all expected the same kingdom in heaven, so they ought not to differ in the celebration of the same mysteries, but rather to inquire what was the truest tradition." The inquiry was conducted with considerable feeling, and the Synod concluded that the Roman Use was to be observed. Cedd was convinced, and, forsaking the practice of the Scots, returned to his bishopric, having submitted to the Catholic (*sic*) observance of Easter. Undoubtedly Bede was influenced by his friend Wilfrid, but there is no reason to doubt the accuracy of his report, especially as he notes the retirement of Coleman and his companions to Scotland to observe their own Celtic rule. The submission of Cedd marks the beginning of a gradual adoption of the Roman customs.

A further insight into the life of Cedd is afforded by the story of the foundation of his monastery at *Lestingeau* (Lastingham) in Cleveland, Yorkshire, on the occasion of one of his visits to his old country, when the son of King Oswald made him a grant of land. According to custom, he cleansed the place for the monastery by prayer and fasting, and obtained permission to reside there for the whole of Lent. "All which days, except Sundays, he fasted till the evening, according to custom, and then took no other sustenance than a little bread, one hen's egg, and a little milk mixed with water. This, he said, was the custom of those of whom he had learned the rule of regular discipline, first to consecrate to our Lord by prayer and fasting the places which they had newly received for building a monastery or church." The monastery was built in due course, and followed the customs of Lindisfarne. It may be observed that a church, with interesting Saxon remains, now occupies the site of the monastery. Doubtless the same pious care was exhibited in the foundation of the churches and religious houses which he may have established in Essex. There is some difference of opinion as to the date of this visit to Lastingham, but it would appear that Cedd returned to his own special work amongst the East Saxons, and continued it till the year 664, when he again visited the monastery over which he had placed a superior. This proved to be his last journey on earth. A great pestilence was then raging, and he fell a victim to it, and was buried first near at hand; "but in process of time a church was built of stone in the monastery, and his body was interred in the same, on the right hand of the altar." So his personal work here came to an end, but not its influence.

A beautiful story is told by Bede of the attachment of the clergy of Essex to their beloved Bishop :—

"When the brethren who were in his monastery, in the province of the East Saxons, heard that the Bishop was dead in the province of the Northumbrians, about thirty men of that monastery came thither, being desirous either to live near the body of their father, if it should please God, or to die there and be buried. Being lovingly received by their brethren and fellow-soldiers in Christ, all of them died there by the aforesaid pestilence, except one little boy, who was delivered from death by his father's prayers. For when he had lived there a long time after, and applied himself to the reading of Sacred Writ, he was informed that he had not been regenerated by the water of Baptism, and being then washed in the laver of Salvation, he was afterwards promoted to the order of priesthood, and proved very useful to many in the Church." [1]

The ten years' mission and rule of Cedd may be rightly accounted as the re-lighting of the lamp which the flight of Mellitus had extinguished. The flame burnt brightly till a visitation of the pestilence fell on Essex, as on many other parts of the land. The faith of a rude and half-taught people is easily affected by such a circumstance, and so it proved in the case of the East Saxons.

The Celtic mission in Essex had its lights and shadows. Mellitus, of the Roman succession, had done something towards its evangelization, but, as we have seen, the people lapsed after his death, and the real founder of its permanent establishment

[1] Bede, Bk. III. chap. 23.

was Cedd. At the close of his ten years' work, the plague, which raged in various parts of the country, and which cost him his life, darkened the prospects of the Church. The two Kings, Sighere and Sebbi, were fortunately subject to Wulfhere, the King of Mercia. Sighere became apostate, and restored in the part of the kingdom under his control the heathen worship and practice " as if by these means he and his people might be protected against the mortality. But Sebbi, his companion and co-heir in the kingdom with his people, very devoutly preserved the faith which he had embraced." Sebbi appears to have ruled the southern part of Essex. At this juncture Wulfhere, the King of Mercia, being over-lord, sent Jaruman, fourth Bishop of Mercia, of the Northumbrian succession, to Essex. Bede goes on to relate how "he proceeded with much discretion, as I was informed by a priest who bore him company in that journey, travelling through all the country, far and near." He succeeded in reconverting Sighere and his people, " so that, either forsaking or destroying the temples and altars which they had erected, they opened the churches, and rejoiced in confessing the Name of Christ."

In short, he produced a revival of religion throughout the province. Having set things in order, the priests and teachers returned home with joy," [1] the mission having lasted about a year. This may rightly be accounted as the third Christian

<hr />

[1] Bede, Bk. IV. chap. 6. ; Haddan and Stubbs, vol. iii. p. 120.

mission to the county of Essex; for, doubtless, the episcopate of Mellitus had been of a missionary character. Jaruman's career from that time is lost in the mist of ages, but it is quite probable that he had some share in the counsels which led to the foundation of the great Saxon Abbey of Mede-hamsted, now Peterborough, which was consecrated in 664. The close of Jaruman's episcopate (667) marks the date of the subjugation of the Saxon Heptarchy (with the exception of Sussex) to the yoke of Christ.

CHAPTER IV

SETTLED DIOCESAN RULE IN ESSEX

" Onward we go, for still we hear them singing,
' Come, weary souls, for Jesus bids you come ; '
And through the dark, its echoes sweetly ringing,
The music of the Gospel leads us home."

FABER.

THE departure of Jaruman marked a period when our local diocesan life was beginning to assume a more definite form. It would appear that Essex, after his departure, was for a little time without a regular Bishop, though possibly it had some oversight from Mercia ; this, however, is not clear. We can hardly think that, when the Mercian Bishop returned from his mission of revival in Essex, he or his successor, St. Chad, would leave that district out in the cold. The county properly fell to the oversight of the Bishop of London, and we see the way opening out for its care from this see.

This is how it came about. Through the influence of Coinwalch, King of the West Saxons, Wini was consecrated (662) to the newly formed see of Winchester, which he only held for a short time. He removed to Dorchester, to which Birinus had been consecrated as first Bishop in 634. After a short time, Wini was expelled from thence, and sought refuge with Wulfhere, the Mercian King. The relation of what happened is neither to the credit of the King nor the Bishop. Wini, being now without a see, Bede tells us, " he purchased for money the see of the City of London, and remained Bishop thereof till his death " (circ. 675). We can glean nothing of his work, nor was it likely, under such circumstances, to be worth recording. We may, however, consider him as the first of the unbroken succession of the Bishops of London, who had *settled authority* over the county of which we are speaking, the works of the Roman Mellitus, and the Celtic Cedd and Jaruman being of a more intermittent missionary character.

Now we come to the first evidence of the grip of the iron hand of the great Archbishop Theodore over this county. On the death of Wini, the Archbishop appointed Erconwald to the vacant see. Erconwald had already made his mark on the neighbourhood of London ; having built two religious houses on the banks of the Thames, one for himself—a monastery at *Ceortesei* (Chertsey), of which he was Abbot, and a convent for his sister at *Berangium* (Barking),[1] for Benedictine nuns ; and placed both under strict rules of life. The Convent of Barking, the first founded in England for women,

---

[1] A deed of gift from Odelred to Barking Abbey is extant, dated circ. 692–93 (" Codex Diplomaticus Ævi Saxoni," vol. i.).

soon became firmly established, and visions and miracles, of which it is reputed to have been the scene, added to its fame. After an existence of two hundred years, it was plundered and destroyed by the Danes. King Edgar rebuilt and re-endowed it a century later, and it again became famous. Its Abbess was entitled, with three others, to bear the rank of Baroness, she herself being the chief Abbess in the kingdom. The only part of the Abbey now remaining is " The Curfew Gate."

We know little of Erconwald's episcopal work. He ruled over the diocese for seventeen years, and, like his predecessor Cedd, he seems to have traversed it on horseback, and " his horse-litter in which he was wont to be carried about when sick " was kept after his death by his disciples, and by its means many wonderful miracles were related to have been effected, the very chips of it being carried to the sick for health. We may perhaps describe him as the " grand old man" of the Essex of his day. On his death (693), Waldhere was made Bishop. He witnessed the last moments of his great patron, Sebbi, King of the East Saxons, "who had received the religious habit," and Bede gives us [1] the usual account of the miracles which marked the occasion.

Waldhere was succeeded by Ingwald (circ. 704). He held the see for about forty years, and was in possession when Bede was writing his great work.

[1] Bede, Bk. IV. chap. 11.

We read of him assisting, with Daniel, Bishop of
Winchester, Aldwin, of Lichfield, and Adwulf, of
Rochester, in consecrating Tatwin, Archbishop
of Canterbury, in June, 731. Alas! the fountain
of information almost dries up in 735, with the
death of Bede, the great ecclesiastical historian ;
and we have now to resort to the little streams,
which only trickle, in comparison with the flow of
his facile pen. It is true that we are not wholly
destitute of sources of information, but for a long
time to come our knowledge extends but little
beyond the mere dry bones of succession. We must
be content, therefore, till a new chronicler arises, to
present some crude facts unbrightened even with a
touch of romance. It is little more than a monoto-
nous tale of succession, from Ingwald's days, through
a line of twenty-nine Bishops, up to the time of
the Norman Conqueror ; though the monotony is
relieved to some extent by occasional glimpses of
interesting characters and facts.

Without professing to enter into many details,
we will draw attention to a few of the more prominent circumstances which affected the county in
common with the Church life of the nation.

The most noted of this long roll of Bishops was
St. Dunstan, who was consecrated to Worcester,
translated to the see of London (959), and raised
to the throne of Canterbury, October 21st, 960.[1]

---

[1] Dunstan is said to have held the see *In commendam* with
Canterbury (*vide* Milman's " St. Paul's ").

After an eventful life which is more of national than of local interest, he died May 19th, 988. Robert was the next Bishop of any importance. He was elevated to the Archbishopric of Canterbury in 1051, having ruled the see of London for seven years. Bishop Maurice, who was consecrated by the Archbishops of Canterbury and York, held the see of London when the Norman Conquest ushered in the new era for the Church and nation.

This account of the settled episcopal rule of Essex would be incomplete without some reference to the incursion of the Danes—an element of confusion which affected so large a part of England. The open seaboard of the Eastern coast rendered it peculiarly liable to attack, and when the Scandinavian storm burst upon it, Essex, like its neighbour, East Anglia, fell before it, and came, by the peace of Wedmore (878), a few years later, into the area of the Danelagh, with Guthrum as its ruler. In the interval, much damage must have been done to the churches ; probably, as so few Saxon buildings remain in the county, many were destroyed, and although Guthrum submitted to baptism, it was more from reasons of state policy than of religion. The men who destroyed the Abbeys of Peterborough, Croyland, Ely, Thorney, and Barking, because they were religious institutions, are not likely to have spared the churches of Essex. It is no wonder that, of all the number of churches which must have been built during the long period

Saxon rule, few, except for instance, Greenstead,[1] Boreham, Felstead, and Holy Trinity, Colchester, can boast of even partial survival. The first of these has a special interest, not only from its rude construction, but from the fact that it afforded a temporary halting-place for the body of St. Edmund.[2]

What was left undone in the way of destruction before the peace of Wedmore was in all probability amply atoned for in the later invasions which led to the submission of all England under Sweyn and Canute. Even when the tide began to turn, and Canute fell under Christian influence, the havoc had been so great that restoration was perforce slow.

The climax of the storm has thus been described—

"Canute, with his armie on board his flete (which lay in the Medway), passed over the Thames into Essex, and there assembled all his power together, and begun to spoil and lay waste the country on each hand. King Edmund (Ironside), advertised thereof, hasted forth to succour his people, and at Ashdone, in Essex, three miles from Saffron Walden, gave battle to Canute, where, after a sore and cruel fight, the Englishmen were beaten down and slaine in heaps. . . . There were also slaine at this battle manie renowned persons of the Spiritualitie, as the Bishop of Lincolne and the Abbot of Ramsey."[3]

[1] "Idem apud Aungre," Registrum Cænobii Sancti Ædmundi.
[2] *Vide* Leland's "Collecteanæ,"vol. i. p. 247 ; Dugdale's "Monasticon," ed. 1655, vol. i. p. 293.
[3] "Historie of England," Holinshed, Bk. VII. chap. 9.

A sixteenth-century writer amusingly refers to the battle thus—

"About this place (Ashdon) Edm.-Ironside had bickerings w^t the Danes." [1]

Holinshed is not accurate in his reference to the examples of the "Spiritualitie." The prelate who was "slaine" was not the Bishop of Lincoln. The episcopal seat was not yet removed there. Nor was the Abbot of Ramsey among the fallen. The Bishop was Eadnoth II., who had been Abbot of Ramsey, and whose remains, after the battle, were conveyed to Ely for burial.

A curious little episode in connection with the incursion of the Danes comes out in the life of Bishop Theodred of London (circ. 926), who seems to have also been Bishop of Elmham. Desiring to do honour to the memory of St. Edmund, "he was found fault with by the Londoners for spending so much money on a shrine over St. Edmund's body at Bury. They were jealous of the favour shown to the Eastern diocese." [2] This little incident serves to show that, even during the days of the Danish occupation, the work of Church building and renovation was not altogether unknown.

Another incident connected with the county throws an interesting light on the gradual restoration of religion even under Danish rule. It has its

---

[1] Norden's "Description of Essex," circ. 1596, last page.
[2] Dr. Jessop's "History of Diocese of Norwich," p. 29.

centre at Waltham Abbey. The first church was built in the time of Canute, by Tofig, a Danish Thane; it was erected for the reception of a crucifix, found at Lutegarsbury, in Somersetshire, and reputed to possess wonderful properties of healing. When the Church was completed, two priests were attached to it, and sixty-six persons, who had been cured, devoted themselves to its honour.[1] This, together with its fame as the burial-place of Harold, by whom it was rebuilt, led to its development in later times into an abbey of great renown. Originally it was intended by Harold as a great educational establishment.[2] The intermittent outbursts of Church progress which had marked the days of Canute, only emphasized the deadness and apathy with which the Church had been smitten during the long days of change and war in the nation.

The restoration of the English dynasty had but little effect in awakening new zeal before the battle blast blew across the field of Senlac. There Harold, the last Saxon King, bowed before the Norman hosts, and, when night fell, the Conqueror "sate down to eat and drink among the dead." It was a night which preceded a new dawn.

---

[1] Murray's " Essex," p. 85.
[2] *Vide* Freeman's " Norman Conquest."

CHAPTER V

CELTIC MISSION TO HERTFORDSHIRE

"The faith of holy men of old,
How much it shameth ours,
Which, aided by a stronger light,
But seldom gains a fuller sight
Of heavenly things and powers."
"The Dove on the Cross."

WE saw in the introductory chapter something of the state of religious life in
both counties prior to the time of the
Saxon conquest. We have told the story of the
various missions to Saxon Essex, and must now
turn to Hertfordshire. To understand the conversion of this county, which formed part of the
newly founded Kingdom of Mercia, we must relate
a few facts of political history. Naturally, from
its inland position, the subjugation of Hertfordshire was somewhat later than that of Essex. We
know, however, that it was firmly established under
the rule of Mercia in the person of the fierce, cruel,
and aggressive Penda. One writer has described
him as the "Anti-Christ of his day." He was a
terror alike to his heathen and Christian neighbours;

but, powerful as he was, and though "five kings fell before him," it was through a member of his own house that the light shone brightly on the kingdom over which he ruled. It came about through the same conditions as those which had brought the Celtic missionary Cedd into Essex.

The great midland kingdom of Mercia was of wide extent. The present Dioceses of Hereford, Worcester, Lincoln, Ely, Peterborough, Chester, Manchester, Liverpool, Gloucester, Southwell, and parts of Oxford and St. Albans were all within its area. Three Saxon Kings had ruled over it before Penda, its fourth and perhaps most celebrated ruler, appeared on the scene, "fierce as a wolf by hunger render'd bold." Whilst the great race strifes were going on, God was working out His ends for these fierce tribes. Northumbria had been won for the faith by the missionaries of Aidan of Lindisfarne. Oswald, its nursing father, was dead, and he had been succeeded on the throne by Oswy, also over-lord of Mercia, whose son Ælfric had married Kyneburga, one of Penda's daughters; and thus the two courts, one Christian, and the other heathen, had become allied. The alliance was shortly afterwards strengthened by another marriage; Peada, the son of Penda, who had been admitted to a share in the government of Mercia, sought the hand of a daughter of Oswy. Oswy consented, on condition that Peada became a Christian.

"When he heard the preaching of truth and the promise of the Heavenly Kingdom, and the hope of resurrection and future immortality, he declared that he would willingly become a Christian, being chiefly prevailed upon to receive the faith by King Oswy's son Ælfric, his own brother-in-law. He was baptized by Bishop Finan, with all his earls and soldiers and their servants that came along with him."[1]

Four priests of Lindisfarne—Cedd, Addi, Betti, and Diuma—were commissioned by St. Finan to accompany Peada back to his home, to conduct a mission to his people. In this connection, a beautiful though somewhat fanciful, story is told.

"While Aidan ruled at Lindisfarne these mission priests were but scholars in the monastery. One day, in the Psalms, occurred the verse—'Tell it out among the heathen that the Lord is King.' The good Bishop detained the two brothers Cedd and Chad, and laying his hands on the fair young heads, he said, 'My sons, 'tis for this high mission I am training you; think you, you will be able to say with the child Samuel—"Speak, Lord, for thy servant heareth"?' 'My father, God helping us, we will.' 'Amen, my sons, may He bless you for the work whereunto you are preparing; wait in patience for the call, yea, though it tarry, wait for it, for it will surely come.' Years passed, but Cedd remained faithful to the rules of the Northumbrian Church, waiting for the call which the great Bishop had foretold, when a messenger came to summon them to the presence of King Oswy. When, after a short time, he came back to his brother, his eyes were full of a strange light, and he took the hand of Chad in a grasp which well-nigh crushed it as he said, 'Brother, it has come! the call of which our Master spoke. Peada,

[1] Bede, Bk. III. chap. 21.

the son of our heathen enemy, has acknowledged Christ, and demands teachers for the people of Mercia. King Oswy has chosen Adda, Betti, and myself to go there under Diuma the Irishman. Brother, do you remember "Tell it out among the heathen"? I go to do his will.' "[1]

So the four started, full of zeal and hope. Arriving in Mercia, they found no warm welcome from the fierce Penda, who never acknowledged Christ to the day of his death. For his son's sake, however, he allowed them to work, and Peada fostered them. This mission resulted, on the accession of Peada to the throne of South Mercia, as viceroy to Oswy, in the consecration of Diuma as the first Bishop of Mercia (656). We have no reason to doubt that the Mercian portion of Hertfordshire received his attention and care.

As we have already seen, Cedd was not permitted to remain long in Mercia, but was recalled by Oswy at the request of his friend Sigebert, King of the East Saxons, to take in hand the reconversion of the people whom the Roman Mellitus had abandoned. I have introduced the part which Cedd took in the evangelization of the new masters of England, to show that whilst we gladly acknowledge the work of Mellitus, so far as it went, it is to Lindisfarne, and the ancient Celtic Church, that we owe the permanent beginning of the revival of the faith in both counties.

To return to Diuma. His was a missionary

[1] Clare, " Foundation Stories of Early Church History," S.P.C.K.

life in its truest sense; he took journeys hither and
thither with no settled centre, unless we may except
Repton, where, having been Bishop for two years,
he died in 658, and where he was buried. The
chief interest of his work lies in the fact that he was
the first episcopal pioneer of the great Church of
Mercia, of which Lichfield became the first see.

Of Adda and Betti we hear no more.

The next Bishop of Mercia was Ceollach.
From what cause it is not stated, but within a year
he retired to the seclusion of the monastery at Iona.
The third was Trumhere, the Abbot of Gilling, in
Yorkshire, a Saxon by birth, taught and ordained
by Celtic Bishops. He was appointed by Wulfhere,
who at this time was reigning over Mercia, as well
as being over-lord of Essex. His episcopate only
lasted three years, and he died in 662 without
leaving any recorded mark of his influence and
work. Next came Jaruman of the same Northern
succession, whose story has been told in a previous
chapter.

CHAPTER VI

DEVELOPMENTS IN MERCIA

" He sitteth o'er the water floods,
And He is strong to save ;
He sitteth o'er the water floods,
And guides each drifting wave."

ANON.

WE must now show how the way was being prepared in Mercia for the coming ecclesiastical changes, and how the old Celtic order was modified by the influence of Rome. We shall see the hand of Theodore at work. After the death of Jaruman, the Mercian Church was affected by the new current of Latin Christianity which was beginning to sweep over the land. St. Chad was destined to fall under its power. He was, as we shall see, to leave as permanent a mark on Mercia as his holy brother Cedd had left upon Essex. By birth he was a Northumbrian, and was brought up under the training of the Celtic Church at Lindisfarne. In 664, three years before the death of Jaruman, and in the same year as that of his brother Cedd, was held the Synod of Whitby, at which Wilfrid, a brilliant

young churchman, who had fallen under the Roman
influence, turned the scale in favour of the Roman
mode as to keeping Easter, and wearing the
tonsure. The decision was one of the first steps
towards Latinizing the English Church. Coleman,
the Bishop of Lindisfarne, who was one of the
chief disputants at this synod, resigned his see
and, together with many of the holy brethren,
went back to Scotland, taking with him the bones
of St. Aidan, thus abandoning the Holy Island,
only leaving there such as conformed to the
decision of the synod. Cedd accepted the decision,
returned to his Bishopric and shortly afterwards,
as we have already related, died at Lastingham.
Wilfrid was selected to fill the long-vacant see
of York, and was sent to France to be consecrated
by Agilbert, the Bishop of Paris. The ceremony
took place at Compiègne, 664, eleven Bishops
assisting Agilbert, thus showing the importance
which was attached to the consecration. According
to the ceremonial of the Gallic Church, Wilfrid
was carried on a golden chair by his brother
Bishops singing hymns of joy. He did not, however,
follow up his victory with promptness, but stayed
too long in France to please his patron the King
of the Northumbrian *Witan.* The impatience
of the King brought St. Chad upon the scene
again, who had by this time succeeded his brother
in the inheritance of the Abbey of Lastingham.
As Wilfrid still delayed his return, Chad was

sent with a priest named Eadhed to Canterbury, to be consecrated, but he arrived too late. Archbishop *Deusdedit* had passed to his rest, and no one had been appointed to succeed him. Bede relates how the difficulty was met. " Whereupon they proceeded to the province of the West Saxons, where Wini was Bishop, and by him was consecrated,"[1] assisted by two British Bishops. This happened at Winchester (A.D. 664). Theodore, the coming Archbishop, had something to say about this later on, when the Bishopric of Lichfield was founded.

However, " Chad, being thus consecrated Bishop, began immediately to devote himself to ecclesiastical truth and to chastity, to apply himself to humility, continence and study, to travel about, not on horseback (as was the custom of his brother Cedd), but after the manner of the Apostles, on foot, to preach the gospel in towns, the open country, cottages, villages, and castles, for he was one of the disciples of Aidan, and endeavoured to instruct his people by the same actions and behaviour, according to his and his brother Cedd's example."

Thus he began his work at York, which he continued for four years, but a new factor now comes in view for our consideration. Theodore of Tarsus, was consecrated to Canterbury on the 26th March, 668, on his arrival in England, and with that determination and vigour which marked his character, made a visitation of " all the island

---

[1] *Vide* note, Bohn's Edition Bede's " History," p. 165.

wherever the tribes of the Angles inhabited." In
due course he came to York. He soon made his
power and purpose felt, and the gentle Chad bent
before him. Theodore questioned the validity
of his ordination. Chad answered with great
humility :—

"If you know I have not duly received Episcopal ordination, I willingly resign the office, for I never thought
myself worthy of it, but though unworthy, in obedience
submitted to undertake it."

He accordingly submitted to a second consecration, at the hands of Theodore, and after
remaining a short time at York, retired to the
monastery at Lastingham. In the meantime Wilfrid
had returned, and finding his see occupied, had to
wait until Chad resigned it. Chad was not destined
to remain long in retirement. Theodore, having
secured to his lieutenant Wilfrid the see of York,
vacant by Chad's retirement, had not lost sight of
the retired Bishop. The see of Mercia had been
vacant about two years, and on the application of
Wulfhere, the Mercian King, Theodore recommended Chad for the office, remembering, no doubt,
not only his piety, but his spirit of gentle compliance.
In 669 he was appointed to the spiritual charge of
the great Mercian Kingdom, including Middle
Anglia, and at least a part of Hertfordshire in its
area. His first work was to found a *sedes*. His
predecessors had had no settled centre, but went
from place to place, as occasioned required. He

fixed upon Lichfield ("the place of the dead"),
consecrated by the holy memory of the traditionary
martyrdom of a thousand British Christians, who
are reported to have been slain here during the
Diocletian persecution.   Lichfield lay near the
junction of the two great Roman roads, known as
Watling Street and Icknield Way, thus affording
easy access to all parts of the Diocese.   Watling
Street runs through the County of Hertford, and,
as we know, passes through St. Albans.   Whether
the Saint ever visited it we do not know; but it
can hardly be likely that a place which was growing into fame can have escaped his attention.   The
great Archbishop kept his eye on him and sym-
pathized with him in his work, in a very practical
way, for—

"seeing it was the custom of that most reverend prelate to
go about the work of the gospel to several places rather on
foot than on horseback, Theodore commanded him to ride
whenever he had a long journey to undertake, and finding
him very unwilling to omit his former pious labour, he
himself, with his hands, lifted him on the horse, for he
thought him a holy man, and therefore obliged him to ride
wherever he had to go." [1]

Theodore knew what he was doing and exhibited the *suaviter in modo* with all his *fortiter
in re*.

Chad was not long permitted to rule over his
diocese.   After his episcopate of two years and a

[1] Bede, Bk. II. chap. 3.

half, he entered into rest on Tuesday, March 2nd, 672.

" A week before his death a sound of angelic melody was heard coming from the south-east until it reached the little oratory where he was praying. This, the good bishop interpreted to be his summons to heaven. The voices, he privately told Ovin his friend (who had come to him from Lastingham), were those of angels. The messenger of death, that 'lovable guest,' was with them. They would come again in seven days and take him. About the same time Egbert, a Northumbrian who had been a fellow-student with Chad in an Irish monastery, dreamt that he saw the soul of Cedd, Chad's brother, descending from heaven with a company of angels to take the soul of Chad with him to the heavenly kingdom. He was laid to rest in the monastery he had founded at Stowe, hard by Lichfield, and his bones were afterwards transferred to Lichfield, in the days of Hedda." [1]

The character of the good Bishop is well drawn by Dr. Bright in the following words—

" If a high wind swept over the moors at Lastingham, —or, we may add, around the little cathedral at Lichfield —he at once gave up his reading and implored the divine mercy for all mankind. If it increased, he would shut his book, and prostrated himself in prayer. If it rose to a storm, with rain or thunder or lightning, he would repair to the Church, and give himself with a fixed mind to prayer and the recitation of psalms, until the weather cleared up. If questioned about this, he would quote the psalmist's words, 'The Lord thundered out of heaven,' and urge the duty of preparing by a serious repentance, for 'that tremendous time when the heavens and the earth should be on fire, and the Lord should come in the clouds with great power and majesty to judge the quick and the dead.'

[1] " St. Chad and the Mercian Church," by Dean Bickersteth.

Yet, with all his dread of Divine judgments, Chad, in his own words, had a 'continual love and desire of the heavenly rewards.' "

" And it was no wonder," says Bede, " if he rejoiced to behold the day of death, or rather the day of the Lord, seeing he had so anxiously prepared for it." His work still lives in the hearts of English churchmen, and his memory is honoured by the dedication of some churches in the Midlands to his name. By his death only three Bishops were left in the Heptarchy, Theodore of Canterbury, Wini of London, Wilfrid of York. So Theodore and the Roman party became by a natural process, as well as by no little political manœuvring, the dominant force in the ancient Celtic Church. Though no special locality in this county is with certainty identified with St. Chad, the story of his episcopate has been recorded to show the gradual change of custom and influence which was creeping over the Mercian Church.

The years after that which witnessed the death of St. Chad brought the county of Hertford into prominence, and added new lustre to the growing fame of Theodore. Having filled the vacant sees of Rochester, Dunwich in East Anglia, and Winchester in Wessex, with men of his own way of thinking, he next consecrated Winfred to the throne of Lichfield.

The air began to clear, and his keen-sighted judgment prompted him to make a grand *coup de main.* He determined to develop the power of the primacy, and to consolidate the church throughout the length and breadth of the land.

The first Synod of the Anglo-Saxon Church was determined on. Hertford, which lay within the borders of the great Mercian see, was the selected place of meeting. Accordingly, on 24th September, 673, the Synod assembled under the presidency of Theodore. It was a notable gathering, whether we consider its constitution or its results. It was attended by the Bishops of Rochester, Lichfield, Dunwich, Winchester, "and many other teachers of the Church who loved and were acquainted with the canonical statutes of the fathers." Wilfrid was not there, but was represented by proxy. With the exception of the kingdoms of Essex,[1] and Sussex which was still pagan, the whole heptarchy was represented. Theodore had his brief in his pocket, and it need hardly be said he won his case. The result of the Synod was the promulgation of the following ten canons. They throw, as we shall see, great light on the state of the Church, both in its ecclesiastical and social aspect, and they are quoted in full.

Chapter I.[2]—" That we all in common keep the holy day of Easter on the Sunday after the 14th moon of the first month.

Chapter II.—"That no Bishop intrude into the diocese of

---

[1] Dr. Browne, Bishop of Bristol, suggests that Theodore "would not recognize Wini as bishop."

[2] Bede, Bk. IV. chap. 5.

another, but be satisfied with the government of the
people committed to him.

Chapter III.—" That it shall not be lawful for any Bishop
to trouble monasteries dedicated to God, nor to take
anything forcibly from them.

Chapter IV.—" That monks do not remove from one place
to another, that is, from monastery to monastery,
unless with the consent of their own Abbot, but that
they continue in the obedience which they promised
at the time of their conversion.

Chapter V.—"That no clergyman forsaking his own Bishop,
shall wander about, or be anywhere entertained without letters of recommendation from his own prelate,
but if he shall be once received, and will not return
when invited, both the receiver, and the person
received, be under excommunication.

Chapter VI.—" That Bishops and Clergymen, when travelling, shall be content with the hospitality that is
afforded them, and that it be not lawful for them to
exercise any priestly function without leave of the
Bishop in whose diocese they are.

Chapter VII.—" That a Synod be assembled twice a year,
but in regard that several causes obstruct the same, it
was approved by all, that we should meet on the first
of August once a year at the place called *Clofeshoch*.
(Cloveshoo).

Chapter VIII.—" That no Bishop through ambition shall
set himself before another, but they shall all observe
the time and order of their consecration.

Chapter IX.—" It was generally set forth that more
Bishops should be made, as the number of believers
increased, but this matter for the present was passed
over.

Chapter X.—" Of marriages ; that nothing can be allowed
but lawful wedlock ; that none commit incest ; no
man quit his true wife, unless, as the gospel teaches,
on account of fornication. And if any man shall
put away his own wife, lawfully joined to him in

E

matrimony, that he take no other, if he wishes to be a good christian, but continue as he is, or else be reconciled to his own wife."

The close of the Synod marked a new era for the Church in its internal regulation, resulting in the establishment of what was practically a national church, which was consolidated under the powerful rule of the chair of St. Augustine, though as yet the nation was politically a battleground of rival kinglets. " Hitherto there had been Churches ; henceforward there was a Church." [1]

It was not till 150 years later (828) that " the English race in Britain was for the first time knit together under a single ruler, and England was made." [2] The unity of the Church preceded the unity of the nation. This splendid triumph of Theodore was not to go unchecked.

[1] Green's " Short History of the English People," sec. iv. p. 44.
[2] " The Saxons in England," Kemble, vol. ii. p. 366. New Edition, London, 1876.

CHAPTER VII

HERTFORDSHIRE UNDER THE BISHOPS OF LEICESTER AND DORCHESTER

"The wind that blows can never kill
The tree God plants ;
It bloweth east ; it bloweth west ;
The tender leaves have little rest,
But any wind that blows is best.
The tree God plants
Strikes deeper root, grows higher still,
Spreads wider boughs, for God's good-will
Meets all its wants."

L. E. BARR.

CHAD'S acquiescence in the Roman customs, and his meek submission to re-consecration, had helped to make things so far go smoothly with Theodore, and prepared the Mercian Church for the impending change. On his death, Theodore, as we have seen, appointed Winfrid to the vacant see of Lichfield, who, though his own nominee, caused him some trouble, and thwarted his purpose. Winfrid, abetted by Wulfhere, resisted one of the Canons of the Council of Hertford, which had reference to the desirability of the increase of the Episcopate, and which specially concerned his huge Diocese. Wulfhere regarded the Canon as an interference with his authority, and his resistance was successful as long as he lived. When the King died in 675 Theodore was equal to the occasion, and deposed the recalcitrant Bishop, who retired and took refuge at the monastery which his great predecessor had founded at Barrow on Humber, and of which he himself had been Abbot before his elevation to his see. The insult, as he considered it, was too much for him, and he determined to appeal to Rome, which however he never reached, being assassinated on his journey. Sexwulf, Abbot of Peterborough, was chosen to take his place, and be became a more pliant instrument in the Archbishop's hands. He gave effect to the spirit of the canons of the Synod in a way which affected the ecclesiastical life of the county we have under consideration. Nineteen counties were comprised in his see, and much as we admire the reverence of Winfrid for his king, we cannot help feeling that Sexwulf was right in his determination to submit to the subdivision of his diocese. Theodore's policy was now to bear its fruit in the following way. The western portion of Mercia, consisting of Herefordshire, was cut off, and a see founded at Hereford (676). The see of Lindsey was established 678 for about a third part of Lincolnshire. In 680, the see of Worcester was erected. Hertfordshire was to participate in the change. The whole of the county was placed under the see of Leicester (680) with the exception of the Deanery of Braughing, a portion of the present county lying eastward of a more or less direct line running from Cheshunt to Royston, which was under the jurisdiction of the Bishop of London. Thus the greater portion of the county was, at least for a time, severed from its former allegiance to Lichfield. Cuthwin was consecrated by Theodore as first Bishop, and exercised diocesan authority over the counties of Rutland, Northampton, Huntingdon, Cambridge, Bedford, Buckingham, Oxford, Leicester, and parts of Hertfordshire and Lincolnshire. The new glory of Leicester was soon to pale before the brightness of Lichfield, and the struggle against the proposal of sub-division began anew. Cuthwin soon dropped out of sight, and though the see was not suppressed, it was united with Lichfield, under Sexwulf.

Whilst the county was subject to the new and temporary jurisdiction of Leicester, it again figured in a council of the Church, summoned at the instance of Theodore. He had been successful at Hertford in laying the foundation of a new diocesan organization, though it is doubtful whether parochial subdivision was one of the immediate fruits of that Synod. His new attempt was directed more especially to the sphere of doctrine. The pretext for the summons of the Council at Hatfield, in 680, when King Ethelbert was present, was the consideration of the prevalence of the Eutychian or *Monotheistic* heresy in the

Church of Constantinople, but the probability is
that he was more concerned in establishing a
Patriarchate of Canterbury. The Council resulted
in the acceptance of the decrees of the four general
councils, at Nicea (325), Constantinople (381),
Ephesus (431), Chalcedon (451). Whatever the
motive may have been, the faith was confirmed,
and the Church declared,

> "We are not divided,
> All one body we,
> One in hope and doctrine,"

though I fear with Wilfrid, the stormy petrel of
York, hovering about the land, it could not with
truth be added—

> "One in charity."

Doubtless these two successive councils, held within
seven years, not only stirred the nation, but awoke
the interests of the priests scattered up and down
the county in which they took place.

On the death of Sexwulf (691), the see of
Leicester was revived; Wilfrid of York was appointed to it, and held the Bishopric till 702, when
he was deprived by the Council of Easterfield. He
afterwards wended his way once more to Rome, to
appeal against the sentence of excommunication.
It is important to notice his action, and the
result of it, as witnessing the growing pretensions
of Rome, and the independence of the English
Church. The Pope ordered his restoration to office,

but the king refused to alter "a sentence issued by himself, the Archbishop, and all the dignitaries of the land, for any writings coming from the apostolic see." In the end Wilfrid accepted the see of Hexham. He died at Oundle in the year 709, his body being removed to Ripon for burial. So at last this pertinacious representative of Rome, this restless and ambitious prelate, found rest. On his death, Leicester was again re-united with Lichfield; Hedda, the founder of the Cathedral, being Bishop at the time. He died in 721, and Aldwin his successor (721–737), was Bishop of both sees. At his death, Leicester was again exalted to independent diocesan rank; Torthelm (or Totta) became Bishop, and the see was finally separated from Lichfield. Then followed as Bishops of Leicester alone, Eadbert (764–circ. 781), then Unwona, the date of whose consecration is doubtful, but who appears as a signatory to a charter in 781, and again in 785.

Unwona's episcopate was remarkable for two events, the first of a temporary character, the second of an abiding influence, both affecting the area of which we are speaking. The first event was the transfer of the allegiance of the Church in Hertfordshire from Canterbury to Lichfield. The reigning Mercian King, Offa, was a man of determined will, and his kingdom "rose to a height unknown since the days of Wulfhere."[1] The title

---

[1] Green's "History of English People," p. 41.

has been given to him of "Emperor of the West."

Amongst his other victories, was the conquest of the Kingdom of Kent. After firmly consolidating his now extended kingdom, he sought its ecclesiastical unification, and having confiscated the Mercian possessions of the see of Canterbury, he successfully persuaded Pope Adrian to raise the Bishop of Lichfield to Metropolitan dignity. The Pope's action was ratified by the Council of Chelsea (785); Lichfield was raised to Metropolitan rank, and Higbert became archbishop.

By the same Council, the new Archbishop of Lichfield was to hold rule over the Mercian sees of Leicester, Worcester, Hereford, Lindsey, and the East Anglian sees of Elmham and Dunwich. As York had been raised to Metropolitan rank fifty years before, embracing the sees of Hexham, Lindisfarne, and Whitherne, with Egbert as first Archbishop (735), Canterbury was now left with the sees of London, Rochester, Winchester, and Selsey. Poor Theodore must have turned in his grave, as the unity for which he had so earnestly laboured was broken, and the dignity of Canterbury impaired.

The second event was of the greatest possible significance to the history of the Church at large, and led in reality, a thousand years later, to the erection of a bishop's throne in the centre of the county of Herts. This was the visit of Archbishop Higbert, accompanied by his suffragan,

Unwona, Bishop of Leicester, and Ceolwulf, Bishop of Lindsey, to St. Albans, in 793. Offa was King of the Mercians at this time, and is reputed to have been guilty of the murder of Ethelbert. According to the custom of the times, he desired to expiate the deed by a religious act. Prompted by a vision, he came in state to St. Albans, accompained by the Bishop of his kingdom. It was a great day for the town, and greater still for the Church. The story is told how the King, the Archbishop, and Bishops, followed by a great multitude of priests and people from far and near, ascended the hill where, five centuries before, Alban had been beheaded, and after diligent search found the martyr's relics. On the site, he built a Church, dedicated to St. Alban. That Church led to the foundation of the Abbey, which a thousand years later, became a Cathedral, the mother Church of the Diocese.

Truly the day of Unwona was the dawn of great things. The next Bishop, Werenbert (802–816), witnessed the abrogation of the Council of Chelsea, by that of Cloveshoo (803), and only remained a short time as Suffragan to Lichfield. Rethun followed (816–839), next Aldred (date uncertain), then came Ceolred, whose profession of faith and obedience to Canterbury has been preserved. It was as follows:—

"In nomine Dei Summi et Domini nostri Jesu Christi. Ego Ceolred humilis licet indignus ad episcopalem sedem

electus Legoracensis civitatis imprimis confiteor tibi, reve-
rentissime pater Ceolnodi Archiepiscope, quod absque
omni ambiguitate credo in Deum Patrem et Filium et
Spiritum Sanctum (Filium) natum ac passum pro humani
generis redemptione et salute, Cujus potestas et imperium
erat ante Sæculum et regni Ejus non erit finis ; et illam
rectam et catholicam fidem, quam priores patres nostri
devote servaverunt, cum omni humilitate et sincera de-
votione, sient prædecessores ipsa sancta sede Dorover-
nensis Ecclesiæ subjuncti sunt, semper servare me velle
humiliter per omnia fateor.   Nec-non et tibi, pater beatis-
sime Ceolnod Archiepiscope, tuisque successoribus, veredico
professione profiteor stabilem obedientiæ præbere præ-
ceptum votorum meorum, sine ullo scrupulo falsi cogit-
ationis, usque ad terminum vitæ meæ.   Ego Ceolredus
mea propria manu perenni signaculo sanctæ crucis Christi
firmando roboravi." [1]

During the quarter of a century which had
preceded his episcopate, the way was gradually
being prepared for the solidarity of the nation.
It had already taken place in the Church, and
when Mercia fell before the power of Wessex, in
828, the unity of the nation was complete, for there
was one king in one country.   The succeeding
years, until 866, witnessed the gradual strengthening of the national consolidation, in spite of the
incursions of the harrying pirates of the north, accompanied with a few flickering but final struggles
amongst the home tribes.   In 866 a new danger
to the Church and the nation arose.   In Mercia,
as in East Anglia and Northumbria, the long-
threatened storm burst in its fury, so that with

[1] "Reg. Cant.," Art. I. fol. 256.   *Vide* Haddan and Stubbs's
" Eccles. Doc."

the closing years of the Episcopate of Ceolred, a
new era of change loomed over the ecclesiastical
history of the county. It was to become now the
scene of struggle for life and death, and the councils
of prelates within its borders were to be followed
by councils of war. The Vikings, with their creek-
men who, for half a century or more, had been
harrying the coasts, emboldened by their success
in the North, soon began to descend on the shores
of Essex and East Anglia, and prepared the way
for the great invasion. In 867 the Danish hosts
poured into East Anglia, where they wintered.
The next spring, they swarmed up the rivers
and soon overran East Anglia, Northumbria, and
Mercia, penetrating to its heart. In four years
they were masters of these three great provinces.
Ceolred fell before the storm, and it was through
this invasion that a new change of diocese was
brought about. The county of Leicester bore the
brunt of the attack for a while, but at last it succumbed. We need only recall the Danish names
of the Leicestershire villages in proof of the assertion, Barkly, Frisby, Hoby, Gaddesby, etc. Its
Bishop was driven from his see (874), which was
then merged into that of Dorchester on the banks
of the Thames, eight and a half miles from Oxford,
in the heart of Wessex, which, by the peace of
Wedmore, in the same year, fell to the rule of
Alfred the Great, while Northumbria, all East
Anglia, and half central England, including part

of Mercia, became subject to the *Danelagh*. How far this Danish invasion affected the Church in the county, beyond the transference of the see, is not precisely known, but it is a feature of diocesan history which cannot be unnoticed. The river Lea afforded the invaders their favourite means of transit, and we find some instances of their ravages. The Abbey at St. Albans narrowly escaped the fate of its sisters in the fens. They contented themselves, however, with sacking instead of burning it, and with stealing the bones of St. Alban, and carrying them off to Denmark.

Ceolred was the last of the Leicester succession, though the title of the see was revived when Dr. Magee, the late Archbishop of York, as Bishop of Peterborough, nominated Archdeacon Thicknesse as Bishop Suffragan to his diocese, under the style of the Bishop of Leicester.

We have traced the birth, growth, fall, and titular resurrection in later days, of the see of Leicester, we have noted the influence of its times on the county, and must now turn our thoughts to a new condition of things.

Guthrum the Dane ruled half of Mercia, while the *sedes* of its Bishop was in the Kingdom of Wessex, far away in the little town on the Thames. Dorchester had been raised to the dignity of a see in the days of Oswald, nearly two hundred and fifty years before, and St. Birinus, the Apostle of Wessex, was its first Bishop. In the course of forty years it became merged with Winchester, but was revived as a separate see when Leicester fell. The memory of Birinus has been handed on through generations. As late as 1781, the glass of a south window in the chancel of Dorchester Church was described as representing Birinus receiving investiture from Cynegils, the King of Wessex and godson of Oswald, who stands behind. One of the ancient bells bore the inscription "*Protege Birine quos convoco tu sine fine.*" [1] All loyal churchmen will be interested in the assertion that Cynegils is the first Christian ancestor of our late most gracious Queen. "His successors, Kings of Wessex, became eventually, when the Heptarchy terminated, sole Monarchs of England. The ultimate heir of their line was James I.; from whom the present reigning house descends." [2]

Of the Bishops of the Dorchester line, in whom we are specially interested, beginning with Alheard, very little is known, and therefore but little can be said. Yet there are some facts of interest, which point chiefly to the hindrance of the work of the Church by the Danish occupation. Alheard succumbed to a plague, after a rule of about twenty-five years. He was succeeded by Ceolwulf (909), Winsy (926), Oskytel (950), who was raised to the see of York in 958, and died on All Saints' Day. Then came Leofwin (958), formerly Bishop of

[1] Hole's "Early Missions to and within the British Isles," p. 176.
[2] *Ibid.*, p. 177.

Lindsey, and Eadnoth I., who signed a charter as Bishop of Dorchester in 975, Escwry (979), Alfhelm (1002), and Eadnoth II. (1006).

During the days of Eadnoth II. Hertfordshire and Essex were again overrun by an invasion of the Danish hordes. The Bishop was slain at the decisive battle of *Assandon*, and Canute was firmly placed on the throne. Ethelric (1016–1034) leaves no trace of his work in the County. He was buried at Ramsey, within the borders of his Diocese.[1]

The third Eadnoth (1035–1049), his successor, witnesses the beneficent effects of the reign of Edward the Confessor, the last King of the old English stock, and passes away with the record in the Anglo-Saxon Chronicle as, " The good Bishop in Oxfordshire."

Ulf, a Norman (1049–53), succeeded for the short period of three years. This appointment does not appear to have redounded to the credit of the Confessor, for it is said, " he gave the Bishopric to Ulf, his priest, and unworthily bestowed it." He was driven from his see, an exile to France, which was not wonderful, considering the record of his appointment and the comment of the Chronicler—" he did nothing Bishop-like therein : so that it shameth us now to tell more about it." He appears to have returned about two years after his banishment, but only to distinguish himself in one of the faction fights of Harold and Godwin, when

[1] " Anglo-Saxon Chron.," 1036.

he, Archbishop Robert and their companions "slew and otherwise injured many young men," after which he fled to Walton-on-the-Naze, where he took ship to the country of his birth. "Wulfwy (1053–1067), obtained the Bishopric which Ulf had, he being yet living, and went over the sea to be ordained Bishop." He ruled fourteen years, and lies buried in Dorchester Abbey. It was during his episcopate that the battle of Senlac was fought, on October the 14th, 1066, and the fate of England was decided. The Earls of Mercia and Northumbria still hold out in support of Edgar Ætheling the boy-king of the old royal line, and the lawful successor of Harold. Hertfordshire was to be the scene of an important event. The Conqueror marched to Berkhampstead, a seat of the ancient Mercian Kings, plundering as he went. Then came to meet him, Archbishop Aldred of York, the child Edgar, and the Earls of Mercia and Northumberland, and " bowed to him for need."

The story of one more prelate brings us to the close of the Dorchester line, and introduces us to the new era. Remigius, a Benedictine monk, and almoner of Fécamp, accompanied the Norman conqueror to England, and if Geraldus be correct, he contributed a ship and twenty armed men, and was himself the leader of ten knights sent by the Abbot of Fécamp. He appears to have been related to the house of the Conqueror. However this may be, his espousal of William's cause raised

him to the throne of Dorchester, to which he was
consecrated by Stigand.

Professor Freeman dismisses the story of
Matthew Paris, in the early part of his episcopate
as to an alleged meeting at Berkhampstead of the
Conqueror, Lanfranc and the abbot of St. Albans
as untrustworthy. His first work was to order
anew the unsettled condition of the Diocese. "He
perambulated the whole of it, so that by his sermons
and instructions he wrought a happy reformation in
every part." Henry of Huntingdon describes him
as *Statura parvus sed corde magnus ; colore fustus
sed operis venusto*. Five years after his consecration, the Pope summoned him to Rome and deposed
him from his see on the ground of an alleged
bargain with the Conqueror in respect to it, but he
was afterwards restored. Like his Norman *con-
frères* he despised the poor buildings of the English
Church, and planned a new Cathedral for Dorchester, but the Council of London (1075) brought
about a new state of things in many dioceses, and
ordered the sees of bishops to be removed from
villes to more important centres. What probably
decided the site of the new see in this case was
the strong position of Lincoln, then the scene of the
building of a royal castle. Dorchester had no such
advantage. It was during his episcopate that
Waltham Abbey again came into prominence, when
Harold pulled down the old church and built
another on a more magnificent scale. It is alleged

that before Harold went to meet the Conqueror at Hastings—

"He went first to Waltham to pray in the church, and offer relics on the altar. Harold's battle-cry on the fatal field was 'The holy Cross,'—a reference, there can be little doubt, to the cross which was the great treasure and glory of the church at Waltham." [1]

[1] Murray's " Herts," p. 2.

CHAPTER VIII

REVIEW OF PERIOD PRIOR TO NORMAN
CONQUEST

" Cloister thee in some religious house ;
Our holy lives must win a new world's crown."
SHAKESPEARE.

" These ancient ruins,
We never tread them, but we set
Our foot upon some reverend history."
WEBSTER, *" Duchess of Malfi."*

OUR previous chapters have stated in detail
the main facts of the changes which, prior
to the Conquest, had affected the diocesan
life of the Church in the two counties. This is
a summary of developments and characteristics.
Diocesan life is in some measure at least an indication of the growth of principles which affect
national character. In truth, the life of the Church
and the life of the nation act and re-act on each other.

There are some points which deserve special
notice as each succeeding phase of government in
the Church and nation presents itself. This period
may be roughly divided, as far as the Church is
concerned, into two parts: the missionary period
up to 673, and the period of organic growth from

673 to the Conquest. With regard to the British Church, we have few materials on which to found very definite statements as to the method of work, but there are enough indications to hazard the opinion that it was apostolic in constitution, and monastic in method. It was Gallic in origin, but Celtic in obedience and inspiration. It was in communion with Rome and for a time acknowledged her primacy, whilst it asserted its insular independence. It was affected to some extent by the civil relations with Rome which paved the way for later ecclesiastical changes. Its churches were of the simplest character, often merely rude huts. It was subject, like other branches of the Church to the storms of persecution and heresy. Our own old Cathedral city witnesses, by tradition at least, to its material building, and to its persecution.

The Saxon age belongs both to the missionary and the organized periods.

In its earlier stage it had its own local customs, such as the observance of Easter, the mode of administering baptism, of celebrating the Eucharist, the tonsure, and a few minor matters. The centre of inspiration was still Celtic, but it operated from the north instead of the west. It was still monastic. It reverenced Rome, but would not cringe to her, and while admitting the claims of primacy for Rome in her own dominions, it refused subordination, looking rather to Jerusalem, " the mother of us all."

On the arrival of Augustine the insular independence was manifestly and firmly asserted, and led to a conflict between the Celtic and Roman Churches which extended through the missionary period and onwards, until the iron heel of the papacy, in later times, nearly crushed the liberty of the ancient Church of the land.

The mission method of the early Saxon Church was bold and definite in its operation. First the court was attacked, and then the courtiers and subjects. It had to combat heathenism rather than heresy. In its missionary stage it evangelized nearly the whole of England, whilst the victories of Rome were confined to the south of the Thames. The Roman attempt on Northumbria was a fiasco. Hertfordshire owes its Christianity to the Celtic Church, and Essex practically so, for the Roman mission there was a failure.

Passing on now to the organized period, during which the old mission methods still prevailed ; while they crystallized round a larger number of centres. Rome constantly renewed her struggle for leadership, the Church of the English protesting, not against Catholicity, but against Rome's interpretation and application of it. The Celtic Church was less cultured, less skilled in dialectics. It was more simple in its conceptions of the alliance of art and worship. It charmed by the sanctity of its life, whilst Rome dazzled and bewitched by the brilliance of intellect, and the attractiveness of greater

civilization. In cardinal doctrines both were one.
The Celt was ruggedly heroic, the Roman was
politely persistent. The Celt set up crosses, the
Roman erected shrines. The Celt had plenty of
Chads, but no Theodores and Wilfrids. As the
Saxon Church became more organized, Rome seized
the helm, and gradually took command of the ship,
but there were always some officers and many of
the crew who refused to obey her orders. The
old order changed inch by inch, giving place to
the new.

The Bishops, as a rule, were of Celtic birth, and
for the most part derived their orders from Canterbury, but succumbed largely to Roman influence.
The Celts left their permanent mark on our two
counties, Mercian Herts being the last to yield to
the foreign yoke, and even while enchained she
struggled still.

The Church of the Saxons extended the diocesan
and founded the parochial system side by side with
the monastic and collegiate centres. She gave the
death-blow to slavery, exalted womanhood, and laid
the foundations of English literature. She taught
the principle of government and held up the example
of an organized unity to a divided kingdom. She
bore her share in defending the kingdom and was
the mother of the liberty which comes of the building up of just and equal laws. Of the progress of
Church-building during this period, we have ample
evidence. The thatched " wattle and daub " gave

way by degrees to more solid structures of wood and stone. The chief glories of the counties were the abbeys of St. Alban and Waltham. By the end of the period, St. Albans had risen to great importance, and had been ruled by a succession of thirteen abbots, one of whom had succeeded to the chair of St. Augustine. Its possessions had increased enormously, and at least three churches had arisen in the town itself. Waltham had been raised by royal patronage to a dignity which made its mark on the whole district, and if tradition be true, as Mr. Freeman asserts in his " Norman Conquest," its honour was enhanced as the burial-place of Harold. We may, on such authority, safely accept the inscription on the reputed tomb of the hapless monarch, " *Hic jacet Haroldus infelix.*" The clergy were for the most part essentially missionary, working from monastic centres such as St. Albans and Waltham. Side by side with these centres the parochial system was growing up. Scattered here and there over the counties, in the little settlements in the forest clearings and by river banks, and in the immediate vicinity of the ancient Roman roads, we find priests working singly or sometimes by two and two, and occasionally married clergy, spreading the light of the Church, and dependent on the good will of the great man of the place for their subsistence.

The monastic order in Saxon times was exclusively of the Benedictine type, disciplined by the most rigid rules, forming a strong contrast to the rising body of the secular order. The monastery was the centre of civilization as well as the cultured teacher of the surrounding people.

The cathedral in other parts of England was, perhaps more than the monastery, the centre of itineration, but it was the monastic system which most affected the church life of our two counties.

The origin of appropriation, that source of endless strife and scandal, may be dated from Saxon times. The founder of a church reserved to himself not only the right of nominating a priest to its charge, but of assigning the endowments, or a portion of them, to the cathedral or monastic church on condition that the altar of the *parochia* was served by the corporation to which the endowments were assigned. At first the duties were performed with some approach to regularity, but the increasing exactions of Rome, and the growth of monastic buildings and officers, led to the impoverishment of the monastic exchequers, and this in turn re-acted on the parish. The responsibilities attaching to appropriation were often unheeded, and the germs of the vicariate system were beginning to work. Thus the Church had its evils, springing out of the difficulties of its environment, but it was an age of heroic faith and of steady progress. The pre-eminent record of the period is the grand fact of the establishment of a united Church in a nation which henceforth was to take her place amongst the great Christian Kingdoms of the earth.

CHAPTER IX

NORMAN TIMES—HERTFORDSHIRE AND ESSEX

These Normans " built as they
Who hoped these stones should see the day
When Christ should come ; and that these walls
Might stand o'er them till judgment calls."

THE knell of Harold was the note of warning for the Church to prepare for a new period of development. Norman feudalism altered the conditions of social life, and for a while put the whole country into a state of ferment, but the iron will of the Conqueror soon enforced submission. Bishops, who had sat side by side with the civil authorities in Saxon times, as they were removed, or died, were succeeded by Norman prelates with Norman ways, often living in baronial style with their military retinue. Though they still had their own courts for ecclesiastical causes, they were soon made to understand that homage must be done to the Conqueror by Bishop and Baron alike, and that the royal prerogative was to be respected in Church and State. The Norman Lanfranc of Canterbury was to the

Conqueror a new Theodore. He consecrated no less than fourteen Bishops in his nineteen years' rule, and Thomas of York, ten, during his Archiepiscopate. These facts, without entering into detail, show the trend of events. The Council of London held at St. Paul's (1075) in the time of William, Bishop of London, convulsed many of the great diocesan centres, and new Sees were formed. The county of Hertford was affected by the change. The see of Dorchester was suppressed, and the allegiance of the county transferred to Lincoln.

Remigius was the last Bishop of Dorchester, signing himself thus as late as 1072.

He was the first Bishop of Lincoln, and so signed himself at the Council of London in 1075, when we have an undoubted instance of the summons to a National Synod. Archbishop Lanfranc was President, with the Archbishop of York on his right, and the Bishop of London on his left. Milman accounts this "the first ecclesiastical parliament of England." [1]

Remigius ruled over the newly founded See of Lincoln for about twenty years. The crowning glory of his life was the erection of a Cathedral Church for his new See. No sooner had he conceived the idea than he set himself heartily to the work, adopting as his model the Church of Rouen, destroyed in 1200. The new Cathedral was consecrated May 9th, 1092, but Remigius

---

[1] *Vide* Milman's "Annals of St. Paul's."

died three days before this consummation of his
work.   He was laid to rest before the Altar of the
Holy Cross in the Church of his foundation, and the
Prelates and Barons who had assembled to assist
at the consecration, attended his obsequies instead,
the consecration being postponed.   The central
portion of the west front of the Cathedral remains
a witness of this great work.   Of the effect of his
rule on the Hertfordshire part of his Diocese, we
learn that, at the entreaty of Paul, abbot of St.
Albans, together with the power of Lanfranc,
and, it is added, with "the influence of a little
money, and through a dreadful fear of the martyr," [1]
he was instrumental in obtaining a restoration
of some of the abbey land, near its Priory of
Sopwell.   During his episcopate, the choir, the
tower, and the north and south transept of the
Abbey Church were erected, mainly out of Roman
bricks, which would abound in Verulam.   The
extent of the pastoral care of Remigius in the
county may be estimated from the fact that when
the Domesday Book was completed, there were no
less than about fifty priests mentioned therein, as
being settled in various parishes, while about twenty
parishes were served directly from the abbey.
Though there are few Saxon, and not many
Norman remains of churches, it is more than probable that every priest represented at least one
church.   Even to this day the remains of three

[1] Matthew of Paris.

Saxon and at least ten Norman churches are known to exist in the county.

I do not propose to refer to the history of the Bishops of Lincoln, except in so far as it relates to the county, or illustrates the course of events under consideration, or gives 'some general illustration of their character.

On the death of Remigius the see was vacant for two years. His successor, Robert Bloett (1094–1123), was consecrated at Hastings by Archbishop Anselm, assisted by seven Bishops, the day after the dedication of Battle Abbey. Among the events of his episcopate which affected this county, we must note his memorable visit to St. Albans for the consecration of the new work of Abbot Paul at Christmas-tide, 1115. It must have been an imposing ceremony. The occasion was graced by the presence of King Henry I., together with his Queen Matilda, the Archbishop of Rouen, the Bishops of London, Sarum, and Durham, besides a great number of abbots and clergy. The new minster of Lincoln was also consecrated during his rule (1095.) He seems to have been guilty of appropriation, the vice of the Bishops of his time, and to have removed the monks from Stow to Evesham, in order that he might annex their revenue for the see. He died suddenly while riding with the King and Roger Bishop of Salisbury in "the deerfold" of Woodstock. His body was removed to Lincoln for burial. It was during his episcopate that the See of Lincoln was first subdivided by the erection of the See of Ely.

Robert was succeeded by Alexander, nephew of the Bishop of Salisbury, and Archdeacon of Sarum (1123–1148). Like his predecessor, he paid an important visit to the county. He was present, 1129, at the translation of the relics of St. Alban to the new shrine erected during the abbacy of Geoffrey Gorham, 16th Abbot, who owned him as Diocesan. In 1145 we read of Alexander dedicating the nunnery of Markgate (Caddington) in the presence of the Bishop of Limerick, Ralph the Dean, Theodoric a canon, Nicholas a clerk, and laying the Charter granted by the Dean and Chapter of St. Paul's on the altar. The Dean of Lincoln, the Archdeacons of Huntingdon, Bedford, and Buckingham were also present, together with the Abbot and many monks of St. Albans, and other canons, clerks, and laity. This recognition of episcopal authority continued through the rule of the next abbot, Ralph, who was one of the domestic officers of the Bishop, through whose influence he had become a monk of the abbey. But the friendly relations of Abbot and Bishop were not long to remain undisturbed. The impending struggle came to a head in the time of Ralph's successor, Robert de Gorham, 18th Abbot.

Robert de Chesney (1148–1167), "a man of great humility," Archdeacon of Leicester, occupied the See of Lincoln at this juncture. Abbot Robert,

when on a visit to Pope Adrian IV. (Nicholas
Brakespeare, himself a Hertfordshire man), having
complained of the troubles and vexations which
(Robert) their Bishop of Lincoln gave his monastery, requested that " the Pope would be pleased to
give them exemption from all other authority than
that of the Pope himself."[1]   The Pope assented,
and the cause came before a council held at Westminster (1163), when it was decided that the church
of St. Albans was freeborn (*ingenua*), and that the
Bishop's rule was founded on prescription, and not
on statute.   The decision was confirmed by Beckett
himself.   The end of the contention was that the
Bishop was compensated for his loss of authority
by receipt of a farm at Fingest, in Bucks, of a yearly
value of £10, and the abbot received a mitre.   It
would seem, however, that ordinations, consecrations,
and the dedication of churches and altars were left
as before to diocesan Bishops, for the next year
a diocesan Bishop, Godfrey of St. Asaph, "consecrated a quantity of oil in the Eucharist at the
great altar, to be distributed as formerly to the
churches belonging to this Abbey ; but that the said
Bishop acted in no respect for the Bishop of
Lincoln."   At the same time he dedicated the altar
of the Holy Cross in the Abbey, and another in the
church of St. Peter in honour of St. Nicholas.
This event forms a marked period in the relation
of the Bishop to many churches in the county,

---

[1] *Vide* Matthew of Paris.

which had been monastic rather than Diocesan in allegiance. Many instruments of endowment at this period required the assent of King and Bishop, and contained a clause recognizing the authority of the latter. The monasteries took special care to secure the greater tithes. If the abbot's appropriation was large in amount, he would not be very much troubled at the loss of authority, at the expense of the smaller tithes for the vicar.

The assumption of the mitre by the abbot of St. Albans actually falls within the Plantagenet period, yet as the dissensions which led up to it were the result of the increasing power of the abbey during the Norman period, I have referred to it, therefore, under that *régime.* Taking a survey of the church work in the county at this time, the following facts may be noticed. The great centre of work was, of course, the Abbey, from which we can picture the monks going forth week by week, either on foot or on horseback, to minister the sacraments, and to evangelize the little "villes" under their charge, often subject to the dangers of flood, storm, and robbers, as they toiled along the country roads or rode through the woods on their way to their appropriated churches.

The Abbey, standing as it does near the centre of the county, dominated. It is not unlikely that, while it was the chief centre of ministration, there were radiations of work round the Benedictine Priory of Hertford which maintained twelve monks.

The Deanery [1] of Braughing appears to have been largely under the influence of the collegiate system in connection with St. Paul's, and to some extent with Waltham. In those parts of the counties which were not subject to monastic rule, we find the secular clergy scattered about here and there (as in Saxon times) in primitive settlements, living in their humble parsonages, and earning their living by tilling the plots allotted to them by the lord of the manor, in the forest clearings. They were also aided by the voluntary offerings of the people. They were often subject to the slights of their superior celibate Benedictine brethren of the monastery. It is interesting to notice that *most* of the churches under the rule of the abbots have come down to us from Norman times as Vicarages, whilst those under the charge of the secular clergy have survived as Rectories. The distinction marks the greedy hand of the monastic appropriator. This is not meant for an attack on the monastic system itself, which was a necessary phase in the ecclesiastical development of the age, and might well be adapted with modifications and restrictions in some districts in the present day.

Reverting to the Diocesan story of Essex, the Bishops of London who succeeded William, the King's Chaplain, came in quick succession. The first, Hugh d'Orivalle (1075–1084), died a leper. He was followed by Maurice (1086–1107), the

---

[1] Browne Willis so speaks of it.

King's Chancellor, who was the munificent founder of the great Norman Cathedral of St. Paul, as Remigius was of Lincoln. He deposited the relics of St. Erconwald in the crypt. Bishop Maurice illustrates the new baronial habits of the Norman bishops. The castle of Bishops Stortford was conferred on him, and he was there surrounded with his baronial retinue. The Castle was subsequently destroyed by King John, in his grudge against Baron bishops, thus bringing to an end the first episcopal residence of the Bishops of London, in the county of Hertford, which, however, was revived at Much Hadham at a later date. This Bishop, also held the manor of Chelmsford, which was afterwards in the occupation of the Bishops of London for a long period.

Richard de Beaumes (1107–1127), Archdeacon of Middlesex, succeeded. To him we owe the revival of the Abbey of St. Osyth, founded by the saint of that name, at which abbey he placed a body of Augustinian Canons.

Gilbert the "Universal" (1127–1134) appears to have made no special mark on the county, whatever he may have done in the world outside. It was something to his honour that he was a friend of St. Bernard.

The chapter was divided in its choice of his successor, some voting for Anselm, the mitred Abbot of Bury. Finally Robert de Segello (1142–1152) a monk from Reading, Archdeacon of London, was chosen instead.

Robert de Beaumes (1152–1162), Archdeacon of Middlesex, a nephew of a former Bishop, was the last prelate ruling the see during Norman times.

However much we may regret the greed and contentions of Norman bishops and abbots, we have to thank them for many things. There were none of those violent "ejections" which marked the crisis of changes in later ages. The simple Saxon priests were allowed to go on with their earnest work, and they quietly submitted to a new race of Bishops as their rulers. The extent to which the work of the Church had already reached, and the way in which that work was being steadily carried on through the changing scene of political conquest, may be gathered from the number of priests whose existence was indicated by the *Domesday Book* for the counties.

A further study of this record reveals the general extent of ecclesiastical influence in the widely extended territorial possessions of the Church. The Bishops of London, the Canons of St. Paul's, the Abbey of Westminster, the Bishop of Durham, the Canons of Waltham, the Abbey of Barking, the Abbey of Ely, the Abbey of St. Edmund, the Canons of St. Martins, Battle Abbey, the Bishop of Hereford, all held lands in Essex, at the time of Survey.

In Hertfordshire, too, there was the same widely extended territorial influence.

G

Foreign ecclesiastical influence was also great at this time, may we not say too great ? Amongst the foreign holders are to be found Odo, Bishop of Bayeux, the Abbeys of St. Valery, Holy Trinity, Caen ; St. Stephen, Caen ; St. Ouen, Rouen.

It is abundantly evident that we have to thank the Normans for extending, and so nobly illustrating the principles of Church Architecture. While there are some undoubted and remarkable remains of the ruder Saxon period, there are some fifty or more churches still existing in the counties with more or less thoroughly marked indications of Norman work.

The simplicity and solid grandeur of the untouched portions of two great Abbeys rejoice our eyes and inspire our faith to-day. The Celtic Mission bore its fruit indeed. New hopes and possibilities for the Church were revived, and by the time the Norman rule had passed away, her mighty influence had gained a firm hold upon the land.

CHAPTER X

PLANTAGENET DAYS—HERTFORDSHIRE

"Ev'n now we hear with inward strife,
A motion toiling in the gloom—
The spirit of the years to come
Yearning to mix himself with Life."
TENNYSON, "*Love thou thy Land.*"

STEPHEN was dead, and Henry II. was now the reigning monarch. Walter de Coutance (1183–1186),[1] Archdeacon of Oxford, was Bishop of Lincoln, and Warren, the twentieth Abbot, was ruling at St. Albans, when the old strife between the Abbey and the See broke out anew. The King, desirous of paying a visit to the celebrated Abbey, went down with a brilliant retinue. There was a great meeting in the Chapter-house, and the King, taking the Abbot's chair, motioned the Abbot to the right, and the Bishop of Lincoln, who was present, to the left.

The Bishop rose and preferred a complaint to His Majesty, which was—

"that he was greatly injured, and the Church of Lincoln shamefully mutilated, by cutting off from it so noble a member as this monastery. With your permission, I

---

[1] The see had been vacant for sixteen years.

must move a question against this Abbot. Whatever my predecessor did, who was simple and easy, he was circumvented in the same ; the world well knows that this Church is subject to the Church of Lincoln ; and whatever hath been done in error, it is fit and expedient that the same should be recalled."

The Abbot resented the intrusion, and the King declared that the matter had been settled—

"when he himself and the most chosen men of the realm were present, what was then done was ratified by writings most incontestible, and confirmed by the testimony of the nobles. The determination stands good, and whosoever sets himself to combat this Abbot and monastery combats me. What seek you ? To touch the pupil of mine eye ? " [1]

Thus the Bishop received his *quietus,* and the year after, his *solatium,* in his appointment to the Archbishopric of Rouen. This story has both a local and a national interest. The event did much towards the final settlement of the recurring contentions of the past as to the relation of Bishop and Abbot, and also illustrates the growing authority of the Sovereign in matters ecclesiastical.

The see of Lincoln was vacant for the next three years, and a terrible catastrophe happened to its Cathedral during the vacancy. In the great earthquake of 1185, which shook the whole country, the minster was rent from top to bottom. "*Ecclesia Lincolniensis metropolitana scissa est a summo deorsum.*" [2]

[1] Newcome's " History of St. Albans Abbey."
[2] Hovenden, *ad ann.* 1185.

The new Bishop, the saintly Hugh of Avalon (1186–1203), better known as St. Hugh of Lincoln, of the Carthusian order, was consecrated the year after this event. The rebuilding of his Cathedral in its noble beauty took up much of his time, but he was not unmindful of his diocesan charge.

Canon Perry informs us " That his first act was to publish certain *Decreta* to remedy some of the most rampant abuses amongst the clergy," viz. : [1]—

" 1. That nothing be given or received for administering or hastening the administration of justice.

" 2. That nothing should be given or exacted of the priest-vicars for their office.

" 3. That the Archdeacons and their officials should not presume to fine any church or any individual without regular trial.

" 4. That no layman or any other person not a priest, should have the celebration of masses inflicted on him as a penance.

" 5. That no annuals or triennials or any other settled masses should be celebrated for temporal gains.

" 6. That no one be admitted to the priestly office unless it shall have been proved that he was ordained canonically by the Archbishop of Canterbury, or one of his suffragans.

" 7. That all who hold benefices should have the tonsure.

" 8. That no clerk sue another clerk in a secular court for matters ecclesiastical." [2]

Among the local incidents connected with a journey through Hertfordshire is the case, at

[1] " History of the Diocese of Lincoln," S.P.C.K. 1897, p. 103.
[2] Benedictas Abbas, S. A. 1186.

Cheshunt, of a "mad sailor, tied in a most inhuman manner, being loosed by the Bishop's order, and who by his calm words and fearless demeanour was so impressed that it is said he was afterwards completely cured of his mania."

Few men have left such an honourable name as St. Hugh. The mark of his episcopate is indelibly engraven on this county in the institution of many vicarages, thus placing the spiritualities of the parish on a sounder basis. The growing wealth and splendour of the Abbey had resulted in the impoverishment of the temporalities of the parishes under its control, whilst the sacred offices were but imperfectly performed. It was to the correction of this abuse that St. Hugh set his mind, and he was in many instances successful. It must be confessed, however, that whilst he secured the appointment of vicars, the habit of appropriation was so strong that the Abbey still clung tenaciously to its custom in this respect, and the evil was not remedied without long and continued effort. For instance, we find that the advowson of the church of King's Walden had been made over to the Gilbertine Priory of Malton, and confirmed during the episcopate of Robert de Chesney by the Neviles, whose family were Lords of the Manor for many years in succession.[1]

The grant was again confirmed by St. Hugh,

---

[1] MS. Cotton Claud. D. xi. "Cartularies of the Priory of Malton," *vide* Clutterbuck, "History of Hertfordshire."

and an interesting series of charters and confirmations is extant concerning this transaction.

It must be observed, as an indication of the gradually strengthening position of vicars that the rights of the Vicar of Walden were to be secured *quâ vicar*, and not merely as the representative of the Abbey. This case came up again on the accession of Bishop Grosseteste.

During the time of St. Hugh, the second Crusade was at its height, and our county saw the first introduction of the Knights Templars, the church of Standon being confirmed to them. We shall have something to say of this brotherhood later on.

The good St. Hugh died in London, November 17th, 1200, and his body was taken to Lincoln for burial, the journey lasting six days. On the route the body rested at Hertford two days after his death.[1] His obsequies at Lincoln, on November 24th, were worthy of the esteem he won in his life. The King of England and the Prince of Galloway assisted as bearers. Three Archbishops (Canterbury, Dublin, Ragusa), thirteen Bishops, and a great company of Abbots and Priors were present.

His honoured name and holy influence have lived on throughout the centuries that followed. The shrine of gold erected to his memory was removed by order of a commission in 1542. Men

---

[1] Digby MSS. 165, fol. 132, Bod. Lib.

may break down "carved work with axes and hammers," but the holy dead still rule the world, in the seeds of life that they sowed. The words of Bishop Fuller, in Restoration days, on the restored tomb, denote the fact :—"it is only marble that we can give, it should have been gold, as it was before the madness of these latter days." At the close of the nineteenth century (Nov. 17th, 1900), the ancient see of Lincoln, again honoured the memory of the holy man in solemnly observing the seven-hundredth anniversary of his call to rest. The Bishop of Lincoln, and the Bishop of Bristol, testified to the power of his character, and the "irresistible humanity" of his life. The one drew out "in his own way the practical lessons of the character of his great predecessor, of his devotion to his home, of his self-discipline, of his moral courage and tact." The other emphasized "his single-hearted devotion to the ideal of what a bishop and a monk should be ; his sternness towards injustice and oppression, only equalled by his tenderness towards helplessness and poverty ; the combination of fearlessness and tact, which won him the respect and admiration of the impetuous monarchs with whom he was so often brought into contact ; the ready wit which tided him over so may crises." [1]

The writer of these sketches is proud to add that the name and work of the saintly Bishop are

[1] For a full account of the Commemoration, *vide Guardian* Nov. 21st, 1900, p. 1642.

kept in memory by a noble figure in a niche on the
pulpit in the parish church of Chipping Barnet.

St. Hugh was succeeded by William of Blois
(1203–6), after a vacancy of three years, who was
followed after another three years' vacancy by
Hugh, Archdeacon of Wells (1209–35), who was
consecrated at Rouen. The kingdom was under
an interdict at this time. This Hugh must not be
confused with St. Hugh, his great predecessor.

We may note in passing that the old contention
between Abbot and Diocesan Bishop receives an
illustration as far as it concerns the services of the
Abbey Church. It was during this episcopate that
Thomas Blumville, Bishop of Norwich, instead of
the Bishop of Lincoln, was requested by the Abbot
to consecrate a cemetery for the Abbey, and for
St. Peters ; and an altar, dedicated to St. Leonard,
"in the great Church." Hugh of Wells, like his
great predecessor, had to face the question of
vicarages, which was still a sore point with the
Abbot, and needed further adjustment. The way
for final settlement seems to have been paved
(as in the case of Luton, where the Abbot had
instituted a vicarage), but the question of endowment and diocesan authority had long remained
under dispute. The Pope appointed the Bishop
of Salisbury and the Abbots of Westminster and
Waltham to act as arbitrators. It was determined
that the abbey should present the priest to the
Bishop for institution, that his maintenance should

be derived from the small tithes and offerings, and that he should be further endowed with a suitable house and glebe ; and that the Bishop of Lincoln and his successors should have full jurisdiction in the church.

As examples of the current method of endowment of the time of Hugh of Wells, Cussans gives the following illustration. When the Vicarage of St. John, Hertford, was instituted in 1209, the vicar was to receive daily "one loaf, three gallons of ale, as much pottage as a monk, a yearly stipend to be paid by the Prior of the Church of 6s. 8d., the corn tithes of a field."

Notes of the constitution, at this period, of many Vicarages are still preserved in the archives of Lincoln.

All through the earlier Plantagenet days the poor vicars were much oppressed, being tributary both to their lay patrons and the various Cathedrals and monasteries who held a lien on their endowments. The Abbots and Priors were the worst offenders. When they saw that public feeling was against the system, "they contrived to obtain indulgence from the Pope, that whatever churches they held in advowson, they should commit them to be served by clerks, who as to the cure of souls should be responsible to the Bishop, but as to the profit should be responsible to the Abbot or Prior and his brethren."[1]

[1] Phillimore's "Ecclesiastical Law," vol. i. p. 269

It is to be feared that, as the Cathedral bodies grew in importance and dignity, they too followed the evil ways of the Abbeys in this respect. It was the outburst of parochial indignation which forced the Bishops to protect the temporal and spiritual rights of parochial cures.

The days of Hugh of Wells saw the Roman pretensions at their height. The death of Stephen Langton, " the champion of the old English customs and law against the personal despotism of the kings," [1] marked a new era of struggle against the Roman claims. The Pope, in conformity with the mediæval theory, regarded the Bishops as his vassals, and the clergy as his liegemen. Under pain of excommunication he over-awed the patrons of benefices, and attempted to flood the country with an Italian priesthood, but the Bishop of Lincoln made a strong resistance. It remained for his remarkable successor, Robert Grosseteste, to deal summarily with the question.

While these dangers were threatening the church within, another from without seemed likely to arrest her progress. The great rebellion of the barons threatened the country with civil war. It was happily suppressed before great harm was done, but in the march of an army in those days the fabrics of the churches were liable to injury and desecration. The army of Henry with 6000 knights and 20,000 soldiers marched through the county

[1] Green's " History of the English People," p. 127.

of Hertford in 1217, and left its mark on at least some of the churches, the Abbey itself narrowly escaping plunder. Matthew Paris tells us, "On 1st May they directed their march for Dunstable, and passed through Redbourne and pillaged the church of *St. Amphibalus*, and stripped the monks of their habits. Laying hands on the relics over the altar, they desecrated them." [1]

When Robert Grosseteste (1235–53), Archdeacon of Northampton, and afterwards Archdeacon of Leicester, came to the see, he found the diocese in a sad state of corruption, and social debauchery reigning in the land. Ministrations at the altar, font, and pulpit were terribly neglected. The churches were scenes of desecration. The lives of the clergy were tainted with the general corruption, while the great officers of the Church were absorbed in all sorts of secular duties. The Abbeys and Collegiate foundations had become little more than great landed corporations. The Pope, in order to extend his interests, had thrust all sorts of worthless nominees into vacant benefices. The King was not slow to follow the evil example, "jobbery" and corruption prevailed everywhere. Grosseteste rose up as the champion for the honour, the purity, and the independence of the English Church.

Grosseteste made a thorough visitation of his Diocese, which is best described in his own words :

[1] Paper on Redbourne by Rev. H. Fowler. "Transactions St. Alban's Archæological Soc., 1887," pp. 53, 54.

"At the commencement of my episcopate, I began to go through the several archdeaconries, and in the archdeaconries through the several rural deaneries, causing the clergy of each deanery to be called together at a certain day and place, and the people to be warned that at the same day and place they should be present with the children to be confirmed, and in order to hear the Word of God and to confess." [1]

On these occasions, as we shall see later, he made use of the Friars as special preachers.

The Bishop was not long before he made his mark on Hertfordshire, and showed the inflexibility of his purpose. He asserted his rights respecting the church at Ashwell.[2] Again, in 1252, he excommunicated a Burgundian Priest who had been collated by the King to the Vicarage of Flamstead (constituted by Bishop Hugh of Wells in 1224).

We find him addressing the Archdeacon of Huntingdon as well as his other officials insisting on reform in various evil customs, and specially against desecration of Sundays and holy days. He denounced plurality and non-residence, which were rife, in the strongest terms.

He was very bold in his denunciation of the system of fleecing the benefices of his diocese by the system of appropriation and the ministry of "middlemen," remarking that "the cure of souls consists not only in the dispensation of the Sacraments, in singing of 'hours' and reading of

---

[1] "History of Diocese of Lincoln," S.P.C.K., p. 136.
[2] *Vide* "Dictionary of National Biography."

masses, but in the true teaching of the word of
life, in rebuking and correcting vice ; and besides
all these, in feeding the hungry, giving drink to
the thirsty, lodging the strangers, visiting the sick
and the prisoners, especially among the parish
priest's own parishioners." This the middlemen,
from their poverty and frequently compulsory non-
residence, could not do, and he set forth all this
and much more in his memorial to the Pope, 1250.[1]

No wonder that the memory and good report
of such a man as he inspired Wicliffe with the fire
of reform.

Grosseteste was succeeded by Henry Lexington
(1254–58), Dean of Lincoln. During the vacancy
which preceded his episcopate, the power of the
Abbot of St. Albans had reached a climax. The
Archbishop desired to hold ordinations in the
Abbey, but the Abbot flatly refused him, and told
him "that he might be considered as representing
the Bishop of Lincoln, the ordinary of that Diocese."
So my lord Archbishop had to proceed to Dunstable,
though my lord Abbot graciously and handsomely
entertained him at the Abbey on his way to and
fro. The Abbot was, however, quite willing to
allow the use of the Abbey buildings when the
conduct of a Bishop of Lincoln was to be called in
question. Matthew Paris tells a story in evidence
of this. The action of Lexington in relation to the
privileges of the University of Oxford, was the

[1] Grosseteste's Letters, 58 ; Lechler's Wycliffe, p. 31, *et seq.*

subject of an inquiry at St. Alban's, in March, 1257, before the King, who listened to the grievances stated by nine representatives from the seat of learning. Much to the chagrin of the Abbot and of the regents of the University, the inquiry settled nothing.

During the rule of Lexington, the Mendicant Friars, encouraged by Grosseteste's patronage, had begun to make their influence felt, for evil as well as for good, but we shall treat of them in a separate chapter, together with other religious orders which obtained a footing in the county.

The Bishop did his best to resist the tax which the Pope proposed to levy, to help pay for the expenses of a war against Sicily. He was also on the side of the barons in their stand for liberty as against the tyranny of the King and the Pope.

Of the work of Richard of Gravesend (1258–79), not much can be related. Like Lexington, he espoused the cause of the barons. In 1262 we find him visiting his diocese, making some attempt to settle the relationship of the religious houses to the parish churches on a more satisfactory foundation. With a view of carrying out this, he summoned the heads of various houses to Lincoln, to exhibit their titles. Their rights were recognized only on condition of their instituting Vicarages in the Parishes where they proved their claim to exercise jurisdiction. Four years before his death, it was found necessary to appoint a coadjutor to assist him.

His successor, Oliver Sutton (1280-99), had among his first acts the privilege of doing honour to the memory of the great St. Hugh of Avalon, at the opening of the Angels' Choir at Lincoln, and the dedication at the same time of St. Hugh's *Golden Shrine*. He took up the work of his predecessor in the better regulation of religious houses. He was not indifferent to church restoration, for we find him granting an indulgence for the rebuilding of the striking central tower of Wheathampstead, during the time of the Incumbency of John de Leicester. He also did much building in his own cathedral city. We read of him passing with the funeral procession of Queen Eleanor through Waltham, and he also took part in her funeral obsequies at Westminster.

John Dalderby (1300-20), like his predecessor, had trouble with the religious houses. It was during his time that the attack was made on the Order of the Templars. He was forced against his will to take action, and to consign the alleged offending knights to various Abbeys for penance and correction. One Thomas, of the Commandery at Temple Bruer, was remitted to the monastery of St. Albans for this purpose.

Dalderby's successor, Henry Burghersh (1320-40), Lord High Chancellor of England, appears in annals as the Pope's messenger to the sick Abbot Richard, and to have revived the old controversy. It is rather a long story, but it shall be briefly told.

One of the monks of Abingdon informed the Pope that the Abbot was incapable of fulfilling the duties of his office. The Pope, in turn, wrote to the Bishop and King for further information, "for he had heard that the Abbot had lost his speech, and was unable to assemble with the brethren." The Bishop despatched the Dean of the Court of Arches. The Abbot, by the person of his Prior, appealed to the King, who was then holding his parliament at York, stating that the monk's accusation had received the imprimatur of the Bishop. The Bishop acknowledged that pressure had been put upon him. The end of the matter was, that the Prior was elected by the Chapter to act as the Abbot's coadjutor. " This being done," adds Newcombe, " there was perfect peace and unanimity restored in the house."

Thomas Bek (1342–47) does not add interest to our annals. We know but little of him, beyond the fact that he is described by Walsingham as "a noble and excellent clerk."

John Gynwell (1347–62), Archdeacon of Northampton, succeeded. His lot fell in anxious times, when men's minds were turned from the quarrels in church and state to the awful visitation of the Black Death, which had commenced its ravages in the time of his predecessor. Knighton, a Canon of Leicester Abbey, records its effects on the ministrations of religion.

"So great was the scarcity of priests, that many

H

churches were desolate, being without divine offices ; but in a short time there was a flocking into orders of many whose wives had died during the pestilence, some of whom were very illiterate, only just able to read after a fashion, and not able to understand what they read."

John Bokyngham (1363–98), another Archdeacon of Northampton, was destined to witness the *Peasants' Revolt* inspired by the growing discontent of the age under the leadership of John Ball, who knew how to use for his purpose the epigrammatic question—

> "When Adam delved and Eve span,
> Who was then the gentleman?"

Bokyngham's attitude toward the Lollards will be noted in a later chapter.

These social and religious disturbances were slow but sure elements, combining in ever-increasing force, to produce the ultimate climax of reform.

CHAPTER XI

PLANTAGENET DAYS—ESSEX

" A slow develop'd strength awaits
Completion in a painful school;
Phantoms of other forms of rule,
New majesties of mighty states."
                TENNYSON'S *" Love thou thy Land."*

LET us now turn to the witness of the Bishops
of London who ruled over Essex during this
period of political and ecclesiastical submission to Papal influence. These were amongst the
darkest days of the Church in the county. It will
be impossible, from lack of opportunity for full
research, from the scantiness of material records,
and partly also from the shortness of some of the
episcopates, to do much more, in several instances,
than to record the names of the successive Bishops.

In the presence of the domination of the Roman
see, and of the ravages of the Black Death which
fell with great severity on the county, a paralyzing
helplessness appears to have settled upon most of
the Bishops, so far as the pastoral side of their
office was concerned. Theirs was one continued

struggle with the circumstances which held the Church of England in bondage. To this it may be added, that the county of Essex was very largely under the sway of monastic influence, radiating from its numerous local centres. Further, there was not a man amongst the successive Bishops of London during this period who possessed the capabilities, tact, and vigour either of St. Hugh, or of Grosseteste, who were such towers of strength in the adjoining Diocese of Lincoln.

Gilbert Foliot (1163-89), formerly a Cluniac Monk, Prior of Abbeville, Abbot of St. Peter's, Gloucester; and afterwards Bishop of Hereford, was translated to the see of London. He was an accomplished linguist, and at one time was in favour with Becket. He seems afterwards to have fallen under his displeasure and excommunication. This was probably the reason that William de Vere, one of his successors in the see of Hereford, consecrated the Lady Chapel at Waltham Abbey in 1188. It may, however, have been that, like his neighbour of St. Albans, my lord Abbot resented the presence of the diocesan Bishop. It is not clear what was the real reason of his absence.

Richard Fitzneal (1189-99), Dean of Lincoln, came to London with the advantage of a close knowledge of the activities of Lincoln, under St. Hugh, whose spirit, however, he does not seem to have caught. He gave himself to literature, and his memory is mainly associated with the fact,

that, as Royal Treasurer, he produced a *Dialogue*
which is recognized as the first work on English
government.

William of St. Mary Church (1199-1221), Dean
of St. Martin's, London, has two memorable incidents connected with his episcopate. First of all
he had fourteen consecrators. Further, in 1208,
he proclaimed the dreaded Papal interdict, which
made the counties tremble with fear. For years
the Papal curse lay upon the land. The unserved
altars, the silent bells, the hasty baptisms, the
unhallowed funerals, the joyless nuptials, must
have cast a worse than heathen gloom upon the
shires, to be lifted only when the light of England's
liberty shone again at Runnymede, and when,
with Archbishop Langton, the Bishop of London
attached his signature to the Great Charter which
declared for ever "the Church of England shall
be free."

William retired from his bishopric to St. Osyth.
A brief from Honorius III. exists in the British
Museum, permitting his retirement and granting
him the Manors of Clacton and Witham.[1] It was
during his day, probably in the interval of his flight
from the fury of King John, that the baronial castle
of the Bishops of London at Bishops Stortford was
dismantled.

The Episcopates of Eustace de Fauconberg
(1221-29), and of Roger de Noir (or Niger)

[1] Milman, "Annals of St. Paul's," p. 51.

(1229–44), were signalized by contentions with the lordly legates of the Papal see. They are too long and too general to describe, but they show that Grosseteste was not standing quite alone in his battle. The former of the two Bishops had a lively quarrel with the monks of Coggeshall, on the subject of the advowson of the parish church of that place.

Fulk Bassett (1244–60), Dean of York, was next in succession. On him was laid by the imperious pontiff the unpopular task of taxing his clergy to the extent of one third of their income if resident, and one half if non-resident, and whilst opposed to the impost, he had no option but to enforce it. It is a curious fact that in a Reformation inventory of goods in the parish church of Therfield in his diocese, to the accounts of the Psalters there is added *The Statutes of Fulk*. These may have been the statutes of the Council held at St. Paul's during his episcopate, or possibly the Papal injunctions enforced by him, much against his will. The latter view is more probable, for in a letter which he addressed to the Abbot of St. Albans in respect to this taxation, he remarks, "if the Pope had known the state of England, he would never have promulgated such a Statute." Eventually the Bishop was true to his convictions, and sided with the Barons against the King and Pope.

The next three Bishops followed in quick succession, and have left but little to record of importance to our purpose. Henry of Wingham (1260–63), ruled but three years, which were signalized only by incompetence and plurality. Henry of Sandwich (1263–74), Archdeacon of Oxford, was excommunicated for his support of Simon de Montfort. John of Chishall (1274–80), Dean of St. Paul's, was called upon to regulate matters at the Nunnery of Barking. His gentle remonstrance in this respect called for the interference of Archbishop Peckham. On February 2nd, in the last year of his episcopate, on account of his growing infirmity, the administration of the diocese was entrusted by the Archbishop to the Dean of St. Paul's, and to Fulk Lovel, Archdeacon of Colchester.

Richard Gravesend (1280-1306), insisted on the reading of the Great Charter in parish churches in his diocese, and thus proved himself worthy of the regenerating spirit of the best of his flock. He is said to have founded the Carmelite Priory at Maldon.

Ralph of Baldock (1306–13) was elevated from the Deanery of St. Paul's to the dignity of its Bishop. If the absence of records may be cited in proof, he cannot be said to have made any special impression on the story of his day.

Gilbert of Segrave (1313–18), Precentor of St. Paul's, kept up the recent tradition of the appointment from the Cathedral body to the bishopric. He is described in the will of Richard of Gravesend, dated September 12th, 1302, as his nephew, and

Archdeacon of Colchester. He died suddenly at
Colchester, August 24th, 1318.

Richard of Newport (1318–19), Archdeacon
of Middlesex, succeeded him.

Stephen of Gravesend (1319–1338) found his
consecration fees a serious matter. They were paid
in kind, viz. "linen tapers 288, and candles 236, 200
loaves, 10 large barrels of wine, 36 small, 1 ox, 1 hog,
4 calves, 24 rabbits, 36 chickens, 200 larks, pro-
vender for 160 horses, 20 marcs, to the servants"
of my Lord Archbishop. He died of the plague,
at his Manor of Copford, and was buried in his
Cathedral.

Richard of Bynteworth (1338–40), another
Canon of St. Paul's, had no time to make episcopal
history.

Ralph of Stratford (1340-55) still kept up the
connection with the Mother Church of the Diocese,
and rose from a Canonry in St. Paul's to the
episcopal chair. It was his sad lot to witness in
the *Black Death* a terror worse than the *Interdict*.
This scourge fell with especial severity on the
eastern counties. It is well-nigh impossible to
depict the havoc it made, not only in its terrible
tale of mortality, but in the panic which seized on
every rank and condition of life. Some idea of
the awful story of its ravages in the diocese may
be gathered when we read that in a burial-ground
for the citizens of London, on the site of the
Charter-House, some fifty thousand bodies are

said to have been buried from its effects. Professor Green tells us that the visitation "fell on the villages almost as fiercely as on the towns."

Of Michael of Northburgh (1355-62), Archdeacon of Suffolk, we have found no record to make beyond his name. During his, and the preceding episcopate, a harvest of religious and social unrest was ripening. *The Black Death* and its attendant miseries, supplemented by the *Statute of Labourers* in 1351, brought matters to a crisis.

The next bishop, Simon of Sudbury (1362-75), was destined to play an important part in the resulting climax of the *Peasants' Revolt,* in which the county of Essex was so prominent. *The Poll Tax*, which included the rustic labourers of England, fanned the flame of an ever-growing social and religious discontent. The outburst which resulted was fierce in the two counties of which we are treating. In the fourth year of Sudbury's episcopate, John Ball, the notorious ringleader, seems to have given trouble to the Essex clergy. Archbishop Langham in this year addressed a mandate to the Dean of Bocking, to warn the people of his deanery, and peremptorily to command them "not to dare to attend the preaching of the said John under pain of excommunication." He was cited to appear before him in person for the correction and safety of his soul. The Archbishop's description of him was *"Johannes Balle presbyterum se pretendens."*

There can be no doubt that Ball was a religious, as well as a social, reformer. An anti-Lollard song of the time, describing their tenets, says :—

"John Balle he foremost such things taught." [1]

The actual leadership of the rising in Essex was assumed by one calling himself " Jack Straw." The peasants of Essex, together with those of Kent and Hertfordshire, poured into London, and, after indulging in rough horse-play, in grim earnestness, demanded their emancipation. They were specially irate with Sudbury, who, by this time raised to the see of Canterbury, had boldly denounced Ball for " errors detestable to pious ears," and had described him as " *Vagabundum Johannes Balle.*" The leader of the Hertfordshire men was a certain Grindecobbe. In the course of the revolt St. Albans suffered, the Abbey buildings and barns at Sandridge, Walden, and Codicote being burnt to the ground. In Essex, Waltham Abbey was threatened, and narrowly escaped serious damage. Though the counties were "gaunt with gallows," it was not before the malcontents had assembled in London, and Wat Tyler of Kent was slain, that they were awed into a submissive acceptance of a verbal promise of redress from the King, who met the assembled forces of Essex and Hertfordshire at Highbury. Inspired by this promise, Grindecobbe set off to

[1] Wright's " Political Songs," I. p. 131.

St. Albans with a multitude from Barnet, swelled by contingents from Watford, Luton, and from surrounding villages, in order to make their demands effective. They required of the Abbot a revocation of the customs by which they considered they were held in bondage. The tramp of the peasant's feet resounded through the peaceful cloisters, and the sound of the hammer rang again as the insurgents smashed in pieces the millstones, which had been in former years placed in the floor as a token that no townsman might grind corn in the demesne of the Abbey; and they carried off the pieces as a witness to the liberties they had won. The liberties indeed were but few, viz. certain rights of pasturage, hunting and fishing, with permission to use hand-mills, together with relief from ale-tax and certain tolls within the Abbot's jurisdiction. The shattered millstones were the precursors of the blows which were to crush the Abbeys themselves, and which well-nigh succeeded in rending the Church asunder.

Grindecobbe, Cadynton, and "John the Barber," the chief local leaders, were brought before the King and Chief Justice Tresilian at the Moot Hall, Hertford, and were condemned to be hanged. The sentence was carried out in the meadows near Sopwell Lane. Meantime Sudbury had fallen a victim to the fury of the mob.

The execution of these ringleaders for a time

quelled the excesses of the insurgents, but the death of Wat Tyler had the effect of enraging the Essex contingent, who, like their comrades of St. Albans, returned to their county, vowing to renew the struggle.

The next Bishop, William Courtenay (1375–82), had no easy task in the presence of the insurrection. He had the exceptional distinction of being only twenty-eight years of age when he was made (by special dispensation of the Pope) Bishop of Hereford, from which see he was translated to London. Of his attitude towards the Lollards we shall have occasion to speak later on. He had a hand in passing the *Statute of Præmunire.* In spite of his nomination by the Pope to the see of London, he was resolute in his resistance to the Papal tax on the clergy, which he described as " an intolerable yoke." In 1380, the Bishop of Pisa acted for him in consecrating the Church of Little Saling. In 1382, the last year of his episcopate, the men of Billericay, Bocking, Fobbing, Goldhanger, Hadleigh, Havering-atte-Bower, Horndon, Mucking, Prittlewell, Rochford, Stanford, Tey Magna, and many other places in the county, were still restless. Numbers of them, as appears from the Assize and Court Rolls of Richard II., were summoned as malefactors. Executions followed, often accompanied by revolting cruelty.

In 1376 Ball came to the front again, and was arrested as an excommunicate person. He is said to have been tried in the presence of the King at St. Albans, and was executed there on July 15th, 1381. The Bishop mercifully obtained for him two days' respite, in order that he might receive ministerial counsel and comfort.

Robert Braybrooke (1382–1404), a Canon of Lichfield, was the last of the Plantagenet Bishops of London. He set his mind, in 1385, to the reformation of sundry abuses which had sprung up in connection with his Cathedral Church, notably in his attempt to suppress buying and selling, playing at ball, shooting birds, etc., within the Precincts. He also reformed the capitular body of the Cathedral, and obtained on April 26th, 1398, a writ from the King, revising the Statutes of that body on the model of those of Salisbury. He is stated to have been "a very devout and zealous pillar of the Church." He decreed St. Paul's Day to be "equal to the highest festival within his Diocese."[1] His injunctions against work on holy days crop up in the presentations in ecclesiastical courts for breach of his orders. He appears to have been sharp in the enforcement of his punishments, and to have kept his prison at Bishops Stortford occupied. In 1388 Bartholomew Kerr and John Grey, his Chaplains, gave him an annual rent of 3 qrs. of corn for the maintenance of his prisoners there.[2] He died

---

[1] "Addit. MSS.," 5833, British Museum.
[2] "London and Middlesex Archæolog. Trans.," 1870, vol. i. (3), pp. 1382, 1383.

August 24th, 1404, and was buried in St. Paul's. In the Great fire of 1666 his coffin was broken open by the fall of the roof, and a long and gruesome story is told of the exhibition of his withered remains as seen December 10th, 1675, by Henry, Lord Coleraine, and two other gentlemen, in the Chapter House of St. Paul's, where the skeleton was preserved.[1] Bishop succeeded Bishop ; but the fuel which Langland had lighted in " The Vision of Piers Plowman," and which was fanned by Ball, Tyler, Grindecobbe, and a host of others, burst out into a consuming and cleansing fire. The engines of popes, bishops, statesmen, were powerless to prevent its spread.

The " phantoms of other forms of rule" became instinct with the breath of life. The Reformation had begun.

[1] " Cole MSS.," vol. xxxii. pp. 123, 124.   British Museum.

CHAPTER XII

DEVELOPMENT OF THE MONASTIC ORDERS— HERTFORDSHIRE

" Yeve us a bushel of whete, or malt, or reye
A Goddes kichel, or a trippe of chese,
Or elles what you list, we may not chese ;
A Goddes halfpenny, or a masse penny ;
Or yeve us of your brawae if ye have eny
A dagon of your blanket, live dame,
Or suster dere (lo, here I write your name)."
CHAUCER.

BEFORE reverting to the story of Episcopal succession, it will be necessary, in order to understand the spirit of the periods discussed in the last three chapters, to review a movement concurrent with that of social unrest, and of yearning after religious liberty. From the days of the first Plantagenet onwards, there had been a gradual and ever-increasing development of the pretension of the Pope, and of the protest of the English Church against it. One of the most marked evidences of the persistence of Rome in her endeavour to subjugate the Church of England was the gradual introduction of a new system of evangelization. The Magna Charta had declared, under the inspiration of Stephen Langton, "that the Church of England shall be free, and hold her rights entire, and her liberties inviolate." Kings had been forced to respect her liberty, and Parliament upheld it by the *Statutes of Provisors* and *Praemunire*, but the Papal See was still persistent.

During all the political struggles of the period, for liberty in Church and State, the spirituality of the former was declining. The older Benedictine monasteries and priories had well-nigh lost their evangelistic influence, though it is true that the monastery was still the centre of industry and of many beneficent developments of art and learning. Agriculture and commerce too thrived under its fostering hand, but the prosperity which surrounded it was largely of the kingdom of this world. Rome, too, often winked at the abuses whilst she filled her coffers. She was at length compelled, by the force of the rising storm of indignation at her methods of exaction, to adopt new tactics. How to retain the masses of the people was the problem to be solved. The older monastic system had outgrown its purpose. Wisely seeing her opportunity, she flooded the land with new orders of evangelists, whose special duty it was to reach the people in town and village alike. England must be retained. There was doubtless a real wish, while seeking to maintain the Papal Supremacy, to revive the spirit of religion, which had so sadly decayed.

It will be necessary, in order to grasp the extent of monastic influence in the past, to give a brief survey of the chief centres of its work in the county before the new development began to make itself felt. Hitherto the Benedictines, who were not at all favourable to the preaching friars, had held the field. We propose only to summarize; too much space would be occupied in any attempt to give many details.

St. Albans Abbey, founded by Offa, was of course the dominating power. We have already referred to its history in various ways, especially in its relation to the Diocesan Bishop. It would require volumes to tell the story of its world-wide renown. We may, however, at this place suitably give an illustration of its attitude towards parochial Church matters within the area of its jurisdiction. The year of the battle of Barnet witnessed an ecclesiastical fight in that parish. The Abbot of St. Albans put an end to the strife in the following way. His decree will explain the subject of contention.

"William, by the grace of God, Abbot of the exempt Monasterie of St. Alban in the diocese of Lincoln, To all and singular persons that this present writinge shall see, reade or heare, sendeth greetings in our Lord God everlastinge, Where of longe tyme diverse strifes dissencons and debates have beene betwixt Sr Richard Bennett, now Parson of Barnett, and his p'decesso^{rs} and the parishoners

I

of Chepinge Barnett, and of East Barnett, of and for
sayinge and singinge Mattines, Masse, and Evensonge on
Sondaies and Holye dayes as well in the Church of St.
John Baptist in Chepinge Barnett, as in the Church of
our Lady in East Barnett, both churches of our juris-
dicton.   The partyes above rehearsed has comprised to
stand to our Lawe and arbitrement in this behalfe.   Wee
therefore in eschewinge and avoiding such strifes, dissencons, discords, and debates, and alsoe for norishinge
of love, peece, and charitie, betwixt the said parson, and
his parishoners, consideringe that in Chepinge Barnett is
more and gre'ater number of people, and also more
recourse of strangers than is in East Barnett, for ease of
all Christian people, and in especiall of the parishoners
above said, by this our writinge, decree and ordeyne that
from hencefoorth the s^d Sr Richard, now parson of Barnett,
and his successors shall singe and say, every Sondaie and
holye day in his owne person or by a deputie, Mattines,
Masse, and Evēsonge in the Church of St. John Baptist in
Chepinge Barnett, and there minister to the parishoners of
Chepinge Barnett, in his owne person, or by his deputie
Sacram^{ts} and Sacramentalls,   And in his owne person
Mattens, Masse, and Evēsonge in the Church of East
Barnett,   If the parson for the tyme beinge may soe attend.
And alsoe at all tymes there shall minister Sacraments
and Sacramentalls to the parishoners of the said East
Barnett.   In witnes whereof wee have made this instrument for to be try partite, the one parte for to remayne
with the parson and his successors, and the other parte
wth the parishoners afore rehearsayd, yeover under
our seale at our Mannor of Tytenhanger, the fourth day
of November, in the year of our Lord, 1471, And in the
eleaventh yeare of Kinge Edward the fourth.

> The Abbott was both patron and ordinarie,
> The Incumbent and parishoners consented,
> This is then a lawfull composicon.

It is likely that the parson before the date hereof did

never serve at Chepinge Barnett as of dutye, but not havinge a house, when the Chappell was builded for the companye of the Chauntrie and brotherhood priests did remayne at Chepinge Barnett, and sometymes served there, and sometymes at East Barnett." [1]

Doubtless, many instances of a like character could be produced from parishes over which the jurisdiction of the Abbey extended. This great foundation was valued at the Dissolution at £1027 7s. 1d. [2]

The Priory of Hertford was founded by Robert de Limesey in the time of the Conqueror. Alas! the old Priory barns were destroyed in 1896. The house was valued at £72 14s. 2d.

There were other houses of the Benedictine order scattered about the county, but they were principally Nunneries. For instance : at Cheshunt, value £14 1s.; at De la Pré, St. Albans, and at Flamstead, sometimes confused with Markgate Street. There was also a Nunnery at Rowney, near Great Munden; this House (value, £13 10s. 9d.) was subsequently occupied by a Chantry priest. At Sawbridgeworth was a cell, probably subject to Westminster.

The Nunnery at Sopwell was one of the most

---

[1] From "History of East Barnet," Rev. F. C. Cass. Extracted from "The Book of 1633" at East Barnet, in possession of the Rector, which was copied verbatim, as was certified by Sir Robert Berkeley, from a paper book which came from Chipping Barnet.

[2] The values at the Dissolution are given according to Dugdale's estimate.

important. A curious story is told of its foundation. It is said that two holy women built a rude hut here, and lived an austere life near to the spring. Geoffrey Gorham, the then Abbot, moved by their piety, in 1140, founded on the same spot a Nunnery for sixteen nuns. The famous " Boke of St. Albans," on English Heraldry and Field Sports, was written by a nun of this House, and was printed at the Abbey Press in 1486. A copy exists in the British Museum. At the Dissolution there were thirteen nuns in the house, which was valued at £40 7s. 10d.

One other Priory may be mentioned, though not then within the border of the county, yet its influence was exercised in that part of it lying on the outskirts of Bedfordshire. Besides which, it supplies an interesting illustration of the dedication of the gift of its possessions. This is the Priory, or Cell, of Markgate Street.

"In 1145 a Charter was granted to it by the Dean and Chapter of St. Paul's. The Charter was laid on the Altar by Ralph the Dean, Theodore a Canon, and Nicholas a Clerk, on the part of the Chapter, at the time of Consecration by Alexander, Bishop of Lincoln. There were also present Patrick, Bishop of Limerick; Alcelin, Dean of Lincoln; the Archdeacons of Huntingdon, Bedford, and Buckingham, the Abbot, the Prior, and many monks of St. Albans, other Canons, clerks, and laity." [1]

Before we proceed to make a few general

----

[1] *Gentleman's Magazine*, Pt. V. p. 259.

remarks on the new method of evangelization, it will be well to refer to the principal orders, viz. the Franciscans, the Dominicans (Mendicants), the Carmelites, the Augustinians. These were the four orders which received special recognition at the Council of Lyons (1274), when it had become necessary to regulate the various bodies which by this time had sprung up in great numbers. These four orders possessed religious houses in several parts of the county.

The Franciscans (Grey Friars, or Minorites) held their first Chapter in England about 1245. They set up a small House at Ware, consisting of five Brethren.

The Dominicans [1] (Black Friars) were introduced into England in 1221. They, too, had one house in the county, at King's Langley, founded by Roger Hele, 1308, and endowed by Edward II., as a place "where Mass should be daily said for ever, for the souls of himself and his antecessors." He further augmented his benefaction, ten years later, by providing for seventy Masses, as a votive offering for his preservation when in danger. It must have been rather a bitter pill for my lord Abbot of St. Albans, who was directed to pay the sum to the Prior, "deducting the same from the annual amount the Abbots were accustomed to pay to the Crown." [2] Further benefactions of wood and lands were made later, together with "the right of taking toll on all

---

[1] Domini Canes, "watch-dogs of the Lord."
[2] *Vide* Cussans' "History of Herts under Langley Regis."

corn ground at the King's mill on the river Gade."
At the Dissolution it was one of the richest of the
Dominican Priories in England, being valued at
£122 4s. This was, no doubt, due to the fact that
it was directly under the patronage of Edward II.,
Edward III., and Richard II., King's Langley
having a royal residence during Plantagenet times.

The Carmelites (White Friars) held their first
Chapter in England in 1245. They possessed a
House at Hitchin, founded in 1316; value,
£4 9s. 4d.

The Augustinian Canons Regular, who came
to this country in the reign of Henry I., had two
locations in Hertfordshire, one at Little Wymondley,
the other at Royston. The Austins knew how to
select attractive sites; the Priory at Wymondley,
is described as—

"almost surrounded with a moat, situated upon the side
of a small hill, encompassed with near four hundred acres
of rich meadow, pasture, and arable land enclosed to
it, with a very fair orchard and garden, yielding the best
sort of fruit. The House is supplied from a conduit, with
sufficient water to turn the spit in the kitchen upon all
occasions." [1]

This Priory was founded in the reign of
Henry III. by Richard de Argentine. Valued
at the Dissolution at £37 10s. 6d. Royston
Priory was founded in 1180, by Eustace de la
Mere. Till the time of Bishop Fitz-James (1509)

---

[1] Chauncy's "Herts," p. 361.

the *Bangor use* had been observed here. The
Prior at this time presented a petition to him to
allow the *Use of Sarum*, alleging that the *Bangor
Use* was imperfect, that the books were worn out
and torn, and that "he was loth to bear the charge
of changing unless for a better." The petition was
granted. On July 12th, 1227, Walter Gray, Archbishop of York, granted an indulgence of thirteen
days to as many as should contribute to the support
of the brethren.

A remarkably interesting cave, which has
puzzled antiquaries, exists here. There seems to
be but little doubt that it was used in mediæval
times, as a Christian Oratory, and was possibly
attached to a Hermitage.

Among other orders were the Gilbertines, of
English origin, who set up a house at Hitchin.

There were several Hospitals, *e.g.* at Baldock,
Berkhamsted, Anstey, Clothall, Royston, and at
De La Pré, St. Albans, for leprous Nuns. The
Knights Templars had a Preceptory at Temple
Disney, which afterwards passed to the Knights
Hospitallers, who possessed a Hospice at Standon.

An estimate of the earlier work of the Friars,
in the Diocese of Lincoln at least, may be best
gathered from the action and words of a prelate,
who was thoroughly in earnest in reforming the
abuses which had grown up. We refer to Bishop
Grosseteste. Describing his method of Visitation
he says—

"When clergy and people were assembled, I myself was accustomed to preach the word of God to the clergy, and some Friar, either Preacher (Dominican) or Minorite (Franciscan), to the people. At the same time four friars were employed in hearing confessions and enjoining penances."

His first Visitation (to which this refers) appears to have been made in each Deanery. His opinion of the work of the Dominicans and Franciscans may be gathered from a letter which he addressed to the Pope, in which he says—

"O, if your holiness could only see with what devotion and humility the people flock together to hear from them the word of life and to make confession of their sins, and how much advantage the clergy and religion have derived from the imitation of their example, your Holiness would certainly say the 'people who walked in darkness have seen a great light.'"

It need hardly be said that the secular clergy were up in arms against his patronage and employment of the mendicant orders, whom they regarded as intruders, and they gave but scant welcome to the members of the orders who accompanied him on his Visitation tours in the several deaneries of the diocese.

Some idea of the territorial and ecclesiastical influence of the Monastic Orders, together with other religious corporations, may be gathered from the record of their custom of appropriating the great tithes of the parishes where they held lands or manors. The instances thus recorded have reference to various Vicarages in the county which were mulcted for the benefit of the Orders.

St. Albans, of course, heads the list, and received the great tithes of 17 Benefices. The Abbey of Colchester, 1 ; Ashridge (Bonhommes), 1 ; Blackmore, 1 ; Charterhouse, 1 ; Elsing Spital (now London Hospital), 1 ; Elstow, 1 ; Priory of the Holy Trinity, London, 1 ; Hertford, 1 ; King's Langley, 1 ; the Knights of St. John of Jerusalem, 3 ; Merton Priory, 1 ; Ramsey Abbey, 1 ; Sheen, 1 ; Westminster Abbey, 2 ; Wymondley, 1. Pensions, which varied in amount, were also granted to 5 other Abbeys or Priories. Besides these, the following were appropriation of parochial tithes : the Bishop of London, 1 ; Dean and Chapter of Lincoln, 1 ; Dean and Chapter of St. Paul's, 3 ; the Precentor of St. Paul's, 1 ; the Treasurer of St. Paul's, 4. It will thus be seen that many benefices lost the great tithes, and others suffered to some extent.

In this instance, as in others, abuses sprang up round the system by which the Friars worked, and though their custom of going out into the highways and bye-ways was right in principle, yet some of the inherent defects of the monastic system are apparent. We shall have something more to say of their methods of work in the next chapter.

CHAPTER XIII

DEVELOPMENT OF THE MONASTIC ORDERS— ESSEX

> "The old order changeth,
> Yielding place to new,
> And God fulfils Himself in many ways."
> TENNYSON.
>
> "Activity and ubiquity."
> F. S. STEVENSON.

THE Religious Houses were very numerous in Essex, where the old order of the Benedictines had been strongly established from early times. It will be well to enumerate their centres.

The glory of Waltham, second only to St. Albans in renown, had shone from the days of Canute. It was regulated by Benedictine rule till the time of its revival in the reign of Henry II., when it was handed to the Augustinians. Its value at the Dissolution was £1079 per annum.[1]

The Abbey of St. John Baptist at Colchester stood next in order of importance. It was founded (1097) by Eudo, completed by his nephew in 1104,

---

[1] Dugdale's figures are those usually quoted.

and consecrated by Maurice, Bishop of London.
Value, £523 17s. 6d. The Priory of Saffron
Walden was founded in 1146 by the first Earl of
Essex of the house of the Mandevilles. In 1191
it was raised to the rank of an Abbey. Value,
£406 15s. 11d. Hatfield Regis, a Priory for nine
monks, founded by Aubrey de Vere in 1135. Value,
£122 13s. 2d. At Hatfield Peveril was a still
earlier house, reputed to have been founded at the
Conquest. It was afterwards turned into a regular
Benedictine Priory, as a cell to St. Albans, with a
Prior and four monks. Value, £83 19s. 7d. The
Priory of Earl's Colne was founded in 1100 by
Aubrey, Earl of Guisnes. It was subject to Abingdon, and had a Prior and ten monks. Value,
£175 14s. 8d.

The following were the chief of the Benedictine
Nunneries.

Barking Abbey, founded (670) by Erconwald,
Bishop of London, who appointed his sister Ethel-
burga as the first Abbess. Value, £862 12s. 5d.
This Convent is said to have had a cell at
Mucking. Castle Hedingham, for five nuns, was
established before 1190 by the first Earl of Oxford.
Value, £29 12s. 10d. Wykes (or Wix) had a
small Nunnery, founded by Walter Mascherell in
the reign of Henry I.

As in the case of Hertfordshire, let us now
glance to the later orders, who were the agents of
the Revival.

The Franciscans had one small house at
Colchester, founded in 1325. The Dominicans
settled at Moulsham, near Chelmsford. Value,
£9 6s. 5d. The Carmelites were located at Maldon
in 1292. This house is said to have been founded
by Richard of Gravesend, Bishop of London. Value,
£1 6s. 8d. The Augustinian Regulars were the most
numerous of the mediæval orders working in this
county. The ancient Abbey of Waltham, after
some hundreds of years of Benedictine rule, passed
into their hands.

Henry II. had vowed that he would found an
Abbey in honour of Thomas à Becket, but instead
of doing so, he turned out the Benedictines from
Waltham, and put Augustine Regulars in their place.
He chose four from St. Osyth, six from Cirencester, and six from Oseney, installing them with
great ceremony under a Prior. Ten years later
the Prior was raised to the dignity of a mitred
Abbot. The gross income at the Dissolution was
£1079 12s. 1d.

The next Priory in point of importance was
that of St. Botolph, Colchester, established there
by Ernulph in the twelfth century. It is believed
to have been the first house founded in England
for the Austin Canons Regular, and, if so, the date
of the foundation would be about 1109. Value,
£113 12s. 8d.

St. Osyth Priory stood on the site of an early
Nunnery, founded about the middle of the seventh

century, and afterwards destroyed.   Richard de
Belmeis built a House here for the Austin Canons
in the reign of Henry I.   It grew into considerable importance, and was valued at the Dissolution at £758 5s. 8d.

The Priory of Little Dunmow was founded in
1104 for a Prior and ten monks.   The memory of
an institution of one of its benefactors is still kept
up by the celebrated custom of the " Dunmow
Flitch."   The holy friars would doubtless be a little
surprised at the modern revel, and would probably
use some stirring language to the Bank-holiday
pilgrims who assemble in their thousands at the
now famous Annual Trial.   Value, £150 3s. 4d.

The Priory of St. Lawrence at Blackmore was
set up by Adam and Jordan de Samford, in the
reign of Henry II.   It passed to Cardinal Wolsey
for the purpose of the endowment of his College
at Oxford.   When he fell, the income was transferred to the Canons of Waltham.

The history of the Priory of Blackmore throws
some interesting light on the relation of a Priory
church to the parish.   The Prior and Canons, not
having appointed a priest for the cure of souls,
Newcourt informs us that the parishioners made
complaint of the omission.   Ralph of Baldock,
Bishop of London, settled the question at a meeting
at the Palace of Stepney in 1309, in the following
way, viz. :—

'on the behalf of the religious that they should cause

divine offices to be performed at the altar, in the body of the Church, which they asserted to be their own, on Sundays and Holy-days, after such a manner as is mentioned in the Agreement, by fit ministers, by them to be presented to the Bishop, and on the behalf of the parishioners that at their own charge they should find one missal, one chalice, one vestment, and several other things therein specified, requisite for the celebrating of Mass, as are found by parishioners in other parishes." [1]

Woodham Ferrers possessed a hermitage of the same order.

Berden owned a small House, which eventually became subject to Walden. Value, £29 6s. 4d. Tiptree Priory, like that of Blackmore, had its revenue appropriated for the collegiate scheme of Wolsey. It was afterwards granted in exchange to the Knights Hospitallers. The Priory of Leighs, founded by Sir Ralph Gernon in 1229, possessed some fine buildings. At the Dissolution there were ten *Religious*, and the value was £141 11s. 8d. Bicknacre cell, near Danbury, belonged to the same order. Thoby was founded by the Capra family in 1141. Value, £75 6s. 10d. Tremhall, (or Trenchale) was valued at £70 19s. 3d.

The Cistercians (from Citeaux in Normandy) now demand our attention.

Little Coggeshall, founded in 1142, was one of their important centres. Value, £251 2s.

Stratford Langthorne was also one of their locations; it was founded in 1134 by William

---

[1] *Essex Review*, vol. viii., No. 30. 1899.

Montfichet for fifteen monks. The frequent floods caused this House to fall into disrepair, and the monks were obliged to seek temporary refuge at Great Burstead, where they held lands till the Dissolution. Value, £511 6s. 3d.

Tiltey Priory was a Cistercian House, founded by Maurice Fitz Geoffrey in 1153. There were seven monks at the Dissolution. Value, £177 9s. 4d. [1]

The Premonstratensians named from Premonstre' (Latine *Premonstratum*, in Picardy) fixed their House first at Great Parndon, whence they removed to Beleigh, where Robert de Mantell founded an Abbey in 1180. Value, £157 16s. 11d.

The Clugniacs settled at three places in the county.

Prittlewell was founded *temp*. Henry II., and was subject to the Abbey of Lewes. Seven monks. Value, £155 11s. 2d. The cell of Stanesgate, in the Parish of Steeple, was also subject to Lewes. Value, £43 8s. 6d. After Wolsey's fall it was granted to the Knights of St. John of Jerusalem by way of an exchange. The Priory of Little Horkesley, founded *cir.* 1142, was dependent on Thetford. Value, £27 7s. 1d.

The Crouched (Crutched) had a small settlement at Colchester, founded 1244. Value, £7 7s. 8d.

Amongst the Houses accounted as Alien, both

---

[1] Its Seal is now in the possession of St. John's College, Cambridge. It bears the legend, " *Sigillum Commune Monasterii Beatæ Mariæ de Tyltey*."

in origin and government, we may reckon Horn-church, which was subject to the Hospital of Monte Jovis in Savoy. In 1245 this house was attached to the Savoy Chapel in London. Eventually it was bought by William of Wykeham, and given by him towards the endowment of New College, Oxford, in 1380.

The house at West Mersea was subject to St. Ouen at Rouen. At the suppression, its endowment was granted to Archbishop Chicheley for his College at Higham Ferrers in Northants. Takeley was dependent on St. Valery, Picardy. The revenues were also applied to New College. Writtle was likewise alien, and its revenues too were purchased and applied to New College. Pan-field was subject to St. Stephen, at Caen.

Hospitals connected with the various orders were scattered up and down the county, as for instance at Barking, for lepers, value, £21 13s. 4d.; Bocking; Colchester, for lepers; Layer Marney, a Warden and two priests; Waltham, Walthamstow. The Hospital of Newport (Birchanger) was held under the peculiar jurisdiction of the Dean of St. Martin's, London. Value, £31 13s. 11d.

There were also several Colleges, consisting of a few Priests living in community, generally under Augustinian rule. These Colleges, to which chantries were sometimes attached, were ordinarily centres both of teaching and of preaching, and were supplementary, though usually subordinate to the existing Parish Churches. They were to be found at Halstead; and at Pleshy, which, at the suppression, had two Clerks and two choristers, and was valued at £143 3s. 10d. At Bishops Stortford was a College of secular priests, governed by a Provost. It was founded by Ralph of Stratford, Bishop of London.

The Knights Templars had a Commandery at Temple Cressing, founded circ. 1150. It came afterwards into the hands of the Hospitallers, and eventually fell to the Crown.

At Little Maplestead is the smallest of the four round churches. It was built for the Hospitallers in 1185, and was dedicated to St. John Baptist.

With this network of the monastic influence covering the county, it is not surprising to find that the custom of appropriation was rife on all sides. The following figures, attached to the names of the various religious Houses both within and without the county, will give a fairly accurate estimate of the number of Essex benefices fleeced of their tithes by the system of appropriation.

The Dean and Chapter of St. Paul's, 10; Prebendary of the same, 1; Westminster Abbey, 10; St. Osyth, 10; Colne, 7; Stoke by Clare, 6; Barking, 6; Waltham Abbey, 5; Stratford, 5; Saffron Walden, 5; Colchester (St. John Baptist), 5; Charterhouse, 5; Little Dunmow, 4; The Knights of St. John of Jerusalem, 4; Prittlewell, 4; Beleigh, 3; Hatfield Regis, 3; Colchester

(St. Botolph), 2 ; Coggeshall, 2 ; Castle Hedingham, 2 ; Thetford, 2 ; Higham Ferrers, 2 ; Holy Trinity, London, 2 ; Lesnes, Kent, 2 ; Blackmore, 2. The following Abbeys or Priories each appropriated one benefice, viz. Abingdon, Berden, Caldwell, Bromley, Hastings, Repton, Stanesgate, Sion College, Latton, Sheen, Tiptree, Tremhall, Bury St. Edmunds, Butley, Battle Abbey, Brusyard, Leighs, Hatfield Peveril, St. Bartholomew's, Clerkenwell ; London, Cobham College, Barnwell. The Bishop of London and the Prior of Horkesley shared the great tithes of one benefice between them. The Bishop of Norwich, a Prebendary of Wells, and the Archdeacon of Colchester, held each the great tithes of one benefice.

Altogether there were in the county about 138 cases of appropriation by various ecclesiastical corporations. Besides these there were 18 benefices which paid pensions, varying in amount, to sundry ecclesiastical appropriators.

It can readily be imagined therefore that the influence of the monastic and mendicant orders was great in these counties.

These latter orders were alien in their origin, though they became naturalized. They came to the country fired with the zeal and success of their great founders on the continent. They were the organized children of Rome's reluctant assent to new methods. The older order of Benedictines, as we have seen, viewed their advent with much disfavour, whilst the parish priests were jealous of their intrusion and influence. Like the Lollards, and the brotherhood of Wesley in later days, "the world was their parish."

A curious light is thrown on the attitude of the older orders and parish priests towards the new mendicants, in the carvings of the great monasteries, and of some parish churches. At Tring, on the corbels of the spandrils, the friars are depicted as pigs, foxes, or monkeys. One of these corbels represents a pig with a friar's cowl, another a fox running off with a goose, indicating the cunning of the friar and the stupidity of the people. Another exhibits a monkey in a cowl, with a bottle in one hand and a book in the other, while on another the legend of St. George and the dragon is reversed—the dragon is killing St. George. Similar carvings are to be seen on the corbels which support the nave roof of Abbot's Langley Church, which was commenced during the time of Abbot John de la Moote of St. Albans, the friars being represented in all sorts of grotesque attitudes.

In Castle Hedingham Church there are, or were, carved *Misereres*, and amongst them a grotesque representation of the devil carrying away a monk, whom he has slung over his shoulder and holds by the heel.

In spite, however, of the scorn with which their more lordly and dignified predecessors in the monastic system regarded the friars, they supplied a

need of the times, erroneous as were some of their
methods and doctrines. They aimed first at the
masses, though, like the Celtic missionaries of old,
they were not afraid to attack the castle and the
court. The slum, the market, the village street,
the abbey or cathedral precincts, the leper hospital,
the universities themselves, were all alike to them.
They had to bear a new witness to the old faith,
to learning as opposed to ignorance, to plainness
as an answer to pomp. Their simplicity of dress,
their unshod feet, their ascetic lives, their words
of burning sympathy with the downtrodden masses,
soon won for them an attentive hearing wherever
they went. The splendour of the old abbeys soon
paled before the men who were content to dwell
in lowlier piles, and had literally to beg their bread
from day to day.

Matthew Paris tells us that "the friar carried
a small super-altar with him, which he laid on a
wooden table, and said mass in private houses." [1]
This custom alone opened the way to endless
abuses which lent themselves to extortion, and
eventually forced the Bishops to act.

For a time, at least, they revived the voluntary
offerings of the people for a nobler purpose than
to feed, through the medium of the abbot and
bishop, the coffers of the Roman see. There was
one man pre-eminently who knew how to use them
for England's Church, Robert Grosseteste. He

[1] "Hist. Major," p. 419, ed. 1640.

allowed them "to drive, whilst he held the reins,"
and it is to him perhaps more largely than to any
man that we owe their best influences in their
purest days. Alas! like their predecessors, though
from different causes, the evil became manifestly
mingled with the good. The Benedictines were
rich, the friars were poor, and they resorted
when the first years of the blush of enthusiasm
were over, to all sorts of questionable ways to eke
out their pittance. They played at length their
part "to the gallery," and by trickery and cajolery
forfeited the good will and respect of the people,
and while for a time they postponed the decisive
climax of Reformation, they were unconsciously
bringing it about. Their liberty grew rapidly into
license, and the bishops, who stood abashed before
their fervour, had at length to lament their excesses;
but alas! too late.

It would exceed our space to describe at any
length or in detail the special features of the work
of each order, but their united influence on the
two counties, especially on Essex, permeated their
whole area. The Franciscan order was the most
learned. The Dominicans were the most active,
and to them especially may be traced the extension
of the *cult* of the Blessed Virgin. The Cistercians
were the least cultivated, and the simplest in their
habits and modes of worship. The rules of the
Augustinians were the least severe; this order
was the most numerous of the four, their canons

(together with the military rules) were the basis
of the religious discipline of both the Knights
Templars, and of their successors, the Hospitallers.

The old order of Benedictines was the most
numerous in Hertfordshire, the new Augustinians
in Essex. The Gilbertines, the only purely English
order, possessed but one house in the borders of
the present diocese, viz. at Hitchin. The friars
have gone, but the Church has found the necessity
of supplying their place to some extent by the
Diocesan and Itinerant Missioners of to-day.

CHAPTER XIV

DAWN OF THE REFORMATION—HERTFORDSHIRE AND ESSEX

> " ' Pilgrimages ? '
> ' Drink, bagpipes, revelling, devil's- dances, vice.
> The poor man's money gone to fat the friar.'
> ' Bread—
> Bread left after the blessing ? ' how they stared,
> That was their main test-question—glared at me !
> ' He veil'd Himself in flesh, and now He veils
> His flesh in bread, body and bread together.'
> Then rose the howl of all the cassock'd wolves,
> ' No bread, no bread. God's body ! ' Archbishop, Bishop,
> Priors, Canons, Friars, bellringers, Parish-clerks—
> ' No bread, no bread ! '—' Authority of the Church,
> Power of the keys ! '—Then I, God help me, I
> So mock'd, so spurn'd, so baited two whole days—
> I lost myself and fell from evenness,
> And rail'd at all the Popes. . . .
> Well—God pardon all—
> Me, them, and all the world."
> TENNYSON, " Sir John Oldcastle."

THE issues of the Plantagenet period were powerful and far-reaching. We regard it as the dawn of the Reformation, in spite of the vigorous effort of Rome to keep her hold on the nation by the new development of the

monastic system. The concurrent struggle for
liberty in Church and State was the birth-throe
of the Reformation. With the close of the Plantagenet period in 1399 we may fairly assert that
the Reformation had begun. It was the work of
an era, not of a reign nor even of a dynasty. The
Bible in English gradually rose in the popular mind
above the *Mass* in Latin. The mingled blood of
the Lollard and the villein was the seed of reform.
Wicliffe shook England, as Luther in later times
shook the world. The Reformation was the child
of discontent, with greedy popes and lustful kings
for its unconscious nurses. The pen of Chaucer
as "he flouted the wallet of pardons hot from
Rome," and of Langland as he sang his breezy
lays, roused a new spirit of freedom. The brokers
of Rome, with their cold calculations and worse than
Jewish exactions, were, in disguise, the saviours
of the Church and the nation. Lordly abbot and
courtly prioress, though they knew it not, were
ringing the death-knell of their order. The hatred
of the regulars and seculars, the impudence and
trickery of the begging friars, were slowly clearing
openings for the new light which was to dawn on
the land darkened with superstition and writhing
under oppression. The Statutes of *Provisors* and
Praemunire were paving the way for the liberation
from the shackles which Rome had forged. The
Black Death had been interpreted as a messenger
of judgment. Grindecobbe in Hertfordshire, Tyler

in Essex, and John Ball in both counties were the rough agents of a new mission of emancipation in the social life, as Wicliffe and Chaucer had been in the world of the Church and of letters.

The fire of reform was well alight in the days of Bishop John Bokyngham of Lincoln, and of Courtenay of London, and all the engines of Rome could not put it out. We are not so much concerned with the social as with the religious aspect of the conflagration.

The dictum of Wicliffe that "dominion depends on grace" was wrested by the leaders of religious and social discontent to the elevation of licensed liberty of conscience. His "poor preachers" succeeded in exposing the tricks of the friars, and the arrogance of the Pope, before they were silenced by the Council of London in 1382, at which Wicliffe was summoned to appear; and his Bible, together with his shower of tracts, much as we may disagree with some of them, spread light throughout the land. His death gave sanctity to his teaching, and the Lollards, of whom he was the foster-father if not the sire, spread their distorted views both of his wholesome and of his strange doctrines far and wide.

Some, like Neander, assert "that before Wicliffe came upon the public stage John Ball had already created a sensation by his preaching."[1]

---

[1] Ball spoke of himself as "sometime of St. Mary Priest of York, now of Colchester." *Vide* Stow's "Annals," p. 294.

The two counties bear some witness to the early character of the movement. In a former chapter we have referred to the successive bishops of the two sees in the general exercise of their office. We renew the chronological order of their succession, and indicate their attitude more especially towards the struggle for religious freedom.

John Bokyngham (1363–98) witnessed, as Bishop of Lincoln, the fury of the storm in the midland counties. The words of his inhibition of one John of Swynderby show what his feeling was towards the followers of Wicliffe. He described him as—

"a man of wolfish capacity, cloaked under sheep-like simplicity, running about in a wandering fashion through various places, assuming the office of preaching without authority, with presumptious temerity, without obtaining a licence, saying many things which are erroneous and contrary to Catholic faith against the state and condition of the Roman Pontiff and other prelates to the opprobrium of the whole clergy."[1]

How many fell under the Bishop's wrath in Hertfordshire it is impossible to say, but William Bilche of Aldbury, Stephen Truebody of Codicote, and William Stable of St. Albans, who, together with one John Coltman of Clavering in Essex, stood accused of heresy—are samples of the number. Bokyngham won the commendation of the Archbishop of Canterbury for his indefatigable zeal against the anti-Christ (Wicliffe) and his adherents.

[1] Wilkins quoted by Lechler in "John Wicliffe and his Precursors," ed. 1884, p. 399.

The authorities of the Abbey of St. Albans were active in the suppression of heresy, a synod being held there in 1382 to consider the steps to be taken against the Lollards.

Henry Beaufort (1398–1405) succeeded, on the retirement of Bokyngham to Canterbury, where he died as a monk. Beaufort was a son of John of Gaunt, and half brother to Henry IV. As a Cardinal of Rome he was no friend to the new doctrine in Church or State. In spite of Shakespeare's dark picture of him he was a great man, but he was no match for John Moot, 31st Abbot of St. Albans, in the old quarrel between the Abbey and the See. On the death of the Duke of Lancaster notice was given to the Abbot that the Bishop would perform the obsequies as the Duke's body passed on its way through St. Albans for burial. The Abbot took the precaution to obtain a letter from the King directing—

"That the Bishop, by his access to the monastery or his behaviour therein, would not do anything to derogate, or injure the rights and privileges of that place, of which his royal progenitors had been founders, and if he should obtain leave to do anything in the monastery, that he would give a special letter of indemnification to the monks."

The Abbot kept the body waiting while indemnity was obtained, but the Bishop, having no seal of Lincoln with him, affixed the seal of the Bishop of London, who was present. The service proceeded, and the day after, the whole monastery attended the funeral procession as far as to Barnet, on its way to London.

It was during Beaufort's episcopate (circ. 1400) that John de Montacute, Earl of Salisbury, caused all the images erected by his predecessor in the manor or chapel of Shenley " to be taken down and hidden away." The said Earl was beheaded at Cirencester the same year.[1]

Philip of Repyndon[2] (Repton) (1405–20), Canon of St. Mary de Pratis, Leicester, comes next; as Chancellor of Oxford, and probably also from his near residence to Lutterworth, he had fallen under the influence of the new teaching. He asserted in a sermon on the feast of Corpus Christi that Wicliffe "was a thoroughly sound and orthodox teacher, and had at all times set forth the doctrine of the universal church concerning the sacrament of the Altar," and referred to Wicliffe's itinerants as "holy priests."[3] His vigorous acceptance of the Lollard tenets was of short duration. In company with Nicholas Herford and John Asheton, he had publicly recanted at St. Paul's Cross (1382), and received the see of Lincoln and a Cardinal's hat as his reward. Doubtless he kept his hand firmly on " the poor preachers " of his former faith, but though the Council of Constance had ordered the remains

1 Walsingham, " Hist. Anglicana," II. p. 204.
2 " Fasciculi Zinianorum," pp. 297–312.
3 Lechler's " Wicliffe " trans. Lorimer, ed. 1884, p. 393.

of Wicliffe to be exhumed and burnt, he was
reluctant to obey, and left his successor in the see
to fulfil the order. Repyndon's episcopate witnessed
the celebrated trial and condemnation of Sir John
Oldcastle (Lord Cobham), once Sheriff of Hertfordshire. His soliloquy, while wandering amongst
the fastnesses of the Welsh mountains, is well
known to lovers of Tennyson, and gives a graphic
description of the thoughts and actions of the times.

A rich brewer of Dunstable, one Murle by
name, jealous of the *largesse* of the monks in the
shape of beer, was one of the local ringleaders of a
movement against the Abbey, and joined a force
under Sir John Oldcastle, who is said to have
promised to have him knighted on the field of battle
and to give him the Abbey lands as his share of
the spoils. Sir John was burnt (1417), and the rich
brewer was subsequently exalted to the gallows
instead. After his escape from the Tower and
before his re-capture in Wales, Sir John is reported
to have taken shelter in one of the Abbey buildings, having left behind him the traces of his
opinions by defacing and mutilating some of the
religious books, "by cutting off the heads of the
Virgin and the saints."

A picturesque light is thrown, by Repyndon,
on the splendour of "the progress" of a mediæval
Bishop. When Henry IV. visited the Abbey of
Bardney, August 22nd, 1406, Repyndon went
to see him. The account is thus recorded :—

"Immediately after noon on Sunday came our venerable lord, the Bishop of Lincoln, from Lincoln on horseback, with a train of 24 horses, and my lord Abbot received him, with his retinue, and in his habit, as was becoming, with some 8 or 10 of the brethren, the rest not knowing of the arrival of so great a prince, and led him honourably as far as the abbot's gate, near the oak, and having explained the business on which he had come, he returned to the place whence he came."[1]

The Bishop's business may have been connected with a writ[2] which he had received from the King earlier in the year ordering him to "apprehend and imprison the fortune-tellers, magicians, enchanters, necromancers, and pythons"[3] (were these names applied to the Wicliffites?) who troubled the diocese. Repyndon resigned his see in 1420.

His successor Richard Flemyng (1420–31), like his predecessor, was in his earlier days favourable to the Lollards. He is reported after he was consecrated Bishop to have met argument with argument by appointing a body of teachers to combat the followers of Wicliffe. The papal authority was in the end, too strong for him, and he became the tool of the persecutors. It is not to his credit that he carried out the decree of the Council of Constance, which ordered the remains of Wicliffe to be dug up and burned. His ashes

---

[1] *Vide* Marratt's "Hist. Lincolnshire," vol. iv.
[2] Rymer's "Fœdera," vol. viii. p. 427.
[3] *Vide* Hearne's Appendix to Leland's "Collectanea."

were then cast into the Swift, which flowed by the Rectory of Lutterworth, and so carried out to sea. As old Fuller remarks, "the ashes of Wicliffe are the emblem of his doctrine, which is now dispersed all the world over." *The Statute of Heresy*, that engine of religious bloodshed, availed for a time, and crushed the activity of the reformers, but the old spirit was still alive. The Bishop, like most of his predecessors, attempted to revive the old claim on the allegiance of the Abbot, and received the same steadfast refusal. A former grievance about the right of pasturage in the Abbot's woods and roads cropped up again, only to be dismissed with a temporizing promise that it should be considered on the production of security against encroachment. Abbot John of Wheathampstead exercised episcopal functions to the exclusion of my lord of Lincoln, in summoning the secular Clergy of his jurisdiction to a Synod, at St. Peters; St. Albans, 1427, when he preached a sermon, condemning the Lollard books. The Abbot's jurisdiction now consisted of 9 Rectories and 28 Vicarages, mostly within the borders of the county. His visitation questions at the Synod related to the subjects of residence, strange preachers, and the existence in the parishes of persons suspected of heretical opinions and of possessing books written in the vulgar tongue. This was aimed at the Lollards. Three persons were suspected and accused. The explanation of two of them satisfied

the Abbot, but William Redhead, a maltster of
Barnet, "infected with the noxious doctrine of the
rector of Tatarigg," confessed, and was sentenced—

"that he should once every year for seven years visit the
martyr's tomb, and approach the same barefoot, and passing through the middle of the choir, should offer on the
great altar a wax candle of one pound weight ; that for
three days succeeding every such visit he should pass
round the Churchyard, every day, in front of a procession,
stripped of his garments, and that at his return to his
parish church he should approach the great altar, bearing
in his hand a wax candle, and present the same on the
altar with bended knees. As a final remission of this
offence, it was enjoined him that he should bring the said
book to the great Cross, and then, with some dry faggot-
wood, consume the same to ashes."

It is conjectured that the book was a Lollard
tract. The Synod dispersed with a caution
against the heretics, and, says John of Amersham
(the chronicler), the Abbot, in tears, closed the Synod,
saying, " *Quis cohibet lacrymas, quis genas non genit
udas ; Cum Lollardinam fectam plus Tigride Sœvam
cernit, et infanam mentem vitam que prophanam* " ?

Of the next Bishop, William Grey (1431–36),
but little can be said to illustrate our present
subject, beyond the fact that he was at variance
with the Dean and Chapter, and had a quarrel
with the Pope about the appointment of a relative
to the Archdeaconry of Northampton, but by
winning the day he encouraged the English
Episcopate to stand more firmly for their rights.

William Alnwick (1436–49) followed. The

disputes with his cathedral body, together with his attendance upon the King, took up most of his time. If we may judge by his sharpness towards heresy in the Diocese of Norwich, from which he had been translated, he was no friend to the Lollards. Marmaduke Lumley (1450–51) ruled for barely a year.

John Chedworth (1452–71) succeeded. His registers bear evidence of the widespread increase of "heresy." As a type of the growing spirit of movement we may quote a few cases. We find that William and Richard Sparke, amongst others, were presented for objection to image worship. Their defence was "Rather man whose extended arms represent a cross as the true image of God ought to be worshipped. Pilgrimages were of no avail. A child born of baptized parents need not be baptized ; the baptism of the parent suffices. Lay persons are not called upon to fast. The dead need not be buried in consecrated ground. The priest has no more power to make the Body of Christ than he has to make straws or reeds. Confession to a priest is needless. Prayer need not be offered in Churches, but is equally valuable everywhere. Consent alone constitutes matrimony. Extreme unction, vulgarly called 'gresying,' only makes a man more dirty and in worse condition. The Pope is Antichrist, and the priests his scholars." [1] Probably Wicliffe would have been as much sur-

---

[1] Perry, "Diocesan History of Lincoln," S.P.C.K., 1897, p. 192.

prised at the development of his teaching, as Wesley might be to-day at the extension of his movement.

Hertfordshire figures in the Bishop's Register, in the person of Thomas Hake of Hertford, who admits that he was in league with " necromancers and heretics." The great offence of the time appears to have been the possession of books on religious subjects, written in English. Chedworth, backed by the strong arm of the law, could not succeed in repressing the tide of change now approaching its flood.

Thomas Rotherham (1472–80) was raised to the see from Rochester. His civil duties were more to his mind than those of his episcopal office, and his opinions and feelings were not favourable to the Lollard party.

John Russell (1480–94) was the last Bishop of Lincoln under the reign of the houses of York and Lancaster. He probably found that persecution was of little avail in quelling the new forces which were growing so strong against the received traditions of the Church, and contented himself with writing a thesis designed to unmask and confute the heretics. It failed in its purpose. The rays of the sun of light and liberty were already streaking the sky with the glow of dawn.

The story of the Bishops of London who ruled during the period of which we are now speaking is much the same as of those who presided over the see of Lincoln.

Robert Braybrooke (1382–1404) was still Bishop of London when the last of the Plantagenet kings passed away and the houses of York and Lancaster became ascendant. We have already said something of Bishop Braybrooke's career. He was not without trouble in the matter of the new opinions. So bold had the Lollards become that they nailed a statement of the principal tenets of their creed on one of the doors of St. Paul's. That he was active in attempting to root out the "heretics" we may infer from the fact that his prison at Bishops Stortford had its occupants in 1382, when Bartholomew Ker and John Grey, his chaplains, "gave the Bishop an annual rent of three qrs. of corn for the maintenance of his prisoners"[1] there. Braybrooke was not indifferent to the details of diocesan life. There had been a great controversy of many years standing between the Bishops of London, the Abbots of St. Albans, and the Priors of Hertford, about the tithe of corn and hay in some fields lying near Amwell and Broxbourne. The Bishop "composed and agreed" the contending parties.[2] We may assume from this that he was a man of tact, when we remember that Bishops, Abbots, and Priors were not easily appeased.

Roger Walden next followed (1405–6), but in his episcopate of a year, made no impression in

---

[1] *London and Middlesex Archæolog. Trans.*, vol. i. (3), 1870, pp. 1382, 1383.

[2] Newcourt Repm., vol. i. p. 809.

the Diocese as Bishop, though he may have done so locally as an Essex Rector. In 1391 he held the Rectory of Fordham, which he subsequently exchanged for that of St. Andrew's, Holborn.[1]

Nicholas Bubwyth (1406–7) had an equally short and uneventful rule. His name, however, still lives in Wells, where, as once its Bishop, he founded almshouses. He was one of the representatives of the English Church at the Council of Constance, and he was no friend to Wicliffe.

The light of liberty was gradually spreading. Essex not only contributed to its glow by its earnest, though turbulent reformer, John Ball, but by many others of its laity and clergy who adhered to the Lollard tenets. We need only instance the martyrdom of John Beckett, of Pattiswick, Thomas Bagley Vicar of Manuden, Richard Wicke, a priest, as typical examples of the victims of the fury of the time.

Bishops Stortford still figured in connection with the Bishops of London during the persecution; though their baronial castle was gone, the prison, which survived as late as Bonner's day, was the receptacle for the Lollard "heretics," for Bishop Clifford, before his death in 1421, writes to the King in relation to the escape of corrected clerks from this prison.[2]

Little is known of the acts of the rest of the Bishops who ruled the see of London during the remainder of the period.

[1] Newcourt Repm., Vol. I. p. 274, Vol. II. p. 270.
[2] *Vide* Ellis, *Letters*, II.

Richard Clifford (1407–21) was translated from Worcester. He was present at the Council of Constance, 1416. John Kempe (1422–26) held first the see of Chichester, after which he became successively Bishop of London, Archbishop of York, and Archbishop of Canterbury. William Grey (1426–31) was advanced to London from the Deanery of York. He is said to have founded a cell at Theale, with a Master and four Canons. The greater income of Lincoln moved him to accept translation to that see, where he did not find much peace. Robert Fitzhugh (1431–36) did not distinguish himself. Like his predecessor, he decided to accept another see, and was elected to Ely, but he died at St. Osyth before the arrangements for his translation were complete. Of Robert Gilbert (1436–50) and Thomas Kempe (1450–89) we have little to remark. The latter Prelate lived through the period of strife, when the Hertfordshire portion of his Diocese was a scene of three of the battles of the Wars of the Roses, and London itself was a centre of constant turmoil.

Whenever opportunity presented itself, these Bishops were active in attempting to suppress the leaders who were bearing aloft the torch of reform.

In spite of the continued spread of Lollard doctrine and influence, the Monastic system had still got a strong hold on the nation, but it was soon to totter to its fall.

CHAPTER XV

GATHERING OF THE TUDOR STORM—ESSEX AND HERTFORDSHIRE

"... *Tinctured trains of latent flame*
Pollute the sky; and in yon baleful cloud,
A reddening gloom, a magazine of fate
Ferment."

THOMSON.

THE Reformation was a process of gradual upheaval, and not a sudden convulsion. Stephen Langton, Chaucer, Wicliffe, Langland (the reputed author of " Piers Plowman "), and John Ball, in their respective spheres, were, as we have seen, its levers. We must not forget that a combination of influences of ever-increasing intensity in the political, religious, literary, and social spheres of the nation's life had long been approaching a climax. It was not the result of the caprice of Henry VIII. He was not the founder of the movement, though he gave it new and violent impetus.

Fifty-seven years had scarcely elapsed since, at the instance of the Pope, the ashes of Wicliffe had been scattered on the waters of the Swift, in the days of Fleming, Bishop of Lincoln, and the battle of Bosworth had raised the first Tudor to the throne of England in 1485. Bishop Russell was then on the throne of Lincoln, fulminating against the Lollards. In 1491 he confesses himself "fatigued and vexed by many heretics," and speaks of "Wicliffists" as those "whose most insane opinions have infected many people in our *Anglican Church*," an expressive and pregnant phrase from a Bishop of the fifteenth century.

Thomas Kempe (1450–89) was closing an episcopate of nearly forty years in the see of London when the nation was racked with the red ruin of war. His two successors, Richard Hill (1489–96), Dean of the King's Chapel ; and Thomas Savage (1497–1502), translated from Rochester, left no special impress on the diocese.

The fire of reform was crackling briskly, but it was not till these comparatively insignificant Bishops had passed away, and Wolsey had appeared on the scene, that the flame burst into a blaze, and began to rage from one end of the land to the other.

William Warham (1502–4), Archdeacon of Huntingdon, ruled the see of London for a short time. He was the friend of the "New Learning," which in turn was the handmaid of the best leaders in the Reformation crisis. He was the patron of men like Erasmus, Colet, and More (said to have

been born at North Mymms, in Hertfordshire).[1]
Professor Green reiterates the praises of Erasmus
in respect of the Bishop's learning, speaking "of
his ability in business, his pleasant humours, his
modesty, his fidelity to friends."[2] He draws a still
brighter picture of him when raised to the Archiepiscopal throne of Canterbury. This is beyond
our present scope, but one thing he remarks
which shows the attitude of the man towards
the subject of our chapter; he says : "Few men
realized so thoroughly as Warham the new conception of an intellectual and moral equality, before
which the old social distinctions were ever to
vanish away." He significantly adds "the New
Learning pressed on the reform of the Church."
While these men of light and leading were kindling a brighter and a purer flame than that which
was to "burn up the Houses of God in the land ;"
instead of being content with cleansing them, the
torches of reckless politicians and iconoclastic
bigots were adding fuel to the fiercer flame of
waste and hate.

When we find the Pope licensing a Dean of
Lincoln at sixteen years of age, profusely granting
dispensations of plurality, casting indulgences right
and left, the secular clergy growing more and more
secular every day, the regular clergy more and

---

[1] It is tolerably certain that he wrote at least a part of " Utopia "
at North Mymms.
[2] Green's " History of the English People," ed. 1891, p. 307.

more licentious and irregular, and lawlessness and profligacy rampant in the religious houses, no wonder that the fire of reform waxed hot, and that the influence of Lollardism, which had been checked by the turbulent times of the Wars of the Roses, became again a power in the land.

No wonder that the fiery tongue of Dean Colet spoke vehement words before the clergy in Convocation.

" Would for once you would remember your name and profession, and take thought for the Reformation of the Church. Never was it more necessary, and never did the state of the Church need more vigorous endeavours. We are troubled with heretics, but no heresy of theirs is so fatal to us and to the people at large as the vicious and depraved lives of the Clergy. That is the worst heresy of all."

The Episcopates of William Barnes (1504–5), once Rector of Therfield, and of Richard Fitzjames (1506–22), translated from Chichester; saw strength added to the rising flame, which was fanned by pulpit, press, and council.

Evidence of its ever-increasing vigour in Essex may be gathered from the fact that, on October 26th, 1526 (before the movement of Reform had been affected by *The Act of Supremacy*), Bishop Cuthbert Tunstal (1522–30) issued a prohibition to the Archdeacons of Essex, Colchester, and Middlesex, peremptorily warning them against Tyndale's translation of the New Testament published in 1525–6. Six thousand copies had been sent from Worms to England for distribution. The Episcopal mandate did not stop here, but commanded such books to be brought in within thirty days. The Bishops' Registers of the time show how the old spirit of Lollardism lived and became recrudescent as a force, asserting itself as more and more distinct from the social and political agitation of Wat Tyler's days, with which it had been strangely mixed. The registers also tell of groups meeting here and there to read "in a great book of heresy, all one night, certain chapters of the Evangelists in English."[1]

During his Episcopate (1527), forty persons were apprehended at Colchester, Witham, Braintree, East Donyland, Boxted, Horksley, and other places as "suspects."

John Stokesley (1530–39), who succeeded Tunstal on his elevation to Durham, carried on the work of repression. In 1531 forty more persons were apprehended at Bumpstead, and forty-one at Birdbrook.

Stokesley's method of persecution may be illustrated by the case of Thomas Patmore, Rector of Much Hadham. Cussans tells the story as given by Fox, who related how

"the newly appointed Bishop, either for malice, not greatly liking of the said Patmore, or else desirous to prefer some other unto the benefice, caused him to be attached and brought before him, and then keeping him

[1] Green's "History of the English People," ed. 1891, p. 351.

prisoner in his own palace, probably at Much Hadham, a certain time afterwards committed him to the Lollard's Tower, when he kept him most extremely alone two years, without fire or candle, or any other relief but such as his friends sent him ; not suffering any of them, notwithstanding, to come unto him, no, not in his sickness."

He deprived him of his benefice, and of all his goods; through the intercession of the Queen, however, he was released at the end of the third year. The principal charges brought against him were, that he had brought into England certain heretical books of Luther, Melancthon, and other reformers; that he had consented to the marriage of his curate, Simon Smith, with Jane Bennore, and had supped with them at the Bell, in New Fish Street. He was further charged with having said at Cambridge, that he did not set "a bottle of hay" by the Pope's or Bishop's curse; "that God bindeth us to impossible things that He may save us by His mercy; that though young children be baptized, yet they cannot be saved except they have faith ; and lastly, that it was against God's law to burn heretics." [1] These allegations having been substantially proved to the satisfaction of the judges, Thomas Patmore was condemned to undergo perpetual imprisonment. Bishop Stokesley, even before the order for the suppression of the smaller Religious Houses was decreed, saw the spirit of destruction begin to manifest itself. In 1532 the Church at

[1] Cussans' "Hertfordshire," vol. i. p. 85.

Dovercourt was desecrated, the rood broken down, and "the wonder-working Crucifix" burnt. In the previous year, many images were cast down and destroyed, such as the image of the Crucifix at Coggeshall, the image of St. Petronel[1] in the church of Great Horksleigh. The Earl of Oxford obtained by gift the most precious of ecclesiastical vestures, and a cope of cloth of gold from Brightlingsea. Sir William Pyrton carried off the bells from Little Bentley church, while Sir John Rayne took the two largest from Bradfield. The bells were usually broken up and sold for gun metal.

Sir William Stafford forcibly carried off the bells from five churches,—Rochford, Ashington, South Shoebury, Hawkwell, and Foulness, in Rochford Hundred, appropriating the proceeds to his own use.

We must now turn to the Diocese of Lincoln. Bishop Russell, of whom we spoke in a former chapter, had lived into the period ushered in by the battle of Bosworth Field, though he had passed to his rest before the Reformation movement had attained the strength of which we are now speaking.

William Smith (1496–1514), Lord-president of the Welsh Marches, and Bishop of Lichfield and

---

[1] The traditional daughter of St. Peter. According to some, she is identified with Drida, the wife of Offa, who styled herself Petronilla. There is a legend respecting Drida, that, in punishment for some crime, she was put out to sea in an open boat without sails or rudder, and at length was rescued by some English seamen. Offa, struck with her beauty and adventure, married her.

Coventry, was selected to succeed him. He was a man of great zeal and generosity. His activity in the matter of ordinations in his old Diocese was amazing. On one occasion, in Tutbury Church, he set apart two hundred candidates for the ministry. His zeal, during his occupation of the see of Lincoln, was directed towards the correction of monastic abuses. At the same time he turned his attention to the Lollards, whom Fox describes as "the new way," and of whom he says, "many abjured, and many were burnt, yet divers he sent quietly home without punishment or penance, bidding them to go and live as good Christians should do. And many which were enjoined penance before, he did release."

His influence must have found many outlets for its exercise, for with the exception of the Deanery and the residentiary Canonries, some seventy stalls were at his disposal in the Cathedral Church of Lincoln. He was lord of forty manors, and had ten episcopal palaces. Fuller says of him, "this man, whithersoever he went, may be followed by the perfume of charity he left behind him." He died at Buckden.

He was followed in 1514 by Wolsey, Abbot of St. Albans, who did but little for the diocese in his rule of eight months.

Bishop Atwater (1514–21) succeeded him. "Bloated pluralism" found its exemplification in him. Archdeacon Perry gives a list of his offices, to which the see of Lincoln was added, November 12th, 1514. He was Dean of the Chapel Royal, Dean of Salisbury, Prebendary of Wells, St. David's, Windsor, and Salisbury, Archdeacon of Huntingdon, Archdeacon of Lewes, Fellow of Eton, Rector of Hawkridge, Pedylinton and Dychet. One is surprised that he found time to bestow any attention upon diocesan matters. Yet, in 1518, he spent three months in the visitation, mainly, though not exclusively, of the religious houses subject to him as ordinary. A sorry record he had to make. The revelations which followed his inquiries seemed to have confirmed his sympathies with reform.

A long account is preserved for us of his itinerary in this visitation tour. In May of this year (1518) we find him in Hertfordshire. The following extract is from his Visitation Book.

> " Die Jovis apud Baldock pro visitatione
> ibidem ; nocte ibidem.
> Die Veneris vig^{mo} Maii apud Wunmeley[1] pro
> visitatione ; nocte apud Hertford.
> Die Sabbati apud Hertford pro visitatione.
> Die Dominico nono Maii ⎫
> Die Lune x^{mo} Maii   ⎪ diebus rogati-
> Die Martis xj^{mo} Maii   ⎬ onum ad plac-
> Die Mercurii xij Maii   ⎪ itum domini.
> Die Jovis xiij Maii   ⎭
> Die Veneris xiiij Maij apud S. Albanum.
> Die Sabbati xv^{to} Maij apud Markiate pro
> visitatione.

---

[1] Probably Wymondley.

Die Dominico xvj^{mo} die Maij ibidem quies-
cendo.
Die Lune apud Hichin pro decanatu ; nocte
ibidem." [1]

His successor, Bishop Longland [2] (1521–1547),
lived right through the period of the violent impact
of the storm. Fox reckons him a fierce persecutor
of the Lollards, but as he was the king's confessor,
it is hardly likely, especially when we are told of
his graphic descriptions of misrule in the monasteries, and read his drastic messages inculcating
reformation. At any rate, it must have been against
his will. However, we find one William Dorset of
King's Langley put to penance by him for saying that
"images stood for nothing, and that pilgrimages
served to spend folks' money and nothing else ; "
also when his wife was going on pilgrimage, he
asked "Whither ?" and she replied, "To our Lady
of Willesden." "Our Lady," said he, "is in
Heaven." [3]

Persecution seems to have been rife at Ware
in Longland's day, but as Ware was in the diocese
of London at this time, we cannot hold him responsible. Bishop Tunstal, who had made his
name famous as a hunter of Lollards in Essex, was
in all probability the moving spirit in the matter

---

[1] From a flyleaf in Bishop Atwater's "Visitation Book."

[2] The direct succession of John Longland has been traced upward
step by step, to apostolic times. *Vide* Mr. C. F. Warren's chart in
Blunt's "Annotated Book of Common Prayer." Ed. 1884, pp. 556,
658.

[3] Fox's "Acts and Monuments," vol. ii. p. 37. Folio Ed.

of Thomas Clerk and his wife, who, in 1521, were
accused of "buying the Bible, reading the Bible,
dissuading from bowing to images, refusing to
believe in the sacrament of the Altar."[1] Longland
was evidently a disciplinarian in parochial matters,
for we read that he urged Archbishop Warham
"to induce his relative the Parson of Tring to
appoint a Curate to Wigginton, which hath of old
time been a Priest's Church."

The most important evidence of the bishop's
views is a letter touching the question of supremacy,
which he addressed to the Hertfordshire clergy, together with the rest of his diocese, commanding it to
be read from the altar. Archdeacon Perry gives
the *ipsissima verba* [2] of this and subsequent orders :—

"Ye shall understand that the unlawful jurisdiction,
power, and authority, of long time usurped by the Bishop
of Rome in this realm, which then was called Pope, is now
by God's law justly, lawfully, and upon good grounds,
reasons, and causes, by authority of Parliament, and by
and with the whole consent and agreement of all the
bishops, prelates, and both the universities of Oxford and
Cambridge, and also the whole clergy of this realm, extinct
and ceases for ever, and is of no value and effect in this
realm of England ; and the King's Highness is acknowledged to be supreme head on earth, immediately under
God, of the Church of England, so ought every Christian
subject of this realm not only to acknowledge and
obediently recognize him to be supreme head on earth
of the Church of England, but also to speak, publish, and

[1] Fox's 'Acts and Monuments," vol. ii. p. 28, *et seq.*   Folio Ed.
1684.
[2] " History of Diocese of Lincoln," p. 209, *et seq.*

teach their children and servants the same, and to show them how the said bishop has heretofore usurped, not only upon God, but also upon princes of this realm and their progenitors. Wherefore to the intent ye should better believe me, and take and receive the truth as ye ought to do, I declare this unto you, not only of myself which I know to be true, but also declare that the same is certified unto me by the mouth of my ordinary, the Bishop of Lincoln, under his seal, which I have here ready to show you."

Then follows a Latin letter, instructing the clergy to see that the schoolmasters taught their scholars the same things, and that the necessary alterations were made in the wording of the Great Curse and the Service Books. Soon after this the Bishop sent to his Archdeacons, Cranmer's letter, *De modo prædicandi et in sermonibus orandi*, with directions as follows :—

"I commend me unto you and send you certain writings, *De modo prædicandi et in sermonibus orandi*, which every Bishop hath in commandment to cause it to be showed and notified to the clergy of his diocese, as well to secular as regulars, exempt and not exempt, with speed, and by them to be put in execution according to the tenor thereof ; and if ye shall know any person refuse this order, and give notice thereof unto me, send ye forth your apparitors that they may call every deanery by themselves, and when they do appear, read ye it openly to them, and if any person will have the copy thereof, let him have it. Ye must have there at the best all the heads or seniors of any religious house of men, and the priests of religious houses of women. These said writings that I now send you are subscribed *manibus episcoporum*. This cause ye to be done speedily throughout your office, and offer an

M

example of these writings to every priest that will write them out."

It seems, however, that the bishop was not satisfied with the way in which these directions had been received, for in the register, immediately after the above, the following passage occurs :—

"I commend me in hearty wise unto you, and when I sent you the last year my letter with certain writings enclosed therein *De modo prædicandi et in sermonibus orandi*, with many other instructions in the same, which I doubt not ye have in your good remembrance, and also in your knowledge, commanding you to give notice and knowledge thereof unto all the clergy within your archdeaconry, as well exempt as non-exempt, and if ye did know any person to refuse that order or otherwise behave himself, to give me knowledge thereof. Yet that commandment notwithstanding, I am informed that some temerous, presumptuous, and indiscreet persons there be, within your office, that doth to the contrary, and doth treat and dispute such matters and doubts as doth rather gender contrariety and difference than necessary things apt for the audience or for the increase of virtue and truth, and many of them not authorized to preach, and yet are by you and the curates permitted and suffered contrary to the said commandment. In consideration whereof I charge you to have such an eye, diligent oversight and inquiry into these premises, that I may with speed be certified the names as well of all such as have trangressed the said order and commandment, as of them who do preach any contentious or doubtful matters, or without authority, and also of all such curates as do admit or suffer any such not authorized persons to preach within their churches, and all such as set forth the Bishop of Rome his usurped jurisdiction and authority, if any such there be. To the intent such transgressors may be known and ordered accordingly, and that to give effectual commandments to all curates from henceforth to note in a bill the names of any other that shall hereafter preach, in their churches, and by whose authority they come, and how they do use themselves in their sermons, and to certify you by these writings once every term, and you to send unto me or my chancellor your said certificates to the intent it may be known how every one doth use themselves. This fail not to do with speed, as ye will answer thereunto." [1]

Few indeed could have foreseen that the doom of the old order was so near, and Longland, busied with the struggle for necessary reforms, little realized how soon it was to come.

Side by side with the agitation for religious reform were eager discussions over the subject of the King's divorce. Cranmer owed his rise to the chair of St. Augustine to his views on the divorce, Herts and Essex being connected in a curious way with the state of affairs.

In his tutor days Cranmer went to stay with the father of one of his pupils at Waltham Cross in Herts. The King was at this time staying at the Romeland, in the precincts of Waltham Abbey, and two of his retinue were "billeted" in the same house with Cranmer. The subject of the King's proposed marriage with Anne Boleyn was discussed, and Cranmer propounded a theory that the first marriage with a brother's widow was null and void, being contrary to scripture, and that therefore the Pope's dispensation was not needed.

[1] " History of Diocese of Lincoln," pp. 219, 220. S.P.C.K. 1897.

Henry, hearing of this at once, took Cranmer into royal favour, and on the death of Wareham raised him to the see of Canterbury.

Thomas Cromwell, a disciple of the New Learning, a man with a purpose, was now well to the front. He solved the Divorce problem by advising the King to declare himself Supreme Head of the Church of England, and to settle the matter in the spiritual courts of his own realm. This advice was accepted, and was followed in 1534 by the Act of Supremacy, which ratified the title the King had already assumed. Henry was now absolute, and became " Master of the Bishops," " Master of Convocation," " Master of the Monastic Orders." The right of visitation, thus transferred from the Pope to the King, was soon brought to bear on the two counties.

These events were but tokens of the storm which had been gathering for a century or more. The climax of the reign came in the fall of the monasteries—the breaking up of a system which for a thousand years had been the dominating force of the English Church.

CHAPTER XVI

FALL OF THE MONASTERIES—ESSEX AND HERTFORDSHIRE

" *Now let us sit in conclave. That these weeds*
Be rooted from the vineyard of the Church,
That these foul tares be sever'd from the wheat,
We are, I trust, agreed. Yet how to do this,
Nor hurt the wholesome crop and tender vine plants,
Craves good advisement."

" *The Reformation.*"

" *The sacred tapers' lights are gone,*
Grey moss has clad the altar stone,
The holy image is o'erthrown,
The bell has ceased to toll.
The long ribb'd aisles are burst and shrunk,
The holy shrines to ruin sunk,
Departed is the pious monk,
God's blessing on his soul! "

" *Rediviva.*"

" *To build large houses pull no churches down.*"

WEBSTER.

WE must now deal with the fall of the
religious houses. Bishop Longland of
Lincoln, and Bishop Stokesley of London,
saw the climax of the monastic crash, which began
with the ruin of the smaller houses. A precedent
had been set in the days of Edward II., in the time

of Dalderby of Lincoln, and Baldock of London, when the Knights Templars were suppressed, and again in the early days of Henry V. (1414), when the Alien priories fell, and their revenues were either pocketed by the Crown, added to some existing English house, or appropriated to some new foundation.

Again, early in the reign of Henry VIII., before the issue of the Commissions, the Pope, at the instance of Wolsey, had decreed by a bull, the fate of the Hospital de La Pré at St. Albans, for the purpose of his proposed colleges, though, as a matter of fact, its funds went to St. Albans. Thomas Cromwell, son of a blacksmith, " traveller, trooper, clerk, and money-lender," was Wolsey's agent. His apprenticeship to Wolsey trained him for a career of plunder, and helped him to reach the zenith of his power. Wolsey was more fortunate in securing, as early as 1523, the Austin Friary of Tiptree for his collegiate scheme.

The next step towards the new outbreak of ruthless plunder was the first general visitation of inquiry into " money and morals," which lasted from October, 1535, to February, 1536, and led up to the *Act of Suppression.* Vicar-General Cromwell made the inspection thorough. Thorough it was indeed, but alas ! inspection with Cromwell spelt destruction, and not reform. In Essex the fair name of Waltham had been tarnished with corruption and exaction, while misrule and neglect reigned at

Colchester. Simony, usury, waste, dilapidation, and profligacy were charged against St. Albans in 1536, as they had been as early as 1489. The lesser houses were the first to come under official condemnation. Though the good often preponderated over the evil, their knell had sounded, and both in Essex and Hertfordshire spoliation had begun, before the Commission was issued.

The Commissioners who especially concern us were the notorious Layton, Lee, Bedyl, and Petre, who started on their infamous errand of ruin, at the King's *ipse dixit*, without waiting for the authority of Parliament. The extant letters of the Visitors are the only reliable evidence of the course of the visitation, for there is a sea of doubt about the existence of any *Black Book* at all, and much about the genuineness of the *Comperta* which is said to have been founded on it. The evidence of the letters, bad enough indeed, is not of that damning character which the machinations of Cromwell and his creatures concocted by the way of report to Parliament. The Visitation produced a very stern document in—

"An Act whereby all Religious Houses of Monks, Canons, and Nuns which may not dispend Manors, Lands, Tenements, and Hereditaments above the clear yearly value of two hundred pounds, are to be given to the King's Highness, his heirs and successors for ever."[1]

It is worthy of notice, in view of the events of

[1] 27 Henry VIII. c. 28. 1536.

three years later, that it was set forth in the Act " that there were divers great and solemn Monasteries of the Realm wherein (thanks to God) religion is right well kept up and observed."

This was immediately followed by a second Commission of Execution, the notorious vagabonds of the previous commission retiring for a while to pull the wires for their puppets in the persons of local laymen, but holding themselves ready to appear on the scene when needed.

By a single stroke of the pen, 376 of the smaller houses throughout England were confiscated, and 10,000 of "the religious" turned out in the cold world.   Our counties staggered under the blow of the greedy hand.   In Essex some 25 priories and nunneries were condemned and sacked, the buildings being given over to grim decay, and to the tenancy of owls and bats.   In Hertfordshire ten of the same class met with a like fate.

The thirst for plunder was whetted by the spoils of the smaller houses, and though the nation and the better of the King's counsellors were against plunder for plunder's sake, that thirst was not satiate as yet, and the greater Houses were to fall a prey to it.   In 1539 came the Act for the Dissolution of the Monasteries.   One after another they were greedily "licked up," as the fury of reform assumed the shape of a devouring beast.

Its overwhelming power fell on the remaining foundations in the counties, viz. Coggeshall,

Stratford, Saffron Walden, St. Osyth, St. John Baptist, Colchester; Barking, St. Albans, and Waltham.

The Cistercian Abbey of Coggeshall was the first to fall. On February 5th, 1538, Capel and Wentworth effected its surrender. The ruins of the old Abbey, until recently used as a barn, have been restored, and were re-opened in 1897 as a Chapel of Ease to Coggeshall.

Stratford fell on March 8th, when Layton appeared at its gates, though the Abbot had been a match for his visitors on a previous occasion, and had excommunicated the brethren for betraying the secrets of the house. Layton, however, overawed him and his monks, and seized the revenue for his Royal master, who granted the site to one Peter Meawles.

A few days later, on March 22nd, Saffron Walden, a great Benedictine Priory, was confiscated by one Ashton, and the whole of its possessions granted to Chancellor Audley, who before had effected some valuable exchange of land with More, the Suffragan Bishop of Colchester, who was the last Prior, and for his pliancy was rewarded with the Archdeaconry of Leicester.

On July 28th a Commissioner visited St. Osyth of Augustinian fame, where he found sixteen Canons.

Chancellor Audley, the year before, possibly in remembrance of the valuable consideration he had already obtained in the matter of an exchange of land, which we have previously mentioned, wrote a pleading letter to Cromwell for the retention of this and the abbey of St. John " as colleges, and not as they be religious," urging in support of his plea " the cause he moved this was" that St. John's standeth in his Grace's own town at Colchester, "wherein dwell many poor people who have daily relief;" adding that "both these houses be in the end of Essex where little hospitality will be kept if they be dissolved. There are twenty houses, great and small, dissolved in Essex." [1] He went even as far as offering him £2000 if the dissolution could be averted. The plea was of no avail, its fate was sealed, and it fell.

The mitred abbey of St. John Baptist followed. It was too tempting a bait to be passed by, though against the venerable Abbot, its guardian, no misgovernment could be alleged. A skilfully concocted charge of treason was brought against him, and it was asserted that he extolled the *Pilgrimage of Grace*, and wished that Cromwell and his crew had fallen in the strife.

After a weary journeying to London for his trial, the good old Abbot Beche was brought back and cruelly executed at his Abbey Gate on December 1st, 1539. [2]

John Beche of Colchester, Hugh Faringdon

---

[1] " Gasquêt Monasteries," vol. i.

[2] The Pectoral Cross of John Beche is now in possession of the Roman Bishop of Clifton.

of Reading, and Hugh Whiting of Glastonbury, stand out as famous, not only among the mitred, but the martyred abbots of a system which, whatever its weaknesses, or even its sins, has contributed to the building up of England's life.

The fall of the Nunnery of Barking was next effected, and the artful Petre arrived on the scene and secured its surrender. The site was granted to Sir Thomas Denny.

Now came to the pirates Petre and Legh the prize of the mighty St. Albans. Fifty years before, in 1489, the Abbey, together with its dependencies, De La Pré, and Sopwell, had received the censure of Archbishop Morton for simony, usury, dilapidation, waste, and profligacy. When the Commissioner arrived on December 5th, 1538, the Abbot was from home, but, on his return, he stoutly resisted the intrusion, declaring "he would rather choose to beg his bread all the days of his life than consent to surrender." The wily Layton was sent for, and the Abbot and thirty-seven brethren at last agreed to quit their beloved house. It appears, however, that the Abbot sat in Parliament in April of the following year. It is therefore probable that the final formalities of surrender were not completed till after the session.

There is a good deal of mystery about the actual relations between the last Abbot and the King, and it comes about in this way.

Wolsey had held the Abbacy in *commendam*, and on his death one Robert Catton was forced, by the King, on the monks as their Abbot, "while the King's agents and secret ministers lived as guests in the monastery and ruled all."[1]

It is thought by some that Abbot Stevenage, the Prior of Norwich, was also the King's nominee, and that his "stout resistance" was for appearance' sake. Newcome directly asserts "that the King granted a *congé d'elire* to the prior and convent with a missive letter, showing the name of the person whom he recommended, and yet under a *præmunire* to refuse. The election thus made, the writ was returned, endorsed with the name, and the King signified his assent under the Great Seal."

One thing is certain, that the fate of the Abbey was sealed by a letter from William Petre on December 10th, 1538, to Cromwell. It is worth quoting as an instance of the method of procedure.

"Please it your Lordship to be advertised :—

"At our comyng to St. Albon's on Thursdaye last, we baganne a visitacion among the monkes, the Abbot being then in London. And because we wolde the more fully knowe the whole state of all things, tarred the longer in the examinacion of theym. And upon Fridaye last we sent a monicion for the Abbot to appere before us, who came hether on Saturday before none: whosom we have likewis as fully examined upon all things as we might. And although, as well by the examination of the monkes,

---

[1] Newcome's " History of the Abbey of St. Albans," p. 429.

as by confession of the Abbot himself, there doth appere
confessed and fully proved, juste cause of deprivacion
against the Abbot, not only for breking the King's injunctions, but also, for manifest dilapidations, making of giftes,
negligent administracion, and sundry other causes ; yet by
what meanes we know not, in all communications or
motions made concerning any surrendre, he sheweth hym-
self so stiff, that as he saith he wold rather choyse to begge
his bredde all the days of his life, than consent to any
surrender. We have everich of us severally, and also
together, communed with hym, and also used all suche
motions as we thought might most further that purpose ;
but he contynueth allweys one man, and waxeth hourly
more obstinate, and less conformable : whether he so doo
upon trust and confidence of any friendshippe, we know
not. The premisses we thought our baunden duetie to
signifie unto your lordshippe, most humbly beseeching the
same, that we maye, by Mr. Doctor Layton, know the
King's highness further pleasure by you ; whether we shall
contyneue in this processe of deprivacion against him, and
so deprive him according to the order of justice without longer
delaye ; which doon the house will be in such debt, that we
think no man will take the office of Abbot here upon him ;
except any doo it only for that purpose to surrender the
same to the King's hands. And by this meanes we thinke
this thing maye most easily be, and with more spede be
brought to the King's highnes purpose ; or else whether
we shall staye in our processe at this tyme and appoynte
some longer daye to hear the sentence of deprivacion,
leaving hym in the meane tyme in utter desperacion of any
favor, which weye maye also be occasioned, that he, when
it shall appere unto hym that he shall be deprived, may
perchance sue to have his surrender taken because he
wolde be assured of some lyving. The premisses we
referre to King's highnes pleasure, which knowen by your
lordeship, we shall, with all our possible diligence, conform
ourselfe to accomplish the same, and in the meane time
travaill with the monks to know how many of theym may

be induced to this purpose. Thus Almighty God have your lordeship in his blessed kepyng. From St. Albans, the xth of December, 1538.

"Your lordships most bounden servant,

"WILLIAM PETRE."[1]

A Charter, dated December 14th, 1539, confirmed pensions of £266 13s. 4d. to the Abbot, and £33 6s. 8d. to the Prior, together with smaller sums to 37 of the brethren. The monastic buildings were granted to Sir Richard Lee, who soon commenced their destruction.

The spoliation of the goods of the Abbey was taken in hand at once, for on December 17th the sacred vessels, together with valuables of the Shrine of St. Alban, were brought into the Royal treasury, viz. "122 ozs. gold, 2990 ozs. gilt plate, 1144 ozs. parcel gilt and silver, 400 ozs. copper. Three Pontifical mitres, golden buckles set with great agates, cameos and coarse pearls, formed part of this plunder."[2]

The Abbey Church itself escaped destruction, and was bought from the Crown by the townspeople for a sum of £400. Waltham, in the county of Essex, was the last to bend to the storm. The visitors arrived on January 23rd, 1540, and proceeded in the usual way.

Sir Anthony Denny, "an ancient favourer of the Gospel," and a gentleman of the bedchamber,

---

[1] Cottonian MSS. Cleop. E. 4.
[2] Monastic Treasures, "Abbotsford Club," p. 429.

received the site of Waltham Abbey as his share, the religious house at Cheshunt, the Hertford Cell and Friary being thrown into the bargain. Gas-quêt gives a full account of the disposal of the plunder.

The Abbot of Waltham received a pension in lands and possessions to the value of £200; the prior and ex-prior each received £20; the *quondam* superior £10; the *quondam* sexton £6 13s. 4d.; and 14 brethren various smaller sums, as witnessed by Thomas Mildmaye, auditor.[1]

It is not a little interesting that the "Romeland" at St. Albans and "Romeland" at Waltham should have witnessed, the one Tankerfield's martyrdom, and the other Cranmer's first step to power, leading him on to the stake.

As we look back on the story of these times, well may we sigh Ichabod! and exclaim for St. Albans and Waltham, and for many another fair fane of praise and prayer, "How are the mighty fallen!" Cromwell had done his task, and well for him, if now, like a useless tool, he had been thrown aside, but God brought him to judgment for the work of his impious hands. Six months after the fall of Waltham (July 28th, 1540), he was led to the block, pleading to an earthly monarch, "Mercy! Mercy! Mercy!" which he had never shown.[2]

---

[1] Stowe's Annals, ed. 1631, p. 577.
[2] Farmer's "History of Waltham Abbey," p. 107.

What became of the spoils of these days of plunder ?

The yearly revenues of the Essex houses alone amounted to about £7500 ; these, as we have seen, were leased to the itinerant banditti, the commissioners, to their friends, or to the King's minions.

A few references and instances will show the fate of the goods and chattels.

" Many private men's parlours were hung with altar cloths, their tables and beds covered with copes instead of carpets and coverlids, and many made carousing cups of the sacred chalices, as once Belshazzar celebrated his drunken feast in the sanctified vessels of the Temple. It was a sorry house, and not worth the naming, that had not some of this furniture in it, though it were only a large fair cushion made of a cope or altar cloth to adorn their windows, or make their chairs appear to have somewhat in them of a chair of state." [1]

The effect of this vast and violent change altered the whole religious system of the country, and, among other things, that of patronage. The religious houses had hitherto, as we have seen, an enormous number of benefices under their control.[2]

The roll of the Crown and lay patronage was now largely increased. In one case, as at Royston, the change resulted in the union of five parishes into one, the people being allowed to purchase the

[1] *Essex Archæological Society Trans.*, New Series, vol. ii. p. 166. *Vide* also Fuller's " Church History," Bk. VII. Sec. 2, vol. ii. p. 347. Ed. 1842, Heylin.

[2] *Vide* Ecton's " Thesaurum Rerum Ecclesiasticarum," Dioc. London, Lincoln.

Austin Priory Church, which had been granted to a courtier.

We have no space to moralize on the effect of the downfall further than to say that prayer, praise, education, hospitality, and learning, received a check. Our readers can trace other effects for themselves in the succeeding years of change, discontent, rebellion, persecution, and chaos.

It is true that certain new sees were erected and more were proposed, but all that our counties got out of the wreck, towards the new sees named, were two ruins, and the two inspiring names of St. Albans, and Waltham Holy Cross. By devotion and sacrifice the dream of the see of St. Albans is to-day a fact. When, and where will Essex have her Bishop's "Stool"?

If *Kennett's Collections* may be relied on, justice demands that Henry's intention of founding a see for each county should be recorded. He arranged that Waltham should be the *sedes* for Essex, and St. Albans for Hertfordshire.

This is illustrated by the following extract:—

" Waltham.

First a Bishoppe.

Item a Presydent, xxxiii^l. vi^s. viii^d.

Item VI. Prebendaries the most part of them to be Preachers.

Every of them by the year xx^{lb}.

Colchestre.

First a Provost of the College xx^{lb}.

Item IIII. Prebendaries the most part of them Preachers.

Every one of them by the yeare, xvi[l]. xiii[s]. iiii[d].
Saint Albans.
First a Bishop.
Item a President of ye College xl[lb].
Item X. Prebendaries every one of them L. marks.
by yere, &c." [1]

It is a sorry story. We may mourn over the wreck, and balance gain and loss, but who can truly tell the tale?

One very odd sequel to the dissolution of the religious houses, and the dispersion of all sorts of small treasures, was the almost sudden revival of witchcraft; so much so that in 1542 a special statute was enacted against it. The statute failed in its purpose, and right down to the end of the eighteenth century witchcraft was rife in the two counties, and many instances occur of its exercise and stern repression.

God has ruled, and will rule all for good; the ancient Church of the land has survived the long and weary years of cleansing fire, which, while it purified much that was evil, destroyed much that was good. God holds the scales.

[1] Bishop Kennett's *Collections*, vol. iv.; Lansdown MS., 938, f. 57; Liber MS., "Continens Foundationes Sedium Episcopalium et Collegionum a Rege Hen. 8, designatus, Anno 1539, et a D. Burnetto memoratus"; Hist. Ref. part i. lvi. p. 262.

CHAPTER XVII

THE DAYS OF EDWARD VI.—HERTFORDSHIRE AND ESSEX

> "CRANMER—
> 'Yet I stood out, till Edward sent for me,
> The wan boy-King, with his fast-fading eyes
> Fixt hard on mine, his frail transparent hand,
> Damp with the sweat of death, and griping mine,
> Whisper'd me, if I loved him, not to yield
> His Church of England to the Papal wolf
> And Mary: then I could no more—I sign'd.'"
> TENNYSON, "Queen Mary."

EDWARD VI. had not been long on the throne when the oligarchy of Somerset, politely called the *Council of Regency*, began to make its power felt, and Parliament took the place of Royal prerogative. The monasteries, great and small, had fallen in the former reign, and by an Act of 1545, two thousand chantries were involved in ruin. The death of Henry had delayed for a time the completion of the design he had in view for their confiscation. A new Enabling Act was introduced in 1547, and soon the first visitation of chantries began ; though before the Act had been passed, many surrendered voluntarily. This new Act came into force at Easter, 1547. Bonner, be it said, voted against it, and to some extent it was modified, but it swept away a vast number of chantries, fraternities, colleges, and hospitals in both counties. The recital of their names only would fill some pages.

The priests and chaplains in some cases received pensions, as in the instance of the chantries of Aldbury, Aldenham, Ashwell, Hemstead, Hatfield, Pelham Furneaux, Bishops Stortford, Wallington, Ware, and the guilds at Baldock, Chipping Barnet, and Hitchin.

There were no less than ten chantries suppressed in Colchester alone, and though for the most part the endowments were small, one chantry in this town possessed one hundred acres of land.

Many more Essex cases might be cited, as at Layer Marney, where the chantry chapel enclosed the founder's tomb. Instances of a different kind were those where the chantry chapel was founded to serve an outlying part of the parish, as at Billericay, and at Foulness. These were allowed in some cases to remain, but the endowments were confiscated, and the fabrics had to be purchased from the new holders. At Romford, the chantry priest was accustomed to preach by consent in eight neighbouring churches each year.

Guilds (the Benefit Clubs of the age) went the way of the chantries. In the busiest centres of population were many guilds, guild altars, and occasionally guild chapels. We note for instance at Maldon there were three guilds, dedicated to " Our

Lady," "Corpus Christi," "St. John." Prittlewell was another case, having its fraternity Altar at the east end of the south aisle of the parish church, known as Jesus Chapel. In this case a Guild House was attached.

We realize now what a power was lost through the abolition of guild life, but use, or abuse, it was condemned, and had to go.

Concurrently, the Colleges were falling right and left. The College of Barking was suppressed. Halstead fell in 1551, and the site went to the Marquis of Northampton. So the work of confiscation and devastation went on.

Whilst this new march of inquisition and plunder was proceeding, the country was in a perfect ferment of confusion as to questions of doctrine and ritual; new acts, injunctions, were flying in all directions. Our own counties, like the other parts of England, were in a state of seething discontent, which was partly agrarian and partly religious in its origin. Edward's *Journal*, 1549, thus refers to the matter :—

"The people began to rise in Essex, Hertfordshire, and because certain Commissions were sent down to pluck down inclosures they did rise again." This is an evident reference to Ket's rebellion, which was rife in the Eastern counties. Dixon forcibly sums up the situation, "To the people it seemed a reformation which let in the rich upon the poor; which, though liberal in putting down doctrines and ceremony, and active in setting up hedges and palings, was not exactly the thing wanted." [1]

Prompt measures were taken to quell the rebellion. Letters were issued " to the gentry of Essex to raise their servants, tenants, and friends, to equip, in especial, as many demi-lances, or light horsemen, as they could," and to meet the Protector Somerset at Walden. One such letter is dated from Walden, August 6th. [2] The motley army met at Walden, August 17th, 1549, and marched on Norwich, Ket's headquarters.

About the same date the Altar war began. Ridley set the example (June 22nd) by breaking down the Altar of the Cathedral Church of St. Paul. The Bishop further sent injunctions by the hand of the High Sheriff of Essex for this purpose. These injunctions were accompanied by *Six Considerations*, which were stated by Fox to be :—

" 1. That in Church there is wanted not an altar but a supper table. 2. That in the Book of Common Prayer the terms altar, table, and board are used interchangeably. 3. The first over again. 4. Sacrifices being ceased, altars are not needed. 5. That no altars are known in the Apostles' time. 6. That if any difficulty arise, the preface of the Book of Common Prayer directs that reference be made to the Bishop of the place."

In the King's *Journal* the following entry occurs under the date of July 15th, 1549 :—

" Sir John Gates, the Sheriff of Essex, went down with

---

[1] Dixon's " History of the Church of England," vol. iii. p. 80.
[2] Strype, iii. 272.

letters to see the Bishop of London's injunction performed, which touched plucking down of super-altaries, altars, and such like ceremonies and abuses."

The most serious part of the whole contention was that the growing spirit of separatism now began to assert itself. Thus the old seed-ground of religious and social discontent was again witness to the appearance of the stubborn blade of social and religious freedom.

On July 15th, 1549, a certain Thomas Puttow, of Berechurch, was to make his recognizance for £100, and "forbear open preaching for any other than his own family between this and the Feast of All Saints, and then to appear before the Council."

The neighbourhood of Bocking appears to have been distinguished for its share in reformation movements as far back as John Ball's time, when the great religious and social revolutions had begun, and as late as the celebrated *Braintree Church Rate Case* in the middle of the nineteenth century.

Dixon has unearthed some important documents which had been only partially quoted by previous writers. They throw a flood of interesting light on church matters in Essex at this period. They are chiefly from the Council Book of Edward VI.

"January 27th, 1550. Upchard of Boking was brought before the Council touching a certain assembly that had been made in his house in Christmas last, who confessed that (there) were certain Kentishmen to the town to have lodged with Goodman Cooke; and because Cooke's wife was in child-bed, they came to this Upchard's house, where Cooke was then at dinner, and by Cooke's entreaty there they were lodged. And upon the morrow, which was Sunday, divers of the town, about XII. of the clock, came in ; and then they fell in argument of things of the Scripture, especially whether it were necessary to stand or kneel bareheaded or covered at prayer, which at length was concluded in ceremony not to be material, but the heart before God was it that importeth, and nothing else.

" And because it seems such an assembly, being of XL. persons or more, should mean some great matter, therefore both the said Upchard and one Simson of the same sort was committed to the Marshallsea till further trial was had ; and order taken that letters should be sent both into Essex and Kent, for the apprehension of these that are accounted chief of that practice."

A letter to Sir George Norton, Kt., Sheriff of Essex, to apprehend " certain persons whose names were sent enclosed in a schedule, and to send them hither, that none of them have conference with other." The persons sent for were of those who were assembled for Scripture matters in Bocking, viz. :—

" John Barrett, of Samford, cowherd ; Robert Cooke, of Bocking, clothier ; John Eglisse, of the same, clothier ; Richard Bagg ; Thomas Pygrinde ; John King ; Myxto ; Boughton ; Robert Woolmer." On February 3rd, " Seven others of Essex appeared . . . which confessed the cause of their assembly to be for to talk of Scriptures. Not denying that they had refused the Communion two years before upon very superstitious and erroneous purposes : with divers other evil opinions worthy of great punishment." [1]

[1] *Vide* Dixon's " History of the Church," vol. iii. p. 209 ; Extracts from Council Book. *Vide* also Burnet's History.

Some were committed, and some were bound to give recognizances.

Soon after this, Hooper was sent into Essex, as one of the King's preachers.

With smashing altars, and hunting schismatics in Essex, Ridley's hands were fairly full, but he had another consideration to attend to, and that was the obstinacy of my Lady Mary, the King's sister, who would have her *Masses*. She was more than a match for "Master Ridley." He was to feel the flame of her tongue now, as he did of her faggots five years later.

We must turn to Hertfordshire, whither Mary had gone, baffled in her attempt to escape to the continent from the Essex coast.

The Bishop was staying at his manor at Much Hadham, and went to visit the Lady Mary at Hunsdon, a short distance away. After the usual courtesies and pleasantries of introduction, Ridley was asked to dine with the officers of the household. Dinner ended, the Bishop was summoned to Lady Mary's presence, and declared the purpose of the visit.

Bishop.—" Madam, considering mine office and calling, I am bound in duty to make your Grace this offer, to preach before you."

Mary.—" Well, I pray you make your answer to this matter yourself, for you know the answer well enough. But if there be no remedy but I must make your answer, this shall be your answer; the door of the parish church adjoining shall be open for you, if you come, and ye may preach if you list, but neither I nor any of mine shall hear you."

Bishop.—" Madam, I trust you will not refuse God's word."

Mary.—" I cannot tell what ye call God's word, that is not God's word now that was God's word in my father's days."

Bishop.—" God's word is one in all times, but hath been better understood and practised in some ages than in others."

Mary.—" You durst not for your ears have preached that for God's word in my father's days that you now do. And as for your new books, I thank God I never read any of them ; I never did, nor ever will do."

After some further conversation on the constitution of the King's Council, the Lady Mary bade him adieu, saying—

" My Lord, for your gentleness to come and see me, I thank you ; but for your offering to preach before me, I thank you never a wit."

So the Bishop was dismissed, and after further refreshment, said with great vehemence—

" Surely I have done amiss ! I have drunk in that place where God's word offered hath been refused, whereas if I had remembered my duty, I ought to have departed immediately, and to have shaken off the dust off my shoes for a testimony against this house."

So he departed.[1]

The next matter of importance arising from the chaos of Acts, Injunctions, and Commissions, was the promulgation of the *First Prayer Book*

[1] For a full account, *vide* Fox, "Acts and Mon.," ed. 1839, p. 521.

of Edward VI., and with it the first Act of Uniformity, while the old diocesan uses were relegated to the archives of their Cathedral. The *Second Prayer Book of Edward VI.*, in which the hand of the foreign Reformers is clearly seen, scarcely influenced our counties before the King died. He survived its issue by only about eight months.

In 1552 the visitation craze was extended to every church in the kingdom by the thirty visitors who were allotted to six circuits. The power of visitation was conferred on local magnates in the various counties. The entries in the King's *Journal* show that the visitation was nothing short of a march of plunder, *e.g.* on April 3rd, " it was agreed that Commissions should go out for to take certificate of the superfluous Church plate to mine use, and to see how it hath been embezzled." The Articles with which the Commissioners were armed produced volumes of returns, which are accessible to every reader.

We give one or two examples of these returns, beginning with Caldecote, one of the smaller parishes—

> " One challeice of silv^r waying x ounces
>   a crosse of latten
>   a vestment of crymsome velvet
>   ij other vestments
>   one cope of red sarsnet
>   iij bells in the steple
>   ij handbells." [1]

[1] Record Office. " Aug.," vol. 497. Published by Mr. Cussans.

Taking the case of the larger and more important parish of Therfield, we find a longer inventory—

"A challeice of sylu^r w^t the cou^r pcell gylt wayenge xj owncs

A cope of purple veluet & ij tunicles of the same one for a deacon wth albe stole amys & phanel another for a subdeacon wth albe amys & phanel a cope of blew satten

a vestmēt of popingeay grene damaske wth albe amys & stole

a vestmēt of red taffita w^t albe amys stole & phan, w^t a corporas clothe and case

a vestmēt of taffita w^t a blewe cross with albe amys stole and phanel

a whyt vestmēt of braunched damaske wth amys stole & phanel

ij whyte vestmēt^s one of satten of brudg^s with albe amys stole & phanell thother of bustien w^t a grene crosse w^t albe stole & phanel

a vestment of blake satten of brudg^s with albe amys stole & phanell

ij hangyng^s f^r hie aulter of blew & red satten of brudg^s

ij curtens of blewe & red sarsnet

A cope of red velvet w^t in a shett

iij copes on of damask ij of taffita

a vestmēt of red sylke w^t albe amys stole & phanel

a tunacle of the same f^r a deacon w^t albe amys stole and phanel & another for a subdeacon w^t albe and amys

a vestment of grene sylke & blak w^t albe amys & phanell

a deacō of the same w^t albe & amys and a subdeacon of the same w^t amys

a vestmēt of grene sylke w^t albe stole & phanel

a deacon & subdeacon complet to the same laking a stole

ij crosses of latten & a pax of latten

In the steple iiij bells & a saunct bell

ix ban^r clothes."[1]

In some inventories we find "itm̄ a pair of orgaynnes," as at Tring, and at St. Peters, St.

[1] "Aug. Off. Misc.," vol. 497, fo. 60. Record Office.

Albans; or "itm̄ a sensor and a shippe of sattene," as at Sandridge; "itm̄ a coffar bound w^t iorne to lay the gear in," as at Sarratt; "itm̄ ij great candlesteks," as at Walkern.

Attached to some of the returns a significant entry is made, as for instance at Hatfield :—

"Itm̄ ffranncis Sothwell of Hartingfordburye gen haythe receyued from the churche of Hatfeld R^s ij challisses of silluer and ij vestments w^t other things, all which good^s he saithe he has received into his hand^s bie vertue of the King^s Mai 'ties." [1]

To a long return for Saffron Walden a typical entry is added :—

"Goods delyvered for the ministration of devyne service.

"To James Corole and Thomas Marten, Churchwardens, a Challis of Silver Gilte, a cope of red velvett, a carpet of blue velvett for the Communyon table, and VII lynen clothes for the same, a little round box to carry the sacrament in with a purse to putt it in, and all the surplices.

GEORGE NORTON,
T. JOSSELYN, } Commissioners.
EDMUND MORDAUNT,

Apart from the questions of ritual and doctrine, it is hardly possible to conceive what we have lost by the wanton destruction of works of mediæval art, as Dixon observes—

"thenceforth began that villainous scraping, coating, or whitewashing of frescoes, and that indiscriminate smashing of windows, which obliterated in countless number the most various and beautiful examples of several of the arts ; and at a blow took from the midst of men the science, the traditionary secrets, which it had taken five centuries to accumulate." [2]

[1] "Aug. Off. Misc.," vol. 497, fo. 60. Record Office.
[2] Dixon, "History of the Church of England," vol. ii. p. 433, 2nd ed. 1887.

Interesting information as to the disposal of Church goods may be found in the Visitation returns, which are now so easily accessible in our public Libraries, and in the Record Office.

The original inventories of church goods in the hundreds of Uttlesford, Freshwell, half-hundred of Clavering, may be found in the British Museum.[1]

A chalice, sometimes a cope, and nearly always a surplice, and "communion cloth," were left for the use of the Church.

Amidst all this zeal for confiscation, the fact must be recorded that Edward confirmed by Charter to the people of St. Albans the permanent possession of the Abbey Church, which they had purchased in the previous reign. He also constituted the Archdeaconry of St. Albans.

These various side-lights on the doings of the seven years of Edward serve to show that it was a time when the leaders in Church and State were seeking not to create a new church, but to evolve, by compromise, a show of order out of the existing chaos. Compromise served its purpose for a time, but party feeling was too strong to ensure a permanent peace, and the Church was yet to be tried by an ordeal of fire.

[1] Stowe MSS., 827.

CHAPTER XVIII

ORDEAL OF FIRE—HERTFORDSHIRE AND ESSEX

"Few remember them; they lived unknown,
Till persecution dragged them into fame,
And chased them up to heaven."

COWPER.

"The mad world sees the world-circling blaze
Vain searching whence it streams, and how to quench its rays."

"Lyra Apostolica."

THE fifty years which followed the climax of the first half of the Tudor times were fraught in our counties with events of thrilling interest, which, owing to the transference in 1550 of the jurisdiction of St. Albans from Lincoln, mainly centred round the see of London. Only sixty-seven parishes, forming a portion of the Archdeaconry of Huntingdon, remained subject to Bishop Taylor, (1552–54), who was on the throne of Lincoln when Mary commenced her reign of blood in 1553. Before the Queen was crowned, an Essex priest, one Bourne of High Ongar, distinguished himself by his vehemence against Ridley and in favour of Bonner, in a sermon on August 13th at St. Paul's Cross, that tryst of fiery tongues.[1]

It is probable that the said Bourne may have

---

[1] Machyn's "Diary Camden Soc.," p. 41 ; Milman's "St. Paul's," p. 234.

come under the personal influence of Princess Mary during her period of residence, either at Beaulieu (now Newhall), near Chelmsford, or at Wanstead.

Her persistent adherence to the Roman rites in her private chapels at these places, must have prepared the Essex folk for what was coming, for though she had been advised by the Council of Edward VI. to command that " *Mass* should be no more used in her house," she refused to listen to the advice, and freely admitted the neighbouring people to the services. When the final order came from the Council, 14th August, 1551, she declared that she would rather lay her head on the block than submit.

One of the first acts of Mary was to reinstate Edmund Bonner as Bishop of London. He had been committed to prison four years before, for his refusal to acquiesce in the instructions of the Council of Edward VI. The Grey Friars chronicles relate how he came forth " from the Marshalsea like a Bishop to St. Paul's, and knelt on the steps and said his prayers, and then the people rang the bells for joy." They little knew what was in store for them.

In forming an estimate of the revolting cruelties of this period and of Bonner's share in them, we must remember that it was an age of fierce persecution. The Bishop was under the influence of Gardiner, Mary, and of Philip, who was imbued with the spirit of Spanish severity towards "heretics."

Bonner does not appear to have taken a delight in "the burnings," and more than once, as in Anne Askew's case, did his best to avert them. He was naturally of quick temper, and doubtless often said more than he meant. He must have smarted too under the remembrance of his own sufferings in the previous reign.

The description of him as a "mitred Nero" is not quite just. Even in the matter of reading the Bible in English he is not fairly dealt with; what he objected to, for instance in St. Paul's, was not the resort of the people there for this purpose, but that they did so, to the disturbance of worshippers, whilst divine service was going on. The following extract from his Register may be quoted in support of this view :—

"An admonition and advertisement gyven by the Byshope of London of this Byble in the Englyshe tongue to the intent that a good and healthsome thinge, Godly and vertuously (for honest intent and purposes) set forth for many be not hindered or maligned at for the abuse, defaulte and evyle behaviour of a few." [1]

"Whereas their hath been given by me, the Byshoppe of London a right honest, charitable, and friendly advertisement and admonition, warn you to read quietly not in time of Divine Service or Sermon, or else the Bibles for the said abuses be taken down." [1]

Mary, with Bonner at her elbow, soon showed her hand. She forced him to proclaim the Reformation preachers, and to license others who would

[1] Lansdowne MSS., 938.   Exts. from Epis. Reg. B. Bonner, ff. 220–242.

support her policy.   Old acts were speedily reversed and new ones substituted.   The climax of legislation was being prepared for by the Act which came in force December 20th, 1553, ordering—

"through London and all England that no man should sing no English service nor communion after December 20th ; nor no priest that has a wife shall not minister nor say mass ; and that every priest to make an altar and to have a cross and staff, and all other things in all parishes all in Latin, as holy bread, holy water, as palms and ashes."

Truly, a negative decree!   Soon we read of processions all round London ; at Stratford, among other places.   As soon as the processions of joy in the neighbourhood of London were over, Bonner determined on the visitation of his Diocese.   He made a "painful peregrination" through Essex, which was not without scenes.   Bishop Bird preached the visitation sermon at Great Dunmow, getting very lengthy and involved, Bonner became very wroth, and gesticulated to him to put an end to his sermon.[1]

A curious story is told by Dr. Morris of the connection of the said Bird with Bonner.   He was once a Carmelite Friar, and was raised to episcopal rank as Suffragan of Lichfield, after which he was elevated to the see of Bangor. During the time he held these appointments he was engaged in the matrimonial concerns of Henry the Eighth.   Subsequently he was translated to

[1] Strype's Annals.

Chester, where he married a wife, much to the disgust of Mary, who by this time had ascended the throne. She promptly ejected him from his see. He, in turn, in the hope of conciliating the Queen, rejected his wife, but Mary was obdurate.[1] Like his ornithological namesakes, he became migratory. The narrative goes on to say, that, having no resting-place, "he was fain to appeal to Bishop Bonner of London for some place of emolument, bringing with him, as a present, a dish of apples and a bottle of wine." He alleged that he had married against his will "to flatter with the time." Bonner eventually instituted him on November 6th, 1554, to the benefice of Great Dunmow, where he died, and was buried on October 15th, 1558.

Hertfordshire also seems to have suffered from Bonner's visitation choler, as Essex did later from his zeal in burning.

The record of his first visitation is preserved for us. We must remember that Fox is the chronicler, and must allow for the value of his evidence, as well as for his bitterly epigrammatic and highly-coloured Protestantism.

"He arrived at Stertford in Hertfordshire, where he rested certain days, solacing himself after that painful peregrination [through Essex] with no small feasting and banqueting with his attendants at the house of one Parsons, his nephew, whose wife he commonly called his fair niece (and fair she was indeed); he took there great pleasure to

[1] *Vide* Dr. Morris, "Diocesan History of Chester," S.P.C.K., p. 108.

hear her play the *virginals* (wherein she excelled), insomuch that every dinner (sitting by his sweet side) she arose and played three several times at his request of his good and spiritual devotion towards her. These certain days thus passed in this bishop-like fashion, he proceeded in his popish visitation towards Hadham."

The churchwardens at Bishops Stortford soon showed their obedience to the new orders, for we read in their accounts :—

" Item for making up of the aulter.   Item to Mr. Vicar for a mass book.   Item pd. for a pyx.   Item pd. for a holye water stope.   Item for makyng of the rood.   Item pd. to Burle for a cross.   Item pd. for a shippe (vessel) for frankincence."

The bells of Stortford " rang him out," and he evidently thought that the bells of Much Hadham, his own manor, should have " rung him in."   The chronicler goes on to relate :—

" Drawing near unto Hadham, when he heard no stirring there in honour of his holiness, he grew into some choler, and the nearer he approached the hotter was his fit and the quieter the bells were, the unquieter was his mood. Thus he rode on chafing and fuming with himself. ' What meaneth,' saith he, ' that knave, the clerk, that he ringeth not? and the parson that he meeteth me not?' . . . At length entering the church, and finding no sacrament hanged up, nor rood-loft decked after popish precept (which had commanded a well-favoured rood (crucifix), and of tall stature, to be set up in all churches), he curtailed his devotions and fell to swearings, calling the parson, whose name was Dr. Edmund Brickett, " knave and heretic.'   The parson humbled himself, saying, ' that as for those things lacking, he trusted in a short time hereafter he should compass that which hitherto he could not bring about.' ' Before God,' replied the furious bishop, ' thou art a knave ; avaunt heretic ! ' and therewith striking at him, the blow came upon Sir Thomas Josseline, who was amongst the rest and stood next the bishop, hitting him full upon the ear, whereas he was somewhat astonied, and said, ' What meaneth your lordship ? ' The Dean of St. Paul's is reported to have apologized for the bishop to the knight, who replied, ' Now that he is come forth from the Marshalsea, he is ready to go to Bedlam.' Leaving Hadham (where he was to have stayed four days) in a rage before dinner, and going to Ware, his chaplains tarried behind, and they dined at Dr. Brickett's as merrily as he rode towards Ware chafingly."

The effect of the visitation was shortly seen, for on October 25th, 1554, he wrote :—

" Edmund, Bp. of London, to all persons within the parish of Hadham. Because some children of iniquity taking from the church the picture of Christ, placing instead certain scriptures on the church walls, upholding the marriage of priests, destroying the sacrament of the altar . . . we charge you, wherever such scriptures have been attempted, to abolish them, that they be razed and be not read or seen." [1]

Some idea may be gathered of the stringent nature of this inquisitorial progress through the counties by a study of his *Articles of Enquiry*, which reached the number of 126. Amongst other things, inquiry was made " whether the ministering priest were married, or not yet separated from his wife ? resident, or having a sufficient

---

[1] Fox's "Acts and Monuments," ii. 87.

deputy ? hospitable and charitable ? whether of suspect doctrine, contrary to the Catholic faith and order of the realm ? whether within any Parish were any foreigner, priest, or others, not formally admitted by the Bishop, serving or ministering ? whether there were any married priests, or naming themselves ministers, keeping assemblies and conventicles with such like as themselves in any office or sect, for private lectures, sermons, playgames, or other unlawful devices ? whether any priests had renewed or reiterated baptism which had been lawfully done before ? whether any said or sung the service in English since the Queen's proclamation ? whether they prayed for King Philip and Queen Mary ? whether there were any serving in cure, and ministering the sacraments, not being priests ? whether they wore priest's apparel, having their heads and crowns shaven, or went like laymen ? " etc.

The Archdeacons of Colchester, Essex, and St. Albans received his attention. He wanted to know " whether they had visited all the Churches in their Archdeaconries, to find how divine service was celebrated, how the ornaments were kept, and what lack of them there might be ? whether they saw to the reservation of the host in a pix hung over the altar ? whether they admonished their parsons to put sick persons in remembrance of the great spoil and robbery that had been lately made of the goods and ornaments and the things of the church ; that in making their wills they might remember both their parish church and the cathedral and mother church of the diocese according to their devotion and power? whether they went frequently to the Chapters of their several Rural Deaneries? and there instructed the priests in 'cure' to live virtuously and to understand and know the words of the *Canon of the Mass*, and the form and order especially of Baptism, and chiefly those words that were of the substance of the Sacrament in any wise?" The churchwardens must have been alarmed at the number of questions which were addressed to them concerning the churches. They were as searching as those asked of the archdeacons and clergy.[1] One of the first effects of these new inquiries was the deprivation of the married clergy. Fox asserts that about one hundred beneficed priests in Essex were thus deprived.

On January 20th, 1555, the old Plantagenet Act, "*De Heretico Comburendo*," and cognate statutes were revived, the Reformation statutes of Henry VIII. and the Acts of Uniformity of Edward VI. were repealed.

Let us turn for a moment to that part of Hertfordshire which was not under Bonner's rule.

Bishop White (1554–57), at the instance of Cardinal Pole, in 1556, made a visitation of the diocese of Lincoln, with which we are still partly concerned.

---

[1] *Vide* Dixon's "History of the Church in England," vol. iv. p. 241, for account of this visitation.

This visitation indicates the general state of the church, including a portion of Hertfordshire. Many churches were in ruins and decay, with the lead stripped from the roofs. Penances were imposed for all sorts of offences, such as "not going in procession;" "for shaving a baby's head in mockery of the razure of the priests;" for calling the church bells "the devil's trumpets;" for asking "whether the vicar would run at the quintin when on Palm Sunday he performed the ceremony of opening the church doors with the staff of a cross." Priests were persecuted for "marrying late nuns," "for ministering the sacrament of the Altar to persons who had not come to confession, for allowing the General Confession of the English service to be used instead of auricular confession before ministering the Eucharist." [1]

The visitations being over, more serious and dreadful work was to begin. Armed with the replies to his visitation questions, and backed by statute, Bonner, in his conscientious but misguided zeal, baptized the counties with blood and fire, and on January 22nd, two days after the proclamation of the new laws, the Commission met to execute them.

Bishops White and Watson of Lincoln, though they issued their Articles of Enquiry, do not appear to have acted on them with the extreme severity of

---

[1] Dixon, abridged from Strype; vi. 389, and Strype, from *Comperta et detecta in Visitat., Patr. Joh. Linc. Epum.*

Bonner in that part of Hertfordshire over which they presided. But the county of Hertford was not without witness to the revolting cruelty of the reign. George Tankerfield was among the first victims of the fury, and after months of weary persecution was condemned. As he waited for the kindling of the fire he sang—

> "Be the day weary, or be the day long,
> At last it ringeth to Evensong."

His martyrdom took place at St. Albans, on a site known as Romeland, " being a green place near unto the west end of the Abbey Church."

William Hale of Essex was burnt at Barnet about the same time, and Thomas Fust, a hosier, at Ware. Neither of the three had any connection with the county previous to their death. Perhaps they were brought into Hertfordshire to overawe the people. Men like George Ferrers, lord of the manor of Flamstead, and subsequently member for St. Albans, the Maynards, the Pembertons, the Bacons of Gorhambury, were all of them staunch friends of the Reformation.

The fires of martyrdom were re-kindled with the fiercest fury in Essex. It would take too much space to attempt to reproduce the story of the heart-rending cruelties, and the wearisome examinations, often under torture, which preceded the climax of the stake. We must be content with an enumeration of the chief sufferers. The vicar of

South Weald informed against one William Hunter, who was burnt at Brentwood. Amongst the rest who met the cruel fate at different places in the county were John Simson, at Rochford ; John Ardeley, at Raleigh ; Thomas Hawkes, at Cogge-shall ; John Newman, at Saffron Walden ; Thomas Watts, George Eagles, at Chelmsford ; — Osmund, at Manningtree ; — Bamford, at Harwich ; Thomas Whittle, John Went ; Robert Drakes, Minister of Thundersley ; William Tyms, Curate of Hock-ley ; Richard Spurge, Thomas Spurge, John Cavel, George Ambrose, all of Essex, at Smithfield.

The chief centres of the pitiless flames were at Stratford, and Colchester, " that Taberah, that place of burning," as Dixon calls it. At Stratford thirteen persons were burned in one day.

"When these thirteen," says Fox, " were condemned, and the day had arrived on which they should suffer, which was June 27th, 1556, they were carried from Newgate in London to Stratford, and then divided into two classes and placed in two several chambers. Afterwards the sheriff, who then attended upon them, came to the one part and told them that the other had recanted, that their lives would therefore be saved, exhorting them to do the like, and not to cast themselves away. Unto whom they answered, that their faith was not built upon man, but on Christ crucified. Then the sheriff, perceiving no good to be done with them, went to the other part, and said the like to them, that they with whom they had been before had recanted, and should therefore not suffer death, coun-selling them to the like, and not wilfully to kill themselves, but be wise. Unto whom they also answered, as their brethren had done before, that their faith was not built in

man, but in Christ and His word. He then led them to
the place where they should suffer, and being then altogether, they most earnestly prayed unto the Lord, and
then joyfully went to the stake and kissed it, and embraced
it very heartily. The eleven men were tied to three
stakes, and the two women loose in the middle without
any stake, and thus they were all burnt in one fire."

There were in all five different "burnings" at
Stratford, and no less than eighteen persons suffered
martyrdom there. The names of the victims of
this mad fury are commemorated on the Martyrs'
Memorial erected there in 1879.

There were also terrible burnings at Coggeshall
and Manningtree.

In August of the same year, at Colchester, five
men and five women met their death. "They all
died," says Fox, "with such joy and triumph that
the spectators, in the midst of their sorrow for them,
burst into shoutings of loud and rapturous applause."

Four months later two men and a woman were
burnt at the same place, and Green asserts that
"seventy-three Protestants of Colchester were
dragged through the streets of London, tied to a
single rope."

As the "*Bloody Reign*" drew to its close, the
red-handed Bonner doubtless willingly slackened
the revolting method of repression to which he
had been forced, and "the people sickened at the
work of death."

No wonder, for during the days of this red glare
of fire it is computed that 277 persons were brought

to the stake; among them were 5 Bishops, 21 Clergymen, 8 lay gentlemen, 84 tradesmen, 100 husbandmen, servants and labourers, 55 women, and 4 children. They suffered with the noblest patience. " Even the commonest lives gleamed for a moment into poetry at the stake." [1] Our diocese stands nearly first with its number of victims. [2]

To the very last Bonner turned his fierce gaze on Essex. As late as April, 1558, he sent Chedsey and Morton, his chaplains, and Boxwell his secretary, into the county on a visit of inquisition. Their report was that they found "a large crop of as obstinate heretics, Anabaptists, and other unruly persons as ever was heard of."

One ray of light brightens the close of these dark days, at least from an architectural point of view.

Towards the end of Mary's reign an effort was made to restore and re-build some of the monastic houses which lay desolate. St. Albans was one of the abbeys contemplated for restoration. The priory of the Blackfriars at King's Langley was actually to some extent restored and re-endowed, and converted into a Nunnery.

We turn from these pages of hate with a sigh of relief, and of fervent thanksgiving that the church has emerged from this and succeeding trials guided and protected by Him who permitted the fire to rage.

---

[1] Green's " History of the English People." London, 1891, p. 366.
[2] Cutt's " Turning Points," ch. xxiv. p. 227.

CHAPTER XIX

THE ELIZABETHAN RE-ACTION—ESSEX AND HERTFORDSHIRE

> " Scarred by storm and foeman's fury,
>   Bathed in high serenest air,
>   See our fortress Church uprising,
>   Based and buttressed strong and fair,
>   Holds aloft the Cross of Jesus,
>   Guards the faithful voice of prayer."
>
> A. C. BENSON.

> " Sir, she would find them[1] by their branching.[2]
>   Their branching sleeves, branched cassocks, and branched doctrine,
>   Besides their texts."
>
> BEN JONSON, " Magnetic Lady."

THE accession of Elizabeth marked the commencement of another era of the history of the Church. The violent actions of the three preceding reigns had wrought great changes in the *personnel* of the clergy, and the policy of Elizabeth in reverting to the standard of Henry VIII. was another step in the consolidation of the Reformation settlement. The first act of her reign restored to the Crown " the supremacy over persons and in causes ecclesiastical," and met with general

---

[1] Protestants.   [2] Branching = embroidered.

acceptance among the rank and file of clergy, comparatively few refusing to comply. Many of the
Bishops, however, refused compliance, and suffered
deprivation. We are only at present concerned
with two, Bonner of London, and Watson of
Lincoln. Bonner's sun had set in a sea of blood,
never to rise again. On his refusal to take the
oath, he was committed to the Marshalsea, where
he dragged out the ten last years of his life, and
where he died on September 5th, 1569. There is
much doubt about the place of his burial; some
assert that he was buried at St. George's, South-
wark; others, with a greater amount of probability,
claim that his burial-place was at Copford, in Essex,
midway between Coggeshall and Colchester, from
whence he had haled men and women to prison,
and where he had burnt them at the stake.

The late Rector of Copford gathered some
interesting facts concerning this latter probability.
He says, in a letter dated December 15th, 1897 :—

"There is no doubt that Copford Hall was his favourite
Manor. There is a walk called *Bonner's Walk* to this
day. About sixty-two or three years ago the Rector of
this parish died, a certain Dr. Kelly ; a grave was being
dug for him under the Altar, when they came upon a
coffin with Bishop Bonner's name upon it. Tradition says
after he died in gaol in London, his body was brought
down to the neighbouring parish of East Thorpe, and was
kept there (apparently secretly), and after ten days it was
removed to his favourite church, probably at night, and
buried under the Altar.

"There is no entry of his burial, nor is there any

monument. It would seem that all was done secretly, and probably his enemies would have torn his body from the grave had they known where to find it. I am not aware that any one knew where it was till the coffin was found accidentally. I know where his coffin is ; I cannot say anything about his bones." [1]

An interesting reference on the subject of the disputed question of his secret burial has been preserved in the correspondence of Grindal, Bishop of London. On September 9th, 1569, four days after Bonner's death, the Bishop wrote from Fulham to Sir William Cecil, secretary to the Queen, to inform her of Bonner's burial by night, but he does not say where. He concludes, " This I write unto you is the veric truthe."

As a lighter touch in the dark story of the close of the unhappy prelate's career, we may add the postscript of Grindal's letter, in which he says, " My grapes this yeare are not yet rype ; about ye end of ye nexte weeke I hoope to send some to the Queen's Majesty." Meantime, however, the plague was reported to have broken out in the Bishop's household, so he wrote again on September 20th, denying this report, though a servant died from a cold (flux), and he excuses himself for tendering the grapes, and says, " Neither would I so far have overseen myself as to have sent to her Majesty, if I had not been more assured that my man's sickness was not of the plague." [2]

---

[1] Letter from the Rector of Copford to the Author.
[2] Lansdown MSS., vol. xi. f. 42, art. 64. See also " Faulkner's account of Fulham," 1813, p. 209.

As it had been in the case of Bishop Bonner of London, so it came to pass with my Lord of Lincoln. When Elizabeth came to the throne, Bishop Watson was deprived, and committed to the Tower, together with John White (of Winchester), who had preceded him.

Dean Hook is very severe on Bonner; he concludes his article in his " Ecclesiastical Biography " thus :—

" Without personal religion he defended the established system ; and had he lived at a later age, he would probably have defended whatever system he found established, while the evil passions of his vindictive mind would have found vent in the anonymous correspondence of a newspaper, or in the conduct of some so-called religious periodical." [1]

The change of tone in Church matters was soon apparent within the jurisdiction of both Bishops.

Resuming the consecutive order of episcopal succession, we will begin with Edmund Grindal (1559–1570), Bishop of London.

He is said to have been a friend of Fox, and to have assisted him in the compilation of his " Acts and Monuments," and it was probably due to his influence that an order was issued by Parliament, that certain books should be kept in parish churches for popular reference, and that we find the " Book of Martyrs " keeping company with " The Paraphrase of Erasmus," " The Bible of the largest Volume," " Bishop Jewell," etc., as at St. Stephen's ;

[1] Hook, " Ecc. Biog.," p. 568. 1845.

St. Albans, Kings Langley, and other places throughout the diocese.

Without discussing either the merits or the accuracy of " The Acts and Monuments," its popularity was undoubted. During the author's lifetime it ran through four editions.[1] On April 3rd, 1571, Convocation ordered that it should be placed in Cathedral Churches, and in the houses of archbishops, bishops, deans, and archdeacons. So much was it esteemed that even a man like Nicholas Ferrar, in his community at Little Gidding, directed that a chapter should be read every Sunday evening along with the Bible. Fox lived for a time within the borders of the diocese of London, and had a son and a daughter baptized at Waltham Abbey.

The entries in the churchwardens' accounts of the period emphasize the effect of the accession of the new Queen and the activity of the Bishops.

At Bishops Stortford, where Bonner five years before had spent his time so gaily, and had passed the days in " bishop-like fashion," his orders were soon reversed, and the churchwardens record, when Grindal ruled—

" For taking down ye hygh aulter-stone. For baryng away ye bryk and yearth of ye aulters. For takynge down of ye roode loft. For ye Boke of Paraphraces of Erasmy. For a deaske for ye polpett, 1569. For a new Bible xxx[s.]

---

[1] The editions were in 1563, 1570, 1576, 1583; they were followed later by editions in 1596, 1610, 1632, 1641, 1684.

1570, Pd. for the Bk. of Marters and Moluments xli[s.] Received for the old bookes, aulter cloths, cross cloths, and such other stuffe, xliv[s.] 1571, Pd. to James Stracy and his father for viii dayes' work in glasing ye church and xii fott of glasse, xviii[s.] 1573, Pd. for defacing of the images in the glasse wyndowes to Alsopp viii[d.] For glasing and glasse to the glasier, viii[s.]"

This is only a single illustration of the turn of the tide. The revival of the Reformation *cult* was soon to show itself in other ways. The purpose of the new leaders was not to form a new sect, but to carry on the work of purification of the old Church.

In 1559 the revived and slightly revised Second Prayer Book of Edward VI., with a fresh Act of Uniformity annexed, established the new order of things, and forthwith led to a visitation for the settlement of religion. Sessions were held at Weald, Chelmsford, Stortford, Dunmow, Colchester. It was generally accepted by the clergy. Gradually recusancy sprang up, and in ten years became common, and the malcontents began to crystallize into sects.

The Independents were the first to detach themselves, under Robert Brown, mainly on the question of church government. The Presbyterian and Puritan party disliked them as much as did the Queen herself, and the result was their voluntary emigration to the continent till better days should dawn. The new Protestantism was thus relieved of its then avowedly separatist element, but it had still to reckon with the Queen and the Bishops.

The rule of Bishop Sandys (1570–1576) scarcely affected the diocese, except that "encouraged by his mildness," and one might add, by his Calvinistic leanings, Puritanism became more aggressive. His days, however, were signalized by an event of the highest importance to the national Church. On the 25th May, 1570, the famous Papal Bull was published, deposing Elizabeth and absolving all who had sworn allegiance to her from their oath. The day for England or her Bishops to tremble at papal bulls had for ever passed, but the event, however, was not without its effect, for while it confirmed many wavering churchmen in their conformity, it was the signal for others who still held the supremacy of the Pope to detach themselves from the Church of England and her ministrations.

The rupture between England and Rome was complete. The new schismatics were comprehended with others under the general term Recusant.

Returns to the archdeacons of Hertfordshire at this date show, almost without exception, "No Recusants;" though here and there instances occurred as in the case of Richard Chambers, Vicar of Hitchin, John Potkyns, Rector of Lilley, and Thomas Wilcocks, Curate of Bovingdon.

In Essex recusancy was sharply dealt with, as, for example, in 1578, when one "Greene was committed to Maldon to be conferred with by two preachers until Michaelmas, and if he do not conform by that time, to be remitted to the gaol." Baddow and Depden figure in the same way.

The Pope, with the persistency which has ever marked the papal see, sent Jesuits from Douay, who flooded the land. But Elizabeth was a match even for the Pope, and in 1576 an Act was passed, directed against treason-mongers, which was followed by persecutions.

Bishop Sandys was succeeded by Bishop Aylmer (1577–95). He was a man of wide learning, a vigorous supporter of Elizabeth, a strong anti-Puritan, unconciliatory in disposition, and with an iron will. He soon made his power felt. He was quick in following up the commission of 1583, which was Elizabeth's answer to objecting Puritans, with a visitation of Essex in the summer of 1584, and threatened to suspend the clergy who would not conform to the use of the surplice and of the cross in baptism. The bloodshed of Mary's reign and the ejectments of the Commonwealth and the Restoration have obscured the persecution of Elizabethan days. It will be interesting, therefore, to record this link in the chain of persecution which is generally unnoticed. Aylmer's threat reached no less than 38 clergy of Essex, and in many cases was put into execution. The names of the parishes are given by Neal in his well-known " History of the Puritans," [1] Panfield,

---

[1] Neal, " History of the Puritans," vol. i. p. 345, *et seq.*

Maldon, Fryerning, Rayne, Coggeshall, Much Totham, Aythorp, Rooding, Tilty, Marks-tey, Leigh, Writtle, Wethersfield, Colchester, Peldon, Dedham, Redewell, Halstead, Wix, Aldham, South Souberry (Shoebury), Tolbury, Little Waltham, Vange, East Hanningfield, Paglesham, Danbury, Langham, Lexden, Colchester (St. Peter's, St. Giles), Easthorpe, Hempsted, Felsted. The names of the clergy are given, and they are described as "the painful ministers of Essex whom the Bishop threatens to deprive for the surplice; saying, 'We shall be white with him, or he will be black with us.'"

One William Dyke or Dix was signatory together with Lawrence Newman, Vicar of Coggeshall, to a petition against Whitgift's Three Articles. It would be interesting to know whether the records of Coggeshall furnish any reference to him. We know that he incurred the wrath of Bishop Aylmer by his "preachings" at St. Michaels, St. Albans; at Redbourne, Shenley, Hemel Hempsted.

Aylmer was as good as his word in the case of the clergy of Easthorpe, Aldham, Fryan (Fryerning), and East Hanningfield, who were indicted at the assizes "for omitting the cross in baptism, for not wearing the surplice once every month, and at every communion." Most of those threatened were deprived and were forced to quit their livings and leave the country. Altogether about 50 clergy are said to have been deprived for not conforming to the Book of Common Prayer. The case of the Vicar of Hatfield Broad Oak was particularly hard. Hoping to excuse himself, he informed the Bishop "that within a compass of 16 miles there were 22 non-residents, and 30 insufficient ministers." The Bishop refused to listen to him, and he fell under suspension and imprisonment. A patron who refused the bishop's nominee met with a like fate. A list is given[1] under date 1584, in which it is stated that in a survey of 16 Hundreds in Essex, containing 335 benefices (Waltham, Beacontree, and half the hundred of Harlow, being omitted), "that there are ' of ignorant and unpreaching ministers 173, of such as have two benefices apiece 61, of non-residents that are single beneficed 10, preachers of scandalous life 12." A long list is given of those suspended for not wearing the surplice, and not using the sign of the cross in baptism.

It would be interesting to trace out in the registers of these Parishes, where they cover the date, how far the assertions gathered by Neal are correct. The state of seething unrest may be gathered from the fact that several of the Hundreds presented petitions against the persecution. The most notable was that from the county, led by Sir Francis Barrington, at the head of 200 gentlemen and tradesmen, householders, complaining in the strongest terms—

" that the greatest numbers of their present ministers were unlearned, idle, and otherwise of scandalous lives, and that

[1] *Vide* David's " Annals of Evangelical Nonconformity in Essex."

those few of whom they reaped knowledge and comfort were threatened and put to silence for small matters in Common Prayer, though they were men of godly lives and conversations."

No wonder that Aylmer complained to the Commissioner, in an appeal for more support, that he was "hated like a dog," and "that he was in danger of being mobbed in his progress at Maldon and other places." He almost rivalled Bonner for petulance and choler, and though he lighted no fires, he was Bonner's counterpart in Elizabethan days.

In 1583 he wrote to the Archdeacon of St. Albans—

"I am given to understand by common information, that many ministers within your archdeaconry do seldom or never wear the surplice, and some of them little or nothing observe the Book of Common Prayer. I do order you to let me know at my visitation who they are, that they may be proceeded against."

The Bishop's activity in enforcing the Acts of the reign, and especially the Commission of 1583, may have something to do with the large returns of communicants at St. Albans in 1584 : at the Abbey 800, at St. Peter's 400, at St. Michael's 260. At Watford, in 1594, as many as 900 were returned.

Mr. Urwick in his "Nonconformity in Herts," a book teeming with interest, gives some of the answers to the Archdeacons of the time, to be found in the "Archdeacon's Acta," *e.g.* :—

"*King's Langley.*—'Our minister (Mr. Lewis) doth not

cross the child in baptism.' *Watford*—'Our font is removed, but by whose orders we know not.' *Northall.*— ' We have not all the service, for he doth preach morning and afternoon, which doth edefie the people very much ' (W. White was the minister). *Ridge.*—' Edmund Peacham, our minister, doth not wear the surplesse. He doth omit the cross in baptism. He doth not, at many times, use the Book of Common Prayer.' *Rickmansworth.*—' Our minister sometimes omits the epistle and gospel. He doth not wear the apparel.' *Hexton.*—' He doth not wear the apparel, but is willing.' *East Barnet.*—' He doth not wear the apparel, but he is willing and ready to wear them.' *Chipping Barnet.*—' We have no preacher but our parson, but we have not known him to wear any cap, for he saith it is hurtful unto his eyes, which indeed are very dimme. Our parson's name is Edward Underne ; he hath not any other living. He is comformable in all good orders. Our Bible is of the largest print and largest volume.' *Watford.*—' There doth come to us divers honest preachers belonging to the right worshipful Charles Moryson, Esq., and others, who, when they do come to preach, help to minister the communion.' *Bushey.*—' No preacher hath preached in our parish save only Mr. Willoughby, parson of Stanmore, whom our parson, Mr. John Singer, hath hired to preach the quarter sermons. Howbeit there was one Richard Costelett, a preacher, licensed as he said by the Bishop of Salisbury, who preached for us the Sunday se'nnight before the Christmas-day.' " [1]

During the episcopate of Aylmer, the Satires of *Martin Mar-prelate* were issued. Aylmer (with Cooper of Lincoln) bore the brunt of the attack, all sorts of epithets and accusations being hurled at him. He was called " the Elmar," in reference to his cutting down timber at Fulham, " Dumb John

[1] " Nonconformity in Herts." William Urwick, pp. 88, 89. London, 1884.

of London," because his sermons were infrequent. Worse accusations, too coarse to repeat, were brought against him.

Aylmer saw the rapidly growing development of the Elizabethan policy, and supported her in it. Dread of Rome, and the foreign influences of Geneva were too strong even for the Queen. The memory of the fires of Bonner and the fear of Spain made men look with suspicion on her Acts insisting on conformity.

Aylmer was not altogether free from the charge of nepotism. He appointed his second son, Theophilus, as Rector of Much Hadham and Archdeacon of London, and we are told of the said Archdeacon that—

"he shut his own eyes with his own hands, dying in the year of the Lord Jesus in the month of January, 1605, a year memorable for a severe pestilence, in which dyed 54 preachers of London. He was buried in his own Parish Church, and honoured with a ffun [funeral] sermon preached by Dr. James Usher, the most learned Archbp of Armagh."[1]

Details are given to us by a contemporary writer of the extent of Aylmer's charge in the Essex portion of his diocese, viz.—

" Number of p̄shes and Chappels that have cure   ... 413
   The whole number of houses of nob-men, gent, and ⎫
       men of accom̄pte observed in the map of this ⎬ 354."
   shire is [2]   ⎭

[1] " Lansdowne MSS.," 984, f. 34.
[2] Norden's " Description of Essex." Probable date of publication, 1596.

Richard Fletcher (1595–97), the son of a Vicar of Bishops Stortford, had too short a time in which to make history as a bishop, though he had succeeded in doing so as Dean of Peterborough, previous to his elevation to the see of Worcester, whence he was translated to London. Whilst Dean, he preached before the Commissioners at the trial of Mary Queen of Scots, at Fotheringhay Castle, 12th October, 1586, and officiated as chaplain at her execution, 8th February, 1587. He was strongly Calvinistic in his leanings.

Richard Bancroft (1597–1604) was more concerned with the question of "divine right" than in attending to the details of church life in his diocese as Bishop of London. He lived to see the death of Elizabeth, and the coronation of James I, whom he declared, in words of servile adulation, to be "such a king as since Christ's time had not been." When he became Archbishop, he enforced the three Articles on Rites and Ceremonies, which became binding on the clergy in 1604, the previous Act in Elizabeth's reign only requiring subscription to those which concerned the faith and the sacraments.

The Bishops of that portion of Hertfordshire, which was still under the episcopal jurisdiction of Lincoln, must be noticed, though but little local information as to their rule can be gained.

Nicholas Bullingham (1560–71) was the first

Elizabethan Bishop of that see. Like all his com-
peers in the throes of great national and ecclesiastical ferments, he was much engaged in questions
of re-settlement. He took a leading part, while
Archdeacon of Lincoln, in the discussion of the 39
Articles. He is said to have been present at the
consecration of Archbishop Parker, acting as Epis-
toler and wearing a silk cope. The robbery, and
consequent poverty of the see of Lincoln left the
Bishop too poor to travel much in his diocese, and
he exercised but little pastoral oversight. He was
not unmindful of others in like distress. One of
the few diocesan matters on record concerning him,
points to this, and gives an indication of his religious
sympathies. In February, 1567, he issued a circular
letter to his diocese, asking for collections for the
refugees from France and Flanders.

Thomas Cooper (1577–87) chiefly distinguished
himself in the *Mar-prelate* controversy. An
Admonition of Parliament, which had been issued
by the Puritan party, produced a rejoinder in an
Admonition to the People of England, which was
generally attributed to Cooper, though the author-
ship belongs to Whitgift. The Bishop was so
intimately concerned in, and so fully in sympathy
with it, that his name was immediately associated
with the reply in the celebrated tract, " Ha' ye
any work for the Cooper? "

Of William Wickham (1584–95) we have been
unable to trace any history of special importance,

in connection with his diocese. He was, however, careful to enjoin the observance of holy days, of Wednesdays and Fridays, and of Rogationtide. After the execution of Mary Queen of Scots, he preached a funeral sermon in her memory on August 1, 1587, in the Cathedral of Peterborough. Two years afterwards he was translated to Winchester.

William Chadderton (1595–1608) was the last of the Elizabethan Bishops of Lincoln. He was " hot against recusants," as his own Visitation Courts, and those of his Archdeacons witness. He supported the Queen in her attempt to enforce the celibacy of the clergy, but his loyalty in this respect was eclipsed by his attachment to one Katharine Revell, whom he married.

In Hertfordshire the *Acta* of the Archdeacons still further illustrate the course of events attending the spread of Puritanism.

We find the Archdeacons imposing penances on various refractory members of their flock—

"not receiving the communion," "opening his shop on St. Luke's Day," "working his horses on holy days." "A clergyman was presented for not reading Litany on Saint's days, for not reading Book of Homilies, for admitting one to be surety for baptism who had not received communion," "omitting the cross in baptism, administering the communion to the people standing."

The greatest of the Puritan leaders was Thomas

Cartwright, a Hertfordshire man, who infused all
the bitterness of Calvin into the growing controversies about matters of ritual, such as the cross in
baptism, the surplice, the ring in marriage, and
kneeling at communion ; he also attempted to set
up a Presbyterian form of church government.
The Commission of 1583 was Elizabeth's main
answer to the spread of the Puritan *cult*. Its
decisions were rigidly enforced, and still further
paved the way to the revolt of the next century.
The effect of the policy of the Queen is thus
summed up by Professor Wakeman—

"The English church found herself in a greater state
of spiritual and intellectual destitution of the beginning
of the reign of Elizabeth than she had experienced since
the coming of the Normans. It was not until a generation
had grown up under the influence of the Prayer-book and
the Bible that, under the leadership of Hooker, the Clergy
of the Church of England began once more to take their
rightful place in the intellectual and religious world."[1]

The newly-found life and power of the clergy
had to reckon with the uprising of an intellectual
and religious power amongst the laity. Sickened
and wearied with a reign of bitter persecution,
which was succeeded by another of bewildering
injunctions, and attempts at compromise, inspired
by the fierce Protestant propaganda of Calvin, they
began to assert themselves with no uncertain voice.

[1] Wakeman's "History of the Church of England," pp. 313, 314.
3rd Ed., 1897.

Despite their subsequent divisions into conforming and non-conforming Puritanism, that force had to be reckoned with.

The succeeding days of the first of the Stuarts delayed, but could not avert, the climax of its strength.

CHAPTER XX

PURITANS OF STUART TIMES—ESSEX

" We do that in our zeal our calmer moments are afraid to answer."—
ANON.

> *" New opinions,*
> *Divers and dangerous, which are heresies,*
> *And not reformed may prove pernicious."*
>
> SHAKESPEARE.

ENGLISH Puritanism must properly be regarded as the child of Lollardism. Its mixed seeds of truth and error were never really thoroughly destroyed as the authors of the *" De Heretico Comburendo"* hoped. Lollardism not only contributed to the beginnings of the Reformation, but was the parent of the excesses which befell the movement in its consummation. The Lollards prepared the way for the later Elizabethan days, and for the whole of the Stuart and Commonwealth period, in which, as Green justly declares, " England became the people of a book, and that book was the Bible." However much national sentiment distorted, misused, and misunderstood that book, the fact remains.

The reaction, from the mediæval view of absolute authority, like all reactions, had unfortunately the tendency to go to extremes. The pendulum swung too far. The choice, as men thought, lay between Rome and the Bible, and the undue exaltation of private judgment brought about the conflict in the Church and nation, the effects of which are only too apparent in the "dissidence of dissent."

There is, however, this difference between the Lollards and the Puritans, that while the one was merely a school, the other eventually became a sect, resulting from an ultimate fusion of Presbyterian and Puritan forces, which combined in their refusal to conform. The Presbyterian power was chiefly fostered by the clergy, the Puritan was more distinctly a lay movement; both were originally opposed to separation, because in combination they hoped to capture the Church. As Lollardism was the parent of Nonconformity, so the Anabaptists of Holland were its nurses, and whilst the Reformation movement was at its height (in 1535), they were quietly training the new force which was to cleave both Church and nation asunder. The broom of Elizabeth, though fairly stubborn, did not, as we have seen, sweep clean, and she had found it necessary to pass an Act in which all persons were required to resort to church, absentees being fined twelve pence for non-attendance. Twenty years later, a fine of £20 a month was imposed. Seven years later still (1593), the first *Conventicle Act* was passed.

The *Recusants*, Roman and Puritan alike, fell under the ban of this imperious Queen. The Puritan movement sprang from the lower and middle classes, rather than from the higher ranks of society, though all were involved in the tumult of its unrest. Its earlier history had more to do with ritual and doctrine than with discipline, and the early Presbyterian Puritan must be carefully distinguished from the later Nonconformist. Aversion to church discipline and ceremony gradually grew into abhorrence, the customs most objected to being, as we have seen, the use of the surplice, the sign of the cross in baptism, the ring in marriage, and the kneeling posture in Holy Communion. In Essex, objection to these symbols was the cause of great severity on the part of Bishop Aylmer. In the latter days of Elizabeth the new power was beginning to make itself more distinctly felt. Though her Royal Arms hung over the heads of the people in church, and her initiatory Uniformity Act (for so it was) had been passed, they only served to irritate the new religionists. William Chadderton was Bishop of Lincoln when James I. came to the throne; Richard Vaughan succeeded to London within a year. They, like the rest of the Bishops, were powerless before the rising storm.

The *Millenary Petition* of 1603 is enough to

show the trend of events. "It asked for no change in the government or organization of the Church, but for a reform of its courts, the removal of superstitious usages from the Book of Common Prayer, the disuse of lessons from the Apocryphal books of scripture, a more rigorous observance of Sundays, and the provision and training of preaching ministers." It was signed by about eight hundred of the Puritan clergy, and led to the Hampton Court Conference.

Having made this preliminary review, let us revert to the episcopal succession of the see of London.

Richard Vaughan (1604–7) succeeded to the see of London, within a year of the accession of James I., and brought with him, from Chester, considerable experience in hunting out *Recusants.* His leanings were Calvinistic, and consequently his relations to the Puritan party were conciliatory, though, as Fuller says, "nothing could tempt him to betray the rights of the Church to sacrilegious hands, not sparing sharply to reprove his own order on that account." There is much interesting information to be found about him in the MSS. of the British Museum.[1]

Thomas Ravis (1607–10) followed, having been translated from Gloucester. It is said of

---

[1] *Vide* Harl. MSS. 6495. f. 51, entitled, "Vaughanus Redivivus"; Lans. MSS. 68, art. 24, 445, f. 34, 983, ff. 60, 61, also in Cat. Hatfield MSS., vols. iv.–vi. ; Brook's "Puritans," ii. 232, 233.

him that as soon as seated he began to persecute
the Puritans, and declared, " by the help of Jesus,
I will not leave one preacher in my diocese who
doth not subscribe and conform." Had he found
time to look round, he would have discovered in
his Essex clergy a very much mixed assembly.
A most interesting account has been preserved
in a curious book published in 1610, entitled, " *A
view of the state of the Clargie within the County
of Essex.*" Even if it be one-sided, its statements
are worth summarizing.

Of the clergy of the county, 94 are described
as " dilligente and sufficiente Preachers," 48 as
" Preachers, some insufficiente some neligente,"
75 as " Ministers which be either non-Residentes,
double beneficed or noe preachers." 21 of these " non-
resident." 26 " dumbe preachers," 11 " negligents."

Some are described as " sufficiente preachers,"
though " non-resident." Among them, " the Vicar of
Witham, Doctor Sterne Lo, Suffregan of Colchester,
a sufficient preacher; he hathe alsoe the p̄sonage
of Bygrave in Harts : shire."

Of the non-residents the Rector " of Topsfield
Mr. —— of Clare Hall, lives at Cambridge, and
hath not come to his Churche theis twelve moneths
last paste." The Rector of Pastwick (? Pattiswick)
" a sufficiente preacher . . . he is the B. of
London's Chaplain, he is p̄son likewise of East
Hanningfield, and non-residente from bothe and
keepethe altogether with the B. of London." Of

the Rector of Bracksted (Braxted) Magna, it is said, "Doctor Blague p̄son there, where he hath not come paste once or twice this eighte yeres last paste, he is alsoe p̄son of Lambhithe (Lambeth), and likewise he is P͞son of Crayford and alsoe Deane of Rochester." The Vicar of Whitcolne "seldom preacheth, then unp̄ffitablie, and for the most part the labr̄s of other men, he beginneth oftetymes to say service as he is goinge to his seate, he readeth the psalmes and chapters un- revēndlie wᵗʰ his hat on his head, gapinge and yaneinge as if he were half asleepe." At Dedham, "Mr. Wright is p̄nted to the Vicaredge thereof by His Majesty, but the B. of London refuseth to admitte him because he refuseth to subscribe. There are above 800 communycants in this cure." At Hadstock, "Doctor Puckeringe p̄son there, he is also p̄son of Newington neere London, a p̄sonage in Wales and Prebende at Norwich, non- residente at Hadstock, and a negligente preacher."

"The p̄sons of Wigborough Magna" is "verie scandalous, for chopinge and changeinge of bene- fices."

Forty-six "are double beneficed." A hundred and six are described as " Ministers which be scandalous, whereof manie double beneficed, manie no preachers, and some non-residentes." In this instance, the names of the parishes are not given, but the values are recorded. Amongst the charges made against these 106, we find the following : "a drunckard," "a

common swearer," "ale-house haunters," " common
gamester," " bowler on the Saboth daies," " common
horseleech, cowleech," "a rediculous, ignorante, and
seldom preacher," " a comōn hunter," "a syllie
preacher," "a common stealer of deare with gray-
hounds," and worse.   Three of them are described
as having been " semenarye pristes."   The "horseleech p̄son" was a " verye imperfect reader, and
omytteth the hard names in readinge or ells readeth
them so absurdlie that he movethe thereby muche
laughter."   Of another it is said that he buried,
" dīvs children born in the p̄ishe not knowne to
have been baptised."   Of another, " an usuall
walker in the streets in the sermon tyme on market
daies."   Of another that he " preacheth seldome,
but is muche given to buye and sell bullocks and
grase them."   Of another that he was " contentious,
a maker of debate, and a deryder of the late
publique faste."

George Abbott (1610–11), Dean of Winchester,
and Prolocutor of Convocation, who had held the
see of Lichfield for about a month, had made
scarcely the record of a year in the see of London
before he was elevated to Canterbury.

We have first given a light sketch of the state
of the clergy, and by way of presenting a picture
of their houses, we quote from two terriers of the
period, relating to Essex parsonages.   Parndon
Parva—

" The Rectorie hath a mansion house newly builded

and repaired by John Nobles, that is to say a hall, a
parler, a kitching, a bruing house, a milk house and
butterie, and other necessarie rooms below, and two fayer
lodging-roomes above the stayers, two garret chambers,
and three other chambers for ordinarie use." [1]

And again at Little Baddow—

"There did then belong to the Vicarage, an old
Vicarage House cover'd with tiles, a little garden, a little
barn, a very little stable, and a little Hay House, all
thatch'd, two little orchards and a little garden plot." [2]

It was during the early episcopates of the period
that the Great Bible, the Geneva Bible, and the
Bishops' Bible rapidly gave way to the Authorized
Version of 1611.

No record remains, as far as I can discover, of
its reception in the counties, but the popularity of
the Geneva Bible amongst Puritans did not smooth
the path for the new version.

John King (1611–21) [3] was raised to the see
from the Archdeaconry of Nottingham, and James,
in his epigrammatic way, spoke of him as " the King
of preachers." Several of his mandates in relation
to the repairs of Essex churches have been preserved, amongst others, one to the vicar and churchwardens of Thaxted, respecting sundry matters in
connection with that church. [4]

Bishop King has the odious distinction of

---

[1] Terrier of 1618.   [2] Terrier of 1610.
[3] *Vide* Grossart's " Life of Bishop King." Edin. 1864.
[4] Add. MSS., 29, 439, f. 190. British Museum.

reviving the Act *De Heretico Comburendo*, in the case of one Bartholomew Leggatt, convicted of heresy. Happily for the church, this was the last "burning" in the diocese, though Neile, the Bishop of Lichfield, burnt Edward Wightman at about the same date.

It was during King's episcopate that "the Book of Sports" appeared.

Strangely enough, this book, prepared by Morton, Bishop of Chester, and issued by royal proclamation on May 24th, 1618, while putting certain limitations on the Sunday pastimes then in vogue, legalized others, and roused far more interest and excitement than did the authorized version of the Bible.

George Montaigne (1621–28) occupied the see of London on the death of Bishop King. He had previously held the Bishopric of Lincoln for about four years. Milton's opinion of him is not very flattering. He described him as "a canary-sucking and swan-eating prelate." The record of his rule is not striking. He is said to have largely occupied himself in his London diocese with the suppression of the popular lay lecturers, and to have sanctioned the erection and adoration of images in churches under his control. I cannot, however, discover any instances of these alleged acts. He affords another instance of rapid promotion, for he shortly became Bishop of Durham, and finally Archbishop of York.

We come now to the commanding figure of the period, William Laud (1628–33). Previously to his appointment to the see of London, he had held the Presidency of St. John's College, Oxford, and the Deanery of Gloucester, from which he had passed to the Bishoprics of St. David's, and Bath and Wells. He held also several rectories *in Commendam*, together with a Prebendal Stall in the Collegiate church of Brecon.

His public life and character are too well known to need repetition here, even if space could be found. His engagements in high affairs of Church and State largely engrossed his time, both as Bishop and subsequently as Archbishop. We can only give one or two local illustrations of his policy.

His attitude towards the question of the removal of the Holy Table from the middle of the Church to the Chancel will be referred to later.

His enforcement of strict discipline among clergy and laity alike, his insistence on the " Book of Sports," promoted very directly the exodus to the far West. The County of Essex was the greatest contributor to the thousands who followed the example of the Pilgrim Fathers. In the colony of Massachusetts Bay, between 1631 and 1641, no less than one-third of the heads of families bore Essex names, and have been distinctly traced to that county. Among the names assigned to the settlements in the new colony, at least thirty-two names of Essex parishes are given, such as Billericay, Braintree, Chelmsford, Colchester, Dedham, East Ham, Hadleigh, Harwich, Maldon, Newport,

Springfield, Toppesfield, Waltham, Wethersfield, etc.

That the "Book of Sports" was one of the greatest Puritan grievances appears from the following quotation from the code of laws, drawn up for the colony of Massachusetts:—

"Whosoever shall profane the Lord's Day by doing unnecessary travelling, or by sports and recreations, he or they who so transgress shall forfeit forty shillings or be publicly whipped; but if it shall appear to have been done presumptuously such person or persons shall be put to death, or otherwise severely punished, at the discretion of the Court. No one shall run on the Sabbath day, or walk in his garden or elsewhere, except reverently to and from meeting. No one shall travel, cook victuals, make beds, sweep house, cut hair or shave, on the Sabbath day."[1]

As an instance of the harsh cruelties to which the advocates of the "Book of Sports" proceeded, Mr. Urwick relates that Prynne, Bastwick, and Burton, who wrote against it, were condemned to the pillory and prison and to lose their ears, to be fined £5000 a piece, and to be branded with the letters " S.L." (*Seditious Libeller*), which Prynne, not unjustly interpreted as "*Stigmata Laudis.*"[2] John Bastwick was born at Writtle, in Essex, in 1593, graduated as *M.D.* at Emmanuel, Cambridge,

---

[1] Dr. Hessey's "Bampton Lectures," p. 285.
[2] Urwick, "Nonconformity in Herts," p. 121.

and practised as a physician at Colchester. Parliament was not long before it ordered restitution of his fine out of the estates of the Archbishop. No wonder that the men of St. Albans and Barnet cheered Bastwick to the echo ; no wonder that this mistaken policy raised the fury of the fire of Puritanism.

Our readers will doubtless be able to supply evidences of Laud's enforcement of his injunction which caused the Altar controversy from various parishes in Essex ; and the *Acta* of the Archdeacons point, as in Hertfordshire, to the same series of presentments and penances for the ecclesiastical offences of the time.

However much we may regret the immediate hardships which fell on Laud's opponents, we must be grateful that largely by his means, as Mr. Gladstone declared, the English Church was saved "from being bound in the fetters of an iron system of compulsory and Calvinistic belief."

William Juxon (1633), Scholar, Fellow, and President of St. John's, Oxford, who had been elected to the see of Hereford, was promoted as Laud's successor to the Bishopric of London. His rule, like his character, was mild and gentle. He was the last episcopal Lord High Treasurer of England, and he had the signal honour of attending " *King Charles the Martyr,*" in his last moments at Whitehall.

Then dark days fell upon the nation. We

shall see shortly how the county of Essex was smitten with the storm which accompanied the darkness. We must first pause to consider what was going on in Hertfordshire during the days of which we have just been speaking.

CHAPTER XXI

PURITANISM OF STUART TIMES—HERTFORDSHIRE

" I know thou art religious and hast a thing within thee called a conscience."—SHAKESPEARE.

" How many things might be tolerated in peace and left to conscience, had we but charity, were it not the chief stronghold of our hypocrisy to be ever judging one another."—MILTON.

THE Elizabethan settlement while it strengthened for a time the position of the Church, had by no means crushed the spirit of the Puritan party, and the struggle between conscience and conformity began to reassert itself early in the Stuart days. The declaration of James I. in respect of the Puritans, " I will make them conform, or I will harry them out of the land," showed clearly enough that a new struggle could not be avoided. Let us proceed with the story of the episcopal succession of Lincoln, and illustrate the course of events from local history. Chadderton was the last of the Elizabethan Bishops of the see, and his episcopate extended five years into the Stuart period, but it produced no personal incident worthy of remark.

There is a matter, which may be mentioned in passing, which must have affected the work of the parochial clergy. During the episcopate of Chadderton, while grave political and ecclesiastical issues were shaping themselves, there appears to have been a great outbreak of the plague. It is often lost sight of, but I expect it was far more wide-reaching than is commonly supposed, and it would be interesting, by a reference to the parish registers of the time, to trace something more of its effects. There can be little doubt that the bills of mortality at this time were very heavy, and that the work of the clergy was correspondingly responsible and difficult ; *e.g.* at Great Amwell, in 1603, there were forty-one interments ; of these nineteen died with plague between August 19th and November 28th. The officiating minister notes, " I buried six of this disease in one daye." Only this one instance is cited, and this by the way, but many others might be produced.

Chadderton's influence was of little account in moulding the course of the controversies of the time, and his immediate successors in the see were, for the most part time-servers and place-hunters.

Of these, William Barlow (1608–13), translated from Rochester, was one of the prominent figures at the Hampton Court Conference, as well as having had a hand in the production of *The Authorized Version*. His absence from his diocese was a consequence of his pre-occupation in these matters ;

but we are indebted to him as the recorder of the doings of the celebrated conference.

Richard Neile (1614–17), his successor both at Rochester and at Lincoln, was a kind of episcopal greyhound leaping rapidly from one see to another. He held in succession the sees of Rochester, Lichfield,[1] Lincoln, Durham, Winchester, finding a resting-place at last on the archiepiscopal throne of York. The story related of him and good Lancelot Andrewes will show the character of the man. The King asked them—

" My Lords, cannot I take my subject's money when I want it, without all this formality of Parliament ? " " God forbid, sir, but that you should ; you are the breath of our nostrils," was the answer of the Sycophant. The reply of Bishop Andrewes was, to say the least of it, clever : " I think, sir, that it is lawful for you to take my brother Neile's money, for he offers it."

After this, the less we say of him, the better.

George Montaigne (1617–21) attempted to rival the rapidity of Neile's promotions, but he only succeeded in running through the sees of Lincoln, London, Durham, when, like his predecessor, he too rested at York. Milton's estimate of him has already been quoted in connection with the see of London.

John Williams (1621–42) makes history. On his promotion from the Deanery of Westminster to the see of Lincoln, we are told of him that he still retained his Deanery, his living of Walgrave,

[1] *Vide*, p. 231.

and a canonry in Lincoln Cathedral. Heylin might well facetiously describe him as " a perfect diocese within himself." His career is very attractive, but we must only single out a few illustrations of his relation to some of the events of the day. The subject of Sunday observance, arising out of the controversy as to " The Book of Sports " issued by Royal Proclamation, May 24th, 1618, was brought to his notice in a very direct manner. It set forth—

"That for his good people's recreation, his Majesty's pleasure was, that after the end of divine service, they should not be disturbed, letted, or discouraged, from any legal recreations, such as dancing, either men or women, archery for men, leaping or vaulting, or any such harmless recreations ; nor of having May games, Whitsonales, or Morice dances, or setting up of May-poles, or other sports therewith used, so that the same may be had in due convenient time, without impediment or let of divine service," etc.

The malcontents, like those of our day, determined to attack the bishop himself. So strong was public opinion, that he was presented at the Archdeacon's Visitation Court at Huntingdon on October 11th, 1631, by the Commissary-General, John Spencer. The ground of the presentment will be gathered from the sentence decreed. Even though the Lord's Day was considered to be at an end at sunset, the proceeding for which the Bishop was presented was not becoming on the part of his lordship. It was certainly not conciliatory, and it must have shocked the good people of Buckden.

The presentment runs—[1]

"John Spencer presents the Bishop of Lincoln for having a play that night in his house, it being the Lord's Day, September 27th, 1631."

The following is a copy of the order or decree of *ex-officio* Commissary-General John Spencer :—

"Forasmuch as this Courte hath been informed by Mr. Commisary Generall of a great misdemeanour committed in the house of the Right Honble. John Lo. Bishopp of Lincolne by intertaining into his house divers knights and ladies with many others, household and servants, uppon the 27th September, being the Sabbath Day, to see a playe or tragidie there acted, which began about ten of the clocke at night and ended about two or three of the clocke in the morning. Wee doe therefore order and decree that the Right Honble. John Lord Bishopp of Lincolne shall for his offence erect a free scoole in Eaton, or else at Great Staughton, and endowe the same with £20 per annum for the maintenance for a school Master for ever."

Sir Sydney Montague, of Hinchinbrook, the ancestor of the Earl of Sandwich, with his lady, were present as spectators, and for this their offence the knight was fined £5, to be given to the poor of Huntingdon, and his lady was to be called on to furnish " five black gounds to five poor widows " on the following New Year's Day. Similar fines were inflicted on other guests, but the most extraordinary sentence was that passed upon a certain

---

[1] The original presentation is among the muniments at Boughton Hall, Northants, *Vide Lincoln Diocesan Magazine*, vol. vii. No. 55, p. 141.

Mr. Wilson. The play enacted seems to have been Shakespeare's *Midsummer Night's Dream*, and the said Mr. Wilson not only got up the performance, but himself sustained the part of Bottom, the Weaver. This is what the court has to say about him—

" Likewise wee doe order that Mr. Wilson, because he was a speciall plotter and contriver of this business, and did in such a brutishe manner act the same with an Asse's head, therefore hee shall uppon Tuesday next, from sixe of the clocke in the morning till sixe of the clocke at night, sitt in the Porter's Lodge at My Lord Bishopp's house with his feet in the stocks and attyred with his Asse head and a bottle of hay sett before him, and this super-scription on his breast :

> " ' Good people, I have played the beast,
> And brought ill things to passe ;
> I was a man, but thus have made
> Myself a silly Asse.' " [1]

The result of the prosecution did not make matters easier for the Bishop in the administration of his diocese.

It was a burning grievance to the Millenarian clergy to be forced by the authority of the Crown, at the instigation of Laud, to read the " Book of Sports " publicly in the churches.

Charles Chauncy, Vicar of Ware, was amongst the clergy who resisted. Cussans gives the story thus— [2]

---

[1] *Lincoln Diocesan Magazine*, 1891, vol. vii. No. 67. Quoted from *St. Neot's Advertiser*.

[2] Cussan's " History of Hertfordshire," vol. i. p. 153.

"He had not long been appointed to the Vicarage, before he also incurred the displeasure of the Bishop, which arose from the protest which Mr. Chauncy made against the Sunday amusements sanctioned in the ' Book of Sports.'

"It was against these amusements that the Vicar protested, and as it was contrary to the Statute to preach in the afternoon, he devoted that part of the day to catechizing and instructing his parishioners. To this it was objected that 'his catechizing was as bad as his preaching.' This and other persecutions induced him to resign his position, and in 1637 he left England for Plymouth, Massachusetts."[1]

Side by side with the authorized encouragement of amusement on Sunday, it is interesting to notice the number of presentments which were constantly being made against work on Sundays and holy days, such as at Hemel Hempsted, " for profaning the Lord's day in killing a bullock ; " for " that the grain they thresh on the week-day, they fan on the Sabbath ;" or, as at Bengeo, " for working at the stock of a tree, and peeling the bark upon Ascension Day all forenoon." " Also on Easter Monday, all the forenoon in felling wood." These latter offenders hailed from Harpenden, and had to do penance in the church. In 1610, a man of Hemel Hempsted was presented for his " irreverent sitting in the Church with his hat on at the *Gloria Patri ;*" he alleged in excuse "that the rain came in." Another man from the same place was

---

[1] Cussan's " Hertfordshire," vol. i. p. 151.

reproved "for that he wrought at his trade, being a bricklayer, on St. Matthew's Day." From Wallington, four were admonished "that they went to cart upon Monday and Tuesday of Whit-week." Scores were of course presented "that they did not receive the Communion on Easter Day according to the 112th Canon." A weaver of Munden Magna was censured "for working at his trade on May-day last," 1611. At Shenley, another was presented for "laying a henne under the book of the parish clarke," and was enjoined to "do penance in the chancel before the Minister and guardians"; another of the same parish was presented "that he went to plough on St. Matthias day."

In further illustration of the activity of the Courts of the Archdeacons of the period, we may note that of St. Albans (1606). One clergyman was presented for "not wearing his surplice always, for not having a cloke with sleeves, and for not having a square cap." In the same year the Vicar of Aldenham was presented "in that he doth not usually wear the surplice, neither doth he use the sign of the Cross in Baptism." The Vicar, in his turn, presented one of his parishioners to the Archdeacon "for playing cards in evening prayer time." Penances and fines for "meeting at a conventicle," which had begun to be imposed in Elizabeth's reign, increased rapidly. The suppression of Puritan lectures, the rigid injunction of the surplice, and other ceremonial matters, added fuel to the fire of discontent.

Side by side with the disputes over the "Book of Sports," and ceremonial uses, was a contention as to the position of the Holy-table, which in the latter days of Elizabeth, had in many places been moved into the body of the Church. Laud's injunction that the Holy-tables should be placed at the east end of the chancel and railed in, gave renewed strength to the storm. His order seems to have been generally accepted, and though Bishop Williams objected to it, his resistance was not very successful in the Hertfordshire part of his diocese. We find it a source of frequent contention that the clergy who had removed their altars eastward refused the Sacrament to those who would not come up to the "rayles" to receive.

The instance of the Puritans at Welwyn, though rather long, is worth quoting, the more so, as it throws an interesting light on the mind of Laud, who has too often been regarded as a mere Romanizer. The following extract from the *Canway Papers*, in the Record Office, will help to remove this aspersion on his character.

" The same week, sixteen men of the parish of Welling, in Hertfordshire, came to their Archdeacon, Dr. Holdsworth, here in London, to complain of the Parson of their Parish, for having refused the three Sundays before, to administer the Sacrament unto them, only because they would not come upp to receive yt at the Rayle about the Communion table. I heare there hath been greate contention betweene the minister and the Parishioners which the Archdeacon not being able to compose, hee therefore, with these sixteen Parishioners, addresseth his complainte to my lord Grace of Canterbury, who haveing heard all the differences, referres all back to Doctor Holdsworth, to settle peace between all parties saying, hee wonders the Parson should exact their comeing upp to the rayle to receave the Sacrament, if soe bee the Pewes be conveniently seated in the Church, to administer in them." [1]

This complaint produced a letter from the Archdeacon to the Rector—

"Mr. Wilshere. It has pleased my Lord Grace of Cant. upon a peticōn delivered to his Grace by some of your pīsh to give order to me to require you not to deny the comn to any of your communicants that present themselves to receive as they ought kneeling in the Chancell although they come not up to the Rayle to which none are to be compelled to come save only those that are willing. These are therefore to require you to take notice of his Grace's Order, the copy whereof I have here sent you enclosed. Sr, I am sorry you should deny theise comforte to soe many conformeable men having noe comand from sup'īours. It might have bred you more trouble than that my Lo : Grace delights in gentlenesse. And, moreover, your pīshoners did not agravate theire greivances against you . . . Sr, there is one thing more that was not represented to his Grace which I must both entreate you & require you to take into consideracōn that you soe order the readeing of the second service [the Communion Service] that your parishoners may conveniently hear it and receive by it edificacōn, for I am informed that at least threescore of them can neither see nor heare you, soe that not

----

[1] Rector of Welwyn, 1606–31.
[2] *State Papers*, Record Office, Dom. Series, Chas. I., 1639, No. 417, 31. *Vide* also Cussan's " Hertfordshire," vol. ii. p. 228.

doubting but that you will accomodate theise things to his Grace's expectation and your pīshoners lawful content, with my hearty love, I commend you to God, and rest,

"Your lo : friend,

". RICH : HOLDSWORTH.

"St. Peter, Bread streete,
  "Apr : 4, 1639.
"Endorsed by Archbishop Laud."

Mr. Urwick has laid us under an obligation in respect to the Altar controversy in Hertfordshire, as well as by the record of many other interesting subjects concerning contentions of the time. He gives the following extract from Laud's "Account of his Province"—

"There are risen some differences in the Southern parts of his diocese (Lincoln) about the ministers urging the people to receive at the rails which his lordship saith he hath procured to be placed about the holy table, and the people in some place refusing so to do. Now because this is not regulated by any Canon of your (*sic*) Church, his lordship is an humble suitor that he may have direction herein. And truly I think ye people will best be won by the decency of the thing itself, and that I suppose may be compassed in a short time. But if your Majesty shall think it fit that a quicker way be held, I shall humbly submit." The King's note is "Try your way for some tyme." [1]

The altar war waxed fierce in Hertfordshire, and led to much violence. It is recorded that—

"the railes in the chancels of tenne Churches in the said two hundreds of Cashio and Dacorum, were pulled down by soldiers, October 5th, 1640. Jo Boteler. Jo Jennings."

[1] "Lambeth MSS.," 943, *Laud's Account of his Province*, p. 253. *Vide* Urwick, "Nonconformity in Herts," 1884, p. 623.

Other witnesses confirmed the statement—

" I did hear Edmund Aylee say that he was captain of those unruly soldiers that did pull down the rails in our Church or chancell, and those were the last of seventeen that he had pulled down and broken with his own hand. . . . *sic testor*, Jo Briggs. *Idem testatus*, Jo Bassill." [1]

The said Edmund Aylee was a glazier of Bishops Stortford, and the climax of his riotous conduct occurred at Rickmansworth, where it was alleged against him, and he confessed that he—

" did come into the church of Rickmansworth, and after sermon ended in the forenoon did then wittingly and suddenly (with seven other soldiers), pull down and break in pieces the rayle about the Communion table, and also in the afternoon of the same day did wittingly and suddenly break down and deface a part of the cover of the font ; " but he went on to state that he was not hired to do the same, and to deny that he had been " at the pulling down of the rayles in the chancells of seventeen churches, or of any other church in the county." [2]

The Parish Church of Hitchin evidently received the attention of the rioters, for we read that a party of soldiers entered whilst the service was going on ; when it was ended, they tore down the rails—

" and having extracted money from the poorly paid minister, invited themselves to the churchwarden's, to dinner.   In the afternoon they brought an excommunicated person into the church, and forced the minister to read evening prayers in his presence." [3]

[1] Record Office, Dom. Series, 1640.   [2] *Ibid.*
[3] Kingston's " Herts during Civil War," p. 6, *State Papers*, Charles I.

To return to Laud; his appearance in the administration affairs of the diocese of Lincoln may appear strange. The fact was that Williams had some years before asserted that "the Puritans were the King's best friends," and had given great offence to the Archbishop in his appointment of the celebrated Lambert Osbaldestone to Wheathampstead, besides having resisted his injunction about the position of the Holy Table. Consequently he had to appear in the Star Chamber, and at the date of Laud's endorsement of the above letter, was a prisoner in the Tower, his episcopal jurisdiction in the meantime having been suspended. The Archbishop, with characteristic vigour, set about a thorough visitation of the diocese of Lincoln, to see that his commands were obeyed. His temporary administration of the diocese prompts a reference to his position. Professor Wakeman thus sums it up :—

"It was his unhappy infirmity that he appeared always to the world as the schoolmaster armed with punishment, rather than the leader and champion of a higher system. The bent of his mind, the peculiarity of his position naturally led him to constrain rather than to persuade. His appeal was to obedience and duty rather than to enthusiasm and zeal. . . . Quick to see the greatness of the Church of England, and to realize her mission to the world, he was slow to recognize the fact that Puritanism was an abiding element in English religious life." [1]

[1] Wakeman's "History of the Church of England," pp. 370, 371, 3rd ed., 1896.

In the course of the Archbishop's visitation to which we have referred, we come across a curious sidelight on the duties of a Stuart parish-clerk. At a Visitation Court held before Laud, in Bramfield Church, on October 15th, 1639, one Richard Burgess was summoned to attend for negligence of duty. The matter ended by John Coaste undertaking that—

"he will be ready and diligent to help the Minister on with surplice and hood, to answer every other verse in the hymns, to say 'Amen' to *St. Ambrose's Creed*, to repeat the Lord's Prayer and the Creed in an audible voice after the minister. To go into the chancel at Communion times, there to answer the praises and thanksgivings according to the Book of Common Prayer, and to meet the minister at burials with the Service Book at the Church Stile or gate."

While the visitation was going on, Williams was still kept a close prisoner in the Tower. He was released in 1640, and, like his two predecessors, was promoted to the see of York. Misfortune once more befell him, a result of his protest against the exclusion of the Bishops from the Upper House, and he had again to suffer imprisonment in 1641. Eventually, after espousing the royal cause, he retired to his native Wales, where he died of quinsy, at Gloddaeth, in the parish of Eglwys-Rhos, March 25th, 1650, and was buried at Llandegai.

The repetition of suspensions and penances, and the determination of Laud to restore to the Church something of its ancient faith and practice, led to the great exodus of the Pilgrim Fathers to the far-off West, where, as they thought, " religion could find a safe and lasting home." Each county contributed its quota to this remarkable exodus. We are told that some sixty-seven persons from St. Albans brought certificates from the minister there, and sailed for Massachusetts in the *Planter* in 1635.[1] The colonizing instinct of the Englishman was doubtless at work, as well as the craving for religious freedom. To these motives may also be added a desire to escape from the heavy imposts which were continually being increased.

Thomas Wynnyffe (1642), Fellow of Exeter College, Oxford, succeeded to the Bishopric. He had previously been Rector of Willingale Doe, to which he was admitted May 5th, 1608, and of Lambourne, to which he was instituted June 15th, the same year.

His ejection from his see followed in three or four years after his appointment to it. We shall speak of his closing days later on. The Hertfordshire part of his Diocese contributed to the numbers of the Westminster Assembly, 1643. Urwick gives their names—

" Divines : Cornelius Burgess, D.D., Watford ; Humphrey Hardwick, M.A., Hadham Magna ; John Lightfoot, D.D., Munden Magna ; Herbert Palmer, B.D., Assessor, Ashwell ; Edmund Staunton, S.T.P., Bushey ; Peter Smith, D.D., Barkway ; Richard Vines, M.A., Watton ; Thomas

---

[1] Urwick, " Nonconformity in Herts," Appendix III. p. 831.

Westfield, D.D., St. Albans ; John Whincop, D.D., Clothall.
Lay members : William Cecil, Earl of Salisbury, Hatfield ;
Sir Thomas Barrington, Flamstead ; John Maynard, St.
Albans ; John White, Bushey." [1]

There appear to have been some forty-one
" Ministers," including those already mentioned,
who gave their adhesion to the principles laid down
by the Assembly. Three of the number migrated
to New England.

The remarkable return, anonymously, on June
4th, 1889, of a lost register of Lambourne, with a
note on a slip of paper, " Found in an old box ;
please acknowledge in the *Standard*," supplies us
with an interesting bit of information about the
Bishop as a country rector. On the second leaf
appears, in Wynnyffe's neat handwriting—

" Memorandum that ye Paraphrase of Erasmus belong-
inge to ye Parish Church of Lamborne is in the custodie
of Thomas Wynnyff, now Parson of Lamborne, and is by
him to be restored againe to the use of ye church." [2]

Wynnyffe of Lincoln, and Juxon of London, each
of them men who vainly strove for peace, lived
through the years when calumny and vituperation
raged on every side. The plea of the Church at
the *Hampton Court Conference*, " No Bishop no
King," had assumed an unexpected form, and
was now the watchword of the Puritanism which

---

[1] Urwick, " Nonconformity in Herts," Appendix VII. p. 835.
Notes and Queries, vol. x. No. 7, p. 5.

Elizabeth and the two succeeding monarchs had fought, but which they had not conquered.

Our shires witnessed to the uprising and the fury of the storm which was soon to shake the ancient church of the land to its very foundations.

The prerogative of the Archbishop had been fiercely resented, but the climax of resentment rose to its height in the more tyrannical exercise by Charles, of the Royal prerogative of the Crown. The forced loans in aid of the impecunious Crown hit the county of Herts with tremendous severity. Names of no less than 167 gentlemen are preserved, who were compelled to appear before the Courts to pay sums varying from £10 to £40. No wonder that the emigrant ships to Massachusetts were heavily laden with their freight of wearied Englishmen.

Exaction followed exaction, and bitterness everywhere reigned supreme. In 1641 the Bishops were expelled from the House of Lords, Strafford was led to the scaffold, Laud was confined in the Tower, soon to meet a like fate. Hampden, Pymm, Hollis rose to the surface. The tramp of Cavalier and Roundhead ushered in the thunder of disruption in Church and State. The Royal banner floated over Nottingham. The Civil War had begun.

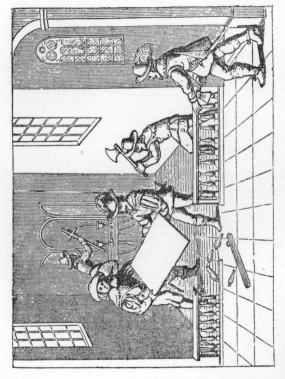

CHAPTER XXII

THE YEARS OF CONFUSION—ESSEX

"Whate'er the Popish hands have built,
Our hammers shall undoe ;
We'll break their pipes, and burn their copes,
And pull down churches too."
"Satirical Ballad," FRANCIS QUARLES.

THE days of Puritan protest in Parliament, from pulpit, and by pamphlet, were to be followed by the more vigorous appeal to the sword. Essex, Manchester, Fairfax, Waller, and Cromwell, came to the front in the great arbitrament of arms. The younger Presbyterianism, encouraged by its successes over "Prelacy and Popery" in the north, now asserted its force, and, in the church of St. Margaret, Westminster, England, through her Commons, swore "with uplifted hands" to the *Solemn League and Covenant.* Then developed such a strife as the nation had never yet known.

The Root and Branch Bill of 1641 had declared the abolition of the Episcopacy, and had paved the way for the wider application of the *Solemn League and Covenant.*

The discipline of Laud was flung to the winds, to be succeeded by a rule of sterner rigour. The language employed by demagogues, pamphleteers, and party preachers of both sides, is often too disgusting to quote. The whole country teemed with the reeking stream of false accusation, while the *Grand Committee of Religion* and its sub-committees were fountains of the vilest accusations for party ends. The charge of purging the Church was entrusted to groups of committees. The seven associated counties of Essex, Norfolk, Suffolk, Hertford, Cambridge, Huntingdon, and Lincoln, were allotted to the Earl of Manchester, who appointed commissioners for each of the counties on February 24th, 1643.

In February, 1644, the *Presbyterian Directory* was forced on the Church. Hundreds of clergy throughout the length and breadth of the land were hounded from their churches and homes under the most cruel and revolting circumstances, all kinds of abominable charges being made against them.

Bishop Juxon of London was amongst the few who escaped the first fury of the storm ; after the execution of his Royal master he fled to his manor in Gloucestershire, but only to be " reserved like Ulysses by the Cyclops, for the last morsel." Happily for the church, he survived the troubles, and saw the sun of the Restoration rise.

The Archdeacon of Colchester was compelled

to resign his living of St. Christopher's, London, " not being spirited for the Cause."

The Archdeacon of Essex was at one time imprisoned at Ely House, at another battened in the hatches of a ship, at another " dragged out of Church, set on horseback with his surplice on, with the Common Prayer Book tied about his neck, and forced to ride through some part of the city of London."

The parochial clergy of the county were not spared. According to Walker, no less than ninety-two of them were ruthlessly ejected. Of course their ejection was based on a show of reason. The charges were sometimes of an abominable character, sometimes trivial, and in most cases were founded on mere hearsay. In those days the proverb that " any stick is good enough to beat a dog with " found abundant illustration.

It is impossible in these pages to recite more than a few specimens of this merciless persecution. The case of Dr. Michaelson, rector of Chelmsford, is a type. The mob fired through the windows of his house, took him in church by the throat and tore his surplice from his back. On another occasion they rushed into the church, sat with their hats on, " and call'd aloud to him to come out of that ' calves coop,' and make an end of his pottage," . . . " tore the prayer-book into shreds, and stuck the leaves on their clubs, and treated the fragments with the vilest indignities." At another time, "when the Doctor was in the chancel to inter a corpse, a party of them rushed into the church, with an intent to have buried him in the same grave, because he made use of the Office in the Common Prayer Book."

When the tidings of the abolition of Episcopacy reached the town, they lighted bonfires in the streets, "most of the fuel being taken from the Doctor's wood-yard." In the end they forced him to flee for his life (of course bringing the usual accusation that he had deserted his charge). "His wife and eight children were left to the mercy of the rebels, who deprived his family of all their livelihood, and exposed them to extreme want."

Walker closes this sad story with the following remarks :—

"I cannot forbear adding that before the calling of the Rebel Parliament, there was not in this great town one to be named either man or woman *who toggled* [*cavilled*] *at the Common Prayer, or refused to receive the Sacrament kneeling;* but within three years after the *Blessed Reformation* was set on foot, the town was so filled with sectaries, especially Brownists and Anabaptists, that a third part of them refused to communicate in the Liturgy, and one half of them to receive the Sacrament in that reverent posture which the Church hath appointed ; nor could it be otherwise expected, when by that time the town was governed by a tinker, two cobblers, two peddlers, etc."

William Osbaldeston, the Rector of Great Parndon, gave offence by asserting that "once hearing of the Common Prayer is better than ten sermons ; " and by affirming that " water in Baptism doth wash away original sin ; " by countenancing the " Book of Sports," and by declaring that he would rather have his throat cut than contribute to *The Association of the Counties,* and so stain his hands with the blood of the rebellion.

The instance of Thomas Wiborow, Vicar of Pebmarsh, presented the usual features of barbarous ruffianism. A party of fanatics, after laying violent hands on him in the prayer desk, used him shamefully in the churchyard, and made him flee for his life. Not content with this, on June 10th, 1643, a troop of rebels came to the parsonage house, broke open the doors, and made their way to the room where Mrs. Wiborow and her children were secreted.

" They violently seize on her, drag her down the stairs, and out of the house into the yard ; the poor children being almost distracted, and at their wits end, for fear what would become of their mother, one of the persecutors offering to provide her his tumbril, that is, his dung cart, to carry her and her children from constable to constable till she came to her husband," and so forth.

As an example of the wanton ferocity of destruction, we may cite the case of the parish church of Chelmsford, where " the mob in a riotous manner, with long poles and stones, beat down the fayre large window at the east end of the Church."

Dr. Stoughton gives a fair estimate of the commission for ejecting scandalous ministers, when he says—

" Commonly, a rather long array of charges was presented on the principle, it would appear, of catching the criminal on a second count of the indictment, if the first should fail. The same person was accused of profaning the Sabbath, of frequenting ale houses, of using the Prayer Book, of playing at cards, of living an unholy life, and of being disaffected to the Government. I cannot help believing, much as I honour the character of the Puritans, that in some cases, they, like their adversaries, yielded to the besetting sin of priding themselves upon their orthodoxy and virtue, and that they took it for granted that the men who differed from them in creed, and whom therefore they considered intellectually wrong, must also differ from them in life, and could not be reckoned morally right." [1]

Some idea of the organized opposition to the Church, and of the spread of Presbyterianism throughout the greater part of the county, may be gathered from an interesting return of the names of the ministers and elders approved by the Committee for Essex. [2]

This return, which is given in our Appendix, appears to have been made at the direction of Parliament by the Standing Committee Meeting at Chelmsford, on March 3, 1646, and is signed by

---

[1] " Religion in England," vol. ii. pp. 101, 102. New and revised edition, 1881.

[2] " The division of the County of Essex into several *Classis*, together with names of the Ministers and others fit to be of each class, certified by the Standing Committee of that County and approved of by the Committee of Lords and Commons appointed by Ordinance of both Houses of Parliament for the judging of Scandal and approving the *Classis* in the several counties of England. Printed at London for John Wright, at the King's Head in the Old Bailey, 1648."

Thomas Honywood, A. Luther, William Collard, J. Barnardiston, Isaac Aleyn. On January 21, 1647, it was ordered by the Committee of both Houses " that the ministers and elders in the 14 Classes shall make one Province." The status of the " elders " is given in the return. There were 3 Earls, 3 Baronets, 6 Knights, 32 Esquires, 1 Lieut.-Colonel, 2 Captains, 84 Gentlemen.

Episcopacy was in suspension, and it was now more than ever impossible, as Wakeman remarks—

"to combine a calvinistic system of Church government, resting upon a *Classis* of Presbyters as the centre of authority, with the system of the Catholic Church, which made the bishop the unit of government and the source of jurisdiction."

In 1648 we find that the ministerial members of the Solemn League and Covenant issued—

" A Testimony of the Ministers in the Province of Essex to the Trueth of Jesus Christ, and to the Solemn League and Covenant ; as also against Errors, Heresies, and Blasphemies of these times, and the Toleration of them sent up to the Minister within the Province of London, subscribers to the First Testimony." [1]

They support—

"The Confession of Faith, Directorie for Worship and Humble advice for Church government, presented by the Reverend Assembly of Divines to the Honourable Parliament."

---

[1] Printed by A. M., for Tho. Underhill, at the Bible, in Wood Street, MDCXLVIII.

We cannot doubt their conscientiousness, however much we may regret its immediate results. The new method of Church government they conceived to be so scriptural that in respect of it they declared—

"We cannot but exceeding blesse the Name of our God," and they went on to say "from our Soules we doe utterly abhor as all former cursed doctrines of Popery, Arminianism, and Socianissme, so likewise the damnable Errors, Heresies, and Blasphemies of these present evill tymes whether of Anti-Scripturists, Familists, Antinomians, Anti-Trinitarians, Arians, Ana-Baptists."

The Testimony is signed by 130 ministers throughout Essex.

A further proof of the extent to which Presbyterianism had become predominant in the county, may be judged from the fact that in 1646 a petition to the Long Parliament, praying for the observance of the Directory, and Church government according to the Covenant, was signed by 63 beneficed ministers, who, by the way, were very severe "on the daring impudence of mechanics preaching contrary to your orders." [1]

From the beginning of the strife our two counties were strongly Parliamentarian. From the date of the formation of the Eastern Counties Association (December, 1642), the Presbyterian movement spread vigorously. An indication of its hold upon the clergy may be gathered from the

[1] *Lond. Journals*, vol. viii. p. 445.

facts recorded in White's " First Century of Malig-
nant Priests," *i.e.* of those most notorious for
opposition to Parliament. He states that there
were but 29 in Essex, and 9 in Herefordshire—
an evidence of the general adhesion of the clergy
to the Parliamentary cause. The financial support
given to the cause was considerable.[1]

The tenor of the doctrine and practice of the
Associated Ministers is fully stated in an agreement
drawn up and printed towards the close of the
period, entitled—

" The Agreement of the Associated Ministers of the
County of Essex, proposed to their particular congrega-
tions, and to all such of the County as love the Church's
Peace." [2]

This Agreement states as to Sacraments :—

" That the Sacraments are Seals of the Covenant of
Grace in the Blood of Christ ; that the Sacraments of the
New Testament are Baptisme, and the Supper of the
Lord ; that the outward elements in the Lord's Supper
are Bread and Wine, and do signify the Body and Blood
of Christ crucified, which the worthy receiver by faith doth
partake of in the Sacrament."

As to the matter of Orders, it says—

" Therefore, when a Minister is to be ordained among
us we agree, that such as are of the Ministry faithful, and
able, be instrusted, and imployed in the tryal and approba-
tion of him, and in the work of ordination, which ordination

---

[1] *Vide* Kingston's " East Anglia and Great Civil War," 1897.
[2] Printed for Edward Brewster, at the Crane, in Paul's Churchyard,
Sept. 28th, 1658. 2nd ed. E. 955, British Museum.

(the most of us judge to be that act of the ministers whereby a fit person, first duly tryed, and approved by them, or some of them), is solemnly set apart, and appointed to the Ministry, and sent into the Lord's work by such acts, and in such manner as is peculiar and proper for that setting apart, appointing and sending, namely, by such suteable prayer, with fasting and laying on their hands on him, as is according to the gospel, which laying on of hands being the universal practice of the Church of Christ, etc."

The "ordination" was to be "in presence of the congregation where he is Minister," or in some place near.

Thus, side by side with the disappearance (or, more correctly, with the temporary abolition) of the old order of Church government, Presbyterianism seemed about to become the permanent religious power of the country. God ordered it otherwise. Though the Puritan influence had made its mark on the tone of religious thought, the Presbyterian form of Church polity did not commend itself to the nation. Towards the close of the period of which we are speaking, a yearning which had long possessed the hearts of the people began to express itself in the watchword of "Church and King."

CHAPTER XXIII

THE YEARS OF CONFUSION—HERTFORDSHIRE

> " We'll exercise within the groves,
> And teach beneath a tree,
> We'll make a pulpit of a cask,
> And hey then ! up go wee."
> " Satirical Ballad," FRANCIS QUARLES.

IT may seem an unwelcome repetition to tell the story of the confusion in Hertfordshire, but the illustrations of it are not without their special interest, and supply some additional indications of the state of chaos. Let us turn first to the tale of ejections. Bishop Wynnyff of Lincoln, though of Puritan tendencies, had to flee from his see for safety. He took refuge in his old country parish at Lambourne in Essex, where he died, September 20th, and was buried within the Altar rails of the Parish Church, September 29th, 1654,[1] just as " many sober and noble patriots did begin to incline to the King's restoration." Walker says, " he had a suitable funeral, and was buried by a collection made among the London apprentices."

---

[1] *Vide* also Smyth's " Obity. Camd. Soc.," No. 44, 638.

Dr. Westfield, Archdeacon of St. Albans, also Bishop of Bristol, and Rector of St. Bartholomew the Great, and Prebendary of Caddington Major, in St. Paul's, escaped with partial deprivation of his emoluments; possibly he could have spared a few, but his will begins with the suggestive remark, "As for my worldly goods, which (*as the times now are*) I know not where they be." He composed his own epitaph, commencing with the words, "*Senio et mærore confectus.*" It is interesting to note that he was among the nine ministers who were selected to represent Hertfordshire at the Westminster Assembly of Divines, when *The Confession of Faith* was drawn up. Perhaps this is the real reason why he, pluralist as he was, escaped lightly.

The Archdeacon of Huntingdon had to submit to plunder and imprisonment, and ended his life as an "ejected minister," in the August after "the bloody January."

The Prebendaries and parochial clergy were condemned to suspension on all sides. It was alleged against the Rector of Aspenden and West-mill, in Herts, that he set the Table altar-wise, bowed to it, forced the people to come to the rails to receive the Communion, heard confessions, possessed a picture of Christ in his parlour, bowed to the cross on the font, profaned the Sabbath, attested his loyalty, refused to preach twice on a Sunday.

One of the offences of Dr. Mountford, Rector of Anstey and Therfield, was that he sang part of Psalm xliii. before the second (*sic*) service, viz. " Then I will to the Altar go,"etc. In his case there was a peculiar hardship ; he had just built a new rectory, and was only suffered to sleep in it "one night at the most." John Clerk, of North Mymms, presumably the Vicar, was banished to the Caribbean islands, and his family was reduced to great poverty.

The cases of ejection in Hertfordshire do not appear to have been accompanied by as much harshness as in some other instances, though there was more than enough of it to show the spirit of the times. According to Walker, there were thirty-three cases of ejection.

At Anstey, the churchwardens and a glazier pulled down "scandalous pictures." Possibly the glazier was Edmund Aylee, of Bishops Stortford, who figured so prominently in the destruction of altar-rails. At Hoddesdon, after the rails had been pulled down, " dogs were turned in, in an offensive manner, under the Communion-table."

Amidst all the work of desecration, there is one redeeming feature in the purposes for which some of the churches were used. St. Peter's ; St. Albans, was converted into a hospital for wounded soldiers ; we can forgive the fact that the windows were taken out to admit air. The church was used for a prison as well as for a hospital.

The following is an extract from the Church-warden's accounts, St. Peter's, 1648–9 :—

"Paid for taking down the windows and moving the things out of the Church when the Colchester prisoners lay there, 4s. ; paid for nailing up the Church door when the prisoners were there, 6d. ; paid a tax for the bread and cheese for the prisoners, 9d. ; paid to a man for making clean the Church when the prisoners were gone, 7s. 6d. ; paid the glazier a bill for work done at the Church, £14."

A like incident occurred at Berkhampstead, of which we read—

"October 8th, 1648. It is agreed att vestry, that in respect the Church windows, by reason of the Colchester prisoners kept in the Church, are pulled downe, that for the repaire of them the above mentioned rate shall be made at twopence an acre." [1]

In St. Albans Abbey, Fairfax, assembled a council of his officers, who sat for five days, "now hearing prayers, now sermons, and now drafting the celebrated *Deed of Remonstrance*," [2] which practically led to the execution of King Charles a few months later.

The Directory and the dictates of the *Solemn League and Covenant* had for some time been in force, and the benefices were being filled by all sorts of illiterate chatterers and itinerant sedi-tionists. We learn something of certain of these

[1] Add. MSS., Brit. Mus., 18, 773, p. 142.
[2] *A Remonstrance* of his Excellency, Thomas, Lord Fairfax, and of the General Council of Officers, held at St. Albans, November 16th, 1648.

men from Mr. Kingston's researches in the State
papers of the time.

"In no part of the county of Hertford were the pulpits
more freely used on the side of the Parliament than along
the northern side extending from Hemel Hempsted, by
Dunstable and Luton to Hitchin. At Kensworth, above
the Downs, Edward Harrison, 'a great demagogue,' is holding forth to crowds of people; at Redbourn, Philip Leigh,
the vicar, had his weakness for drinking the King's health
in a very poor surplice cut short, and Master Rotheram
put in his place; at Harpenden the Puritans have unani-
mously chosen a Puritan Minister; at Kimpton, Thomas
Faucett, a violent Royalist incumbent, has got put in
prison, and is replaced by another; while Benjamin King,
of Flamstead, a very Boanerges in the pulpit, who had been
formerly one of the lecturers in Dunstable Church, is
now one of the band of fifteen lecturers appointed in turn
to preach in Hitchin Parish Church on market day." [1]

Doubtless many of them were "painful preachers,"
but all were violent Puritans.

The parishes were overrun with all sorts of
strange preachers, many of them drawn from the
lowest of the people. The Rev. Thomas Edwards,
once curate of All Saints, Hertford, in his
"*Gangræna:* a catalogue and discovery of many
errors of the Sectaries," classifies the sects who
were let loose upon the counties as Independents,
Chiliasts or Millenaries, Antinomians, Ana-Baptists,
Manifestarians or Arminians, Libertines, Formalists,
Enthusiasts, Seekers and Waiters, Perfectists,
Socinians, Arians, Anti-Trinitarians, Anti-Scripturists, Sceptics, and Questionists. He further

---

[1] Add. MSS. 15, 670, fo. 206, Brit. Mus.

says of them, " All kinds of sectaries and mechanic preachers from London, and from the army, preach and corrupt the people, and of those practices there are manie sad examples in Hertfordshire and Essex."

John Bunyan was one of the better sort of mechanic preachers who stirred up a few of the Hertfordshire villages, especially in the neighbourhood of Hitchin. Edwards speaks of others, " as he had it from sure hands," *e.g.* Heath, "a collarmaker," of Watton; Rice, "a tinker," of Aston; Field, "a boddies-maker," of Hertford; Crew, "a tailor," of Stevenage.

Amongst those who were thrust into the vacant benefices were several noted men, who caused great trouble, even to the Assembly of Divines— *e.g.* Baldwin, the "deputy preacher" of Hemel Hempsted; "Master Freake," of All Saints, Hertford; and Dr. Burges, Vicar of Watford, who became an active supporter of the Parliamentary cause, and one of the leading figures in the Assembly of Divines. This Burges bought the Palace, the Deanery and Chapter House of Wells, from the Parliamentary Commission, and wrought much havoc there.

Midst all this tumult and faction, one story must be told of Josias Byrd, the aged and loyal rector of Baldock.[1] On June 26th, 1647, hearing that the King was to pass through the town, he

---

[1] Kingston, " Hertfordshire during the Civil War," p. 71.

"got together his parishoners, and in full canonicals marched at their head to the town's end, where the two strange processions met. Armed with the communion cup, from the Parish Church, filled with wine, the old Rector saluted the King with a fervent 'May God bless your Majesty!' The King, touched at receiving such a demonstration of loyalty, inquired the name of his loyal subject, to which the old Rector proudly replied, 'I am Josias Byrd, the Parson of Baldock, and I offer you this cup for your refreshment.' Whereupon the King drank, and replied with ready wit, 'Mr. Byrd, I thank you; I did not think I had so good a bird in all my kingdom.'"[1]

These sketches demand at least some reference to the fate of the churches, as well as of the clergy who were in so many instances ejected from them.

It must not be forgotten that the Reformation and the Rebellion treated the churches in different ways. The robbery of Henry was the robbery of endowments, the seizure of shrines and vestments, and of anything which could produce revenue. The reformers were only anxious to efface all evidences of Roman superstition; the rebels were only too willing to obliterate the Church of England itself, and to turn her fabrics into mere preaching-houses. Purification was the motto of the reformers, desecration marked the path of the rebels. The earlier reformers did undoubtedly desecrate, but the rebels were ruthless destroyers. The monastic institutions and buildings were the special mark of the reformers, the

[1] Kingston, "Hertfordshire during the Civil War," p. 71.

parish churches suffering less at their hands. Their protest was against misuse and abuse. They dealt unsparingly with images and the like, but in most cases respected the fabrics. For instance, in 1560, Archbishop Parker procured Letters under the Great Seal to certain commissioners, "to take remedies about decays of Churches and unseemly keeping of Chancels, and for the comely ordering the East part of Churches."[1] However much we may admit and regret the violence of their methods of purification, the mischief was nothing like so deplorable as the havoc wrought during the Great Rebellion. The satirical ballad of Francis Quarles (an Essex man by birth), quoted at the head of this and the preceding chapter, gives the keynote to the aims of the Roundheads.

The Ordinances of 1643–1644 ordered that Altars and tables of stone should be destroyed, basins, crucifixes, organ-frames, and cases should be taken away and defaced, and that no rood lofts or holy water font should remain. The axes and hammers of depredators rang through the Cathedrals and churches, no horror was too shocking to be committed in the House of God; the perpetrators were even represented as doing the work of God. It was not done even at the instigation of an impulse, but it was the climax of a licence which falsely called itself liberty, and

---

[1] *Vide* Markland's "Remarks on English Churches" (Parker Ox., 1842), p. 8, *et seq.*

which resulted in acts of wanton malice and vengeance. D'Israeli sums up the story in his " Curiosities of Literature."

" What occurred in the French Revolution happened here ; an age of impiety ! Society itself dissolved : for every tie of private affection and of public duty was unloosened. Even nature was strangely violated. From the first opposition to the decorous ceremonies of the National Church by the simple Puritans, the next stage was that of ridicule, and the last of obloquy. They actually baptised horses in the churches at the fonts ; and the jest of that day was, that the Reformation was now a thorough one in England, since our horses went to church."

The insignia of Royalty were almost more repulsive to the Parliamentarians than the " Popish gewgaws." There is no lack of thoroughness in the following letter addressed to the corporation of Hertford :—

" Gentlemen,
" We are informed that in several Churches and other publique places, in your counties, there remayne standinge the arms and picture of the late King, which have been ordered to be taken away in other publique places.
" We therefore desire you to appoint some fitte persons, to make a due and stricte searche in all Churches, halles, and other publique places, and to returne to you an account of all such as shall be so standinge, and therefore to gyve your expresse order for the takinge awaye and destroyinge all the same arms and pictures, and that you certifie the councell of your proceedinge herein before the last of the instant December. Signed in the name, and

T

by order of the Counsell of State, appointed by the Authority of Parliament.

"Jo. Bradshawe, President
"For the Commissioners of the Militia for
"the County of Hertford."

"Whitehall,
"3rd December, 1650."

It is to the honour of the Commonwealth period that an attempt was made, in 1656, to remedy the social evils arising from the number of inns, and to regulate their conduct.

"At the General Quarter Sessions of the public peace of the county of Hertford, holden at Hertford, for the county aforesaid, on Monday next after the Feast of the Translation of St. Thomas the Martyr; that is to say, the fourteenth and sixteenth dayes of July, in the year of Our Lord, One thousand six hundred and fifty and six.

"Forasmuch as his Highness, the Lord Protector of the Commonwealth, etc., hath taken special notice of the mischiefs and great disorders which daily happen and are committed in Taverns, Inns, and Ale-houses, which are extremely multiplied in this nation, etc. . . . Therefore, it is thought fit and accordingly ordered, That no person whatsoever living in any house within this county, shall from henceforth be licensed to keep any Ale-house or Victualling-house, unless his house be in the common road, or open street, and not standing alone; and that such persons so to be licensed, be of honest life and conversation, and of good ability, well affected to the present Government, and of persons who have not adhered to the late King and his party, etc. Justices of the Peace are enjoined to suppress all such ale-houses which may be opened for the 'reception of company on the Lord's day,' or of which the Landlords shall be guilty of swearing, drunkenness, suffering disorders, tippling, gaming, or playing at tables, Billiard-Table, Shovel-board, Cards, Dice,. Nine-pins, Pigeon-holes, Trunks, or of keeping of Bowling-Alley or Bowling-Green, or of any of them, or of any other games, etc., etc." [1]

Another curious phase of the county's life is illustrated at the same sessions of Hertford. The following persons were to be severely dealt with :

"All persons calling themselves scholars, going about begging, all sea-faring men, pretending losses of their ships or goods on the sea ; all idle persons going about the country begging or using any subtle crafts, in unlawful games, playes, or feigning themselves to have knowledge in Physiognomy, Palmistry, or other like crafty sciences, pretending that they can tell Destinies, Fortunes, or such other phantastical imaginations. All Collectors for Gaols, Prisons or Hospitals ; all Fencers, Bear-wards, Common Players of Interludes, and Minstrels ; all Juglers, Tinkers, Pedlers, Petty Chapmen wondering abroad, and Ballad Singers ; all wandering persons and Common Labourers, using loytering and refusing to work for such reasonable wages as is taxed ; or commonly given in those parts. . . . All persons, not being Felons, pretending themselves to be Egyptians, or wandering in the form, habit or attire of Counterfeit Egyptians ; and all such persons as wander up and down in the country to sell Glasses, etc."

Before closing our account of some of the features of the Commonwealth period, we may quote a page of local history in connection with General Monk, whose vigorous march from the north led to the consummation of the " Happy Restoration." Dr. Price, the General's chaplain (writing of this march), gives many interesting

[1] British Mus. Lib., 190 g, fo. 106, s—h.

particulars of the five days' halt at St. Albans ; he says of one incident :—

"There we spent one day extraordinary at the church, the famous Mr. Hugh Peters, Mr. Lee of Hatfield, and another carrying on the work of the day, which was a fast day. Peters *supererogated*, and prayed a long prayer in the general's quarters, too, at night. As for his sermon, he managed it with some dexterity at the first, allowing for the cantings of his expressions. His text was Psalm 107, v. 7. 'He led them forth by the right way, that they might go to a city of habitation.' With his fingers on the cushion, he measured the right way from the Red Sea through the wilderness to Canaan, told us it was not forty days' march, but God led Israel forty years through the wilderness before they came thither ; yet this was still the Lord's right way, who led His people, *crincledum crancledum*,"[1] etc.

Then he reviewed our Civil Wars, our intervals of peace, and fresh distractions and hopes of rest. And though the Lord's people, he said, were not yet come to the city of habitation, He was still leading them on the right way, how dark soever these dispensations might appear to us. Before he concluded his sermon, he seemed to me to preach his own funeral sermon. Eight months afterwards he was cruelly executed as a " regicide " at Charing Cross.

A few days after the rest at St. Albans, the General entered London. " From the moment of his entry, the restoration of the Stuarts became inevitable."[2]

---

[1] Kingston's " Herts during Civil War," p. 99.
[2] Green, " A History of the English People," 1891, p. 600.

CHAPTER XXIV

RESTORATION JOY—ESSEX AND HERTFORDSHIRE

TREBLE.

" *Now that the Lord hath re-advanced the Crown*
Which thirste of spoyle and frantick zeal threw down :

TENOR.

" *Now that the Lord, the miter hath restored,*
Which, with the Crown, lay in the dust abhorr'd.

TREBLE.   TENOR.

" *Praise him, ye kings,*   *Praise him, ye priests,*
Glory to Christ our High Priest, highest King.

TREBLE.

" *May Judah's royal scepter still shine clear :*

TENOR.

" *May Aaron's holy rod still blossoms bear.*

TREBLE and TENOR.

" *Scepter and rod rule still, and guide our land,*
And those whom God anoints feel no rude hand ;
May love, peace, plenty, wait on Crown and Chair,
And may both share in blessings as in care.

CHORUS.

" *Angels look down, and joy to see*
Like that above, a Monarchie ;
Angels look down, and joy to see
Like that above, an hierarchie." [1]

THE fierce hate of war, which had desecrated churches and filled the land with blood, had done something worse; it had driven out, for

---

[1] Anthem composed by Fuller, Dean of St. Patrick's (afterwards Bishop of Lincoln), on the occasion of the consecration of twelve bishops in St. Patrick's Cathedral, Dublin, Jan. 27, 1660.

the most part, the best instincts of religion.   The
narrow, but pious Puritan had largely given way to
the new political Presbyterian.   By the time of
Cromwell's death, in 1658, Presbyterianism had
become the dominant civil and religious force.   Its
spirit is quaintly summed up by a modern historian
—it had become " flat popery to eat a mincepie."
The truth concealed under this epigram (together
with political rancour), brought about the inevitable
reaction, resulting finally in the Restoration of 1660,
and with it the return to Episcopacy.

The days of confusion sickened the people of
unrest and bigotry, and they began, as one writer
observes, "to dote after prelacy and the Service
Book."   In other words, they longed for order in
the Church.   The watchword of the first general
election of the reign of Charles II. was "Church
and King."   The result showed that the tide had
turned.   Dean Fuller's anthem, quoted above, is a
quaint but striking expression of the national joy.
The news of the Restoration was the signal for great
rejoicing in our own counties.   Here are some
records.   At Hertford the ringers received 5s.,
while the soldiers were paid 9s. 6d. for bonfires.
The Arms of the Commonwealth were taken down,
and the Royal Arms erected.   At Berkhampsted
the Royal Arms were cleaned, and the ringers
received £1 when the King was proclaimed.[1]   At
St. Peter's; St. Albans, the ringers were paid

[1] Add. MSS., 18,773, pp. 168, 169, British Museum.

£1 with an additional 3s. 6d. "to drink at the bonfire." One "Robert Babbs, the painter, for the setting up the King's Arms in the Church, and writing the Commandments," received £2 10s. The Vicar of the same place came in for a share of the *largesse* of the Churchwardens, as there appears in the account, "paid to Mr. Hanslope for three sermons, one whereof was preached upon Thanksgiving Day for the King's most happy return to England." Bonfires were blazing at Waltham Cross, and as the faggots were successively placed on the fire, the crowd shouted in exultation, "Here is a Roundhead! Here is an Anabaptist!"

The record of the manifestations of joy in Herts and Essex alone would fill pages, but we have to do with more serious indications of the triumph. One of the first matters of importance in the necessary re-organization, was the re-settlement of Diocesan rule. Accordingly we find Gilbert Sheldon was raised to the see of London, while Robert Sanderson was appointed to Lincoln.

These two Bishops saw in their dioceses, in common with England at large, a new era of religious change, which was permanently to affect the whole status of the Church and her worship. Their appointment was the signal for re-action and retaliation. The legal enactments which enforced the new order of things are too well known to need more than a few words. The first of these laws was the *Corporation Act* of 1661, applying severe religious tests in qualification for Civil office. The places of the clergy ejected during the Commonwealth had been filled by Presbyterians, Independents, Baptists, etc. Many of the ejected and persecuted sufferers had died in the interval of confusion. The occupants of the benefices were allowed to remain in possession till the *Act of Uniformity* came into force (St. Bartholomew's Day, 1662). Then came the tug of war. It was a question whether the eight or nine thousand clergy would "reconcile themselves to renounce their covenant obligations to destroy the episcopal form of government, to accept ordination, and to use the Prayer Book in their ministrations." There is considerable uncertainty as to the number of the *ejected* ministers, but it is tolerably clear that about two thousand refused to conform, and had to give up their benefices. It is doubtful whether the whole two thousand were ejected, for both Calamy and Palmer speak of "ejected or silenced." The distinction is important. It is, however, undeniable that there were hardships in the ejectment, but no one can with justice assert that there was the same brutal want of consideration which was exhibited in the time of the Rebellion. The new *Act of Uniformity* led to the ejectment of some thirty nonconforming ministers in Hertfordshire, and about one hundred and twenty in Essex—Calamy says that seven in Essex and six in Herts afterwards conformed.

Bitter as was the new persecution, a Declaration of Indulgence by the King in 1662 might have softened its edge, had it been accepted. The refusal to accept it brought about the *Conventicle Act* in 1664 and the *Five Mile Act* in 1665, their object being to prevent the Nonconformists from forming congregations, as they had already begun to do.

These blasts, which were intended to sweep away Nonconformity from the land, only served to fuse the separate bodies into closer religious and political union, and to revive the strength of their cause; in fact they laid anew the foundations of Dissent.

The *Conventicle Act* was aimed specially at the Nonconforming laity; the *Five Mile Act* was directed more particularly against the ministers, with a view to separating them from their flocks. Fines, penalties, banishments were the result of these Acts, but they failed in their object. Mr. Urwick has unearthed a private return of Conventicles which was made in the year 1669, and which exists among the *Lambeth Manuscripts*. From this it appears there were then in existence in St. Albans alone Conventicles of the Presbyterians, with a congregation numbering a hundred, of Anabaptists fifty, and of Quakers six. The Congregationalist numbers were described as "great." At Redbourne, Quakers had congregations of sometimes two or three hundred, Anabaptists of sixty or eighty. Quakerism received a special impulse in the county of Hertford from the residence in Rickmansworth (from 1672–1678) of William Penn, who, by the way, received his early education at Chigwell in Essex. The tenets of this sect were also further spread by visits of George Fox to Hertford, who in his *Journal* [1] speaks of "having much service for the Lord there, both among Friends at their meetings and in conferences." Nine years later he paid a second visit to Hertford, "then he journeyed to Ware and had a little stay among friends there." The Quakers seem to have suffered persecution at the hands of both Roundhead and Royalist. As many as ninety-four were committed to prison in one month ; whilst we read of seven Quakers of Hertford who were sentenced in 1664 to transportation for seven years.

In 1669 we find Quaker Conventicles at Norton, Markgate Street, and at Hemel Hempsted. The feeling here was evidently strong, for a party of Quakers and Anabaptists joined in burying a Quaker in an orchard. The Vicar reported that many were thus buried there. They appear also at Hoddesdon, where, it is said, William Penn's wife died. At Baldock, in 1660, their meetings were " violently disturbed, and many were fined and imprisoned." [2] Sawbridgeworth and Hitchin were also centres of their activity.

The persecution of this sect seems to have

---

[1] P. 531.   [2] Besse, " Sufferings of the Quakers," i. 241.

attained its object, for it eventually dwindled into insignificance in the country, though, generally speaking, force proved no remedy against conscience. Whatever the motives of Charles II. may have been, he was wiser than Parliament, which rejected the new Declaration of Indulgence of 1672. The worst blunder which the State committed in this reign of blunders was the imposition of the *Test Act*, 1673. The effect of it was, says Wakeman, to lower "irretrievably for generations the whole conception of the Sacraments." The same writer goes on to remark that "it admitted the hypocrite, the blasphemer, the libertine, and made the moral discipline of the Church a very byword of shame.[1]

Having made this general reference to the restoration of the Episcopate and the immediate results of the new order of things, we will revert to the chronological line of Episcopal succession.

Gilbert Sheldon (1660-63), Warden of All Souls, Oxford, and Prebendary of Gloucester, was, as we have seen, the first Bishop of London under the Restoration. In churchmanship he was of the type of Laud. To Bishop Sheldon is largely due the *Act of Uniformity*, which once and for all decided the cause of the Puritans, and which forced them (many unwillingly) into schism. He had, while at Oxford, suffered severely at the hands of the Puritan fanatics, and it is not surprising that he did not forget it when he was restored to power.

[1] Wakeman, "History of the Church of England," p. 393.

It is asserted that, whilst he was Bishop of London, he held no confirmation in Essex. It is no wonder that he found but little time for the exercise of the pastoral side of his office, concerned as he was with pressing matters of ecclesiastical policy and organization. His Archdeacons made up for his lack of time in respect of the matter of parochial organization, for we read that the Right Worshipful John Hanslow (? Hansley), Archdeacon of Colchester, " a Person of very meek and sweet temper," in his *Articles of Enquiry*, in 1662, asks for particulars not only as to the clergy and the state of their churches, but includes the parish clerk.

" 1. Have you belonging to your church or chapel, a parish clerk aged 21 years at the least ? Is he of honest life and conversation ? and sufficient or able to perform his duty in reading, writing, and singing ?   Is he chosen by your Minister, and doth he duly attend him in all Divine services at the Church ?   Are his wages duly paid unto him ?   Or who withholdeth the same from him ?

" 2. Doth he diligently doe his duty in keeping the church clean and decent, in tolling and ringing the bells before Divine service, and when any person is passing out of this life, doth he upon notice, toll a bell, that the neighbours may thereby be warned to recommend the dying person unto the grace and favour of God ? "

Humphrey Henchman (1663–75) was translated

from Salisbury to succeed Sheldon. His personal
efforts in assisting Charles II. to make a safe
retreat to France, after the battle of Worcester, no
doubt furthered his promotion. He is described as
" giving no trouble or disturbance to the Nonconformists."

It should be remarked that while many of his
officials deserted him in the time of the *Great
Plague*, he and some of the " more sober clergy "
remained at their posts. The *Great Fire*, and its
disastrous effects on his Cathedral, and on the city
churches, occupied his thoughts. He lived to hear
of the foundation of new St. Paul's, laid on June
21st, 1675, though he was not present.

At least one of his Archdeacons was active in
reform, judging from the Articles to be inquired
into by the Archdeacon of Essex, in 1672. He
asks, amongst other things—" Have timber or bells
ever been sold ? Whether font with cover stands
at the neather end of your church in such a manner
as Fonts have anciently and usually stood ? Is
there a Chalice or Communion Cup with a cover ?
A decent surplice and hood ?

" Does your Minister observe the Holy-days and
Fasting days, the Ember-week, and the yearly
Perambulation in Rogation week, as is appointed
by the Rubrick ? And give warning thereof the
Lord's day before ?

" Hath your Minister taken upon him to appoint any public or private Fasts, prophecyings or

exercises not appointed by authority? or, doth he, or any other Minister, or lay person, hold any Conventicles or meetings in private houses within your Parish, for people of several families to resort unto, under the pretence of preaching, praying, thanksgiving or humiliation, contrary to the Laws and Canons in that case provided?"

He also inquires as to "the names of those [parishioners] who refuse to come to public Assemblies, Prayers, or Service of the Church, as required;" whether those who come to church "demean themselves reverently, uncovering their heads, kneeling at prayers, standing up when the Creed and Gospel are read?" Is there any person "of 16 years of age who doth not receive the Sacrament three times in the year?"

He inquires particularly as to thanksgiving of women after childbirth, attendance at church "on Sundays and holidays, in the afternoon, obediently to hear and be ordered by the Minister until they have learned the Catechism."

There are also questions as to Licences to Schoolmasters, public and private, Physicians, Chyrurgeons, Midwives. He adds: " Is there sufficient quantity of fine white bread and good wine according to the number of Communicants ? "

The Archdeacon of Essex was more explicit than his brother of Colchester. We find him giving authority for his inquiry by side notes of reference to the Prayer Book, Canons, and Articles.

Henry Compton (1675–1714), the successor of Bishop Henchman, was popularly and irreverently called *Jack Boots*. He had been a cornet in the army. Even when he was Bishop, he accompanied Princess Anne to Northampton, dressed as a soldier, and he subsequently took the command of a small body of troops. He was the last Bishop to bear arms. As a theologian, he was a strict Anglican, standing firm against both Rome and Nonconformity. He voted in favour of the *Exclusion Bill*, which was brought before the House in 1679. When one Dr. Sharp preached a sermon against the Church of Rome, and the King ordered him to suspend the preacher, he flatly refused to do so, and was himself suspended for his refusal. He was not a man to be driven to act against his principles. A little later on, we shall see, that in spite of his suspension, he was not silent in the presence of an impending danger of a renewal of the Roman pretensions. The Bishop took a firm line in dealing with Nonconformists, and was attacked by the Rector of All Saints', Colchester, for his attitude towards them. The latter was cited to Doctors' Commons for conducting marriage without banns or licence, and was temporarily suspended. He was also brought before Chelmsford Assize for slandering the Bishop, and was mulcted in the sum of £2000.[1]

During Bishop Compton's episcopate, the custom of wearing a surplice for the sermon began to be

[1] " Nat. Dic. of Biography."

revived in the county. Strype, in a letter dated April 7th, 1696, writes :—

"Yesterday I saw in Low Leighton church that which to my remembrance I never did see in a church in England but once, and that is a minister preach in a surplice for Mr. Harrison, whereas other ministers on Fast days do not so much as wear any surplice, he, by way of supererogation, preached in his. The sight did stir up in me more of pity than anger to see the folly of the man ; but if he preach in a fool's coat we will go and hear him."

We come now to consider the rule of Lincoln over a portion of Hertfordshire.

Robert Sanderson (1660–63), Prebendary of Lincoln, Regius Professor of Divinity at Oxford, was the first Restoration Bishop of the see of Lincoln, from which poor Wynnyff had been so ruthlessly driven. Sanderson, like Sheldon at Oxford, and like Wynnyff, his own predecessor, had tasted the bitterness of persecution. While rector of Boothby Pagnell (1648), the soldiers entered his church and tore the Prayer Book from his hands, submitting him to other merciless indignities. Perhaps it was partly in reward for his patient suffering that the King nominated him to the see, but it is more probable that his elevation was due to his power as a preacher, and to his high character. The King's opinion of him in the pulpit is evident from his trite remark : " I carry my ears to hear other preachers, but I carry my conscience to hear Mr. Sanderson." As in the case of Sheldon of London, his activities were largely directed to the re-establishment of order after the years of chaos.

Good old Izaak Walton, his lifelong friend, gives a delightful account of him. He tells, referring to the Revised Prayer Book of 1662, among many other charmingly recorded details, how in Convocation—

"the Common Prayer was made more complete, by adding three new necessary offices, which were '*A Form of Humiliation for the murder of King Charles the Martyr,*' '*A Thanksgiving for the Restoration of his Son our King,*' and '*For the baptising of Persons of riper Age.*'" He adds: "I cannot say Dr. Sanderson did form or word them all, but doubtless more than any single man of the Convocation ; and he did also by desire of the Convocation alter and add to the forms of *Prayers to be used at Sea* (now taken into the Service Book)."[1]

He touchingly closes his account of the bishop with these words—

"Thus this pattern of meekness and primitive innocence changed this for a better life. It is now too late to wish that my life may be like his; for I am in the eighty-fifth year of my age ; but I humbly beseech Almighty God that my death may ; and do as earnestly beg of every reader to say Amen."[2]

Walker, in summing up his character, remarks : "I cannot forbear to add that modesty and humility were two gems which shin'd with a peculiar brightness in it." Neal, even in spite of himself, gives him his due when he relates "that he had a roll of

[1] Walton's "Lives," S.P.C.K. London, 1847, p. 354.
[2] Ibid., pp. 299–375.

Nonconformist ministers in his eye, but when he was near his end he ordered the roll to be burnt, and said he would die in peace."[1]   In his will he declares that he is "abundantly satisfied, that the schism which the Papist, on the one hand, and the superstition, which the Puritan, on the other hand, lay to our charge are very justly chargeable upon themselves respectively."   He directs—

"As for my corruptible body, I bequeath it to the earth whence it was taken, to be decently buried in the Parish church of Bugden, towards the end of the chancel, upon the second, or (at the farthest) the third day after my decease; and that with as little noise, pomp, and charge as may be, without the invitation of any person, how near soever related unto me, other than the inhabitants of Bugden; without the unnecessary expense of escutcheons, gloves, ribbons, etc., and without any blacks to be hung anywhere in or about the house or church, other than a pulpit-cloth, a hearse-cloth, and a mourning gown for the preacher; whereof the former (after my body shall be interred), to be given to the preacher of the funeral sermon, and the latter to the curate of the parish for the time being.   And my will further is, that the funeral sermon be preached by my own household chaplain, containing some wholesome discourse concerning mortality; the Resurrection of the Dead, and the Last Judgment; and that he shall have for his pains, £5, upon condition that he speak nothing at all concerning my person, either good or ill, other than I myself shall direct; only signifying to the auditory that it was my express will to have it so."

Benjamin Laney (1663-67) ruled but a short time.   Like Henchman of London, he had been a

---

[1] Neal's "Puritans," vol. iv. p. 315.

faithful Royalist, and as chaplain to the King, had waited on him in his exile. He was rewarded first with the throne of Peterborough. He evidently did not like enforcing the *Act of Uniformity*, and when obliged to take action, he sheltered himself under the phrase, "Not I, but the law." He was an old man when he came to Lincoln; his rule was mild, and when twitted with not exercising greater severity towards Nonconformists, he said he could "look through his own fingers." Near Buckden (where he usually resided) he allowed a Nonconformist to preach publicly every year for some years.[1] He was translated to Ely in 1667.

Next to Laney came William Fuller (1667–75), Bishop of Limerick, one of the comparatively few Irish Prelates translated to an English see. His views may be gathered from the anthem composed by him, and quoted at the heading of this chapter. We can quite understand that his appointment delighted the heart of the loquacious Pepys, who thus refers to it—

"I met with Bishop Fuller, who, to my great joy, is made Bishop of Lincoln—come to dine with us—and there mighty good company. But the Bishop is a very extraordinary good-natured man, and one that is mightily pleased, as well as I am, that I live so near Bugden, the seat of his Bishopric, where he is like to reside, and indeed I am glad of it."

If the admiration of good men is any index of

---

[1] Calamy, "Mem.," pp. 92–94.

high character, that of Bishop Fuller is illuminated
by his reverence for the life and work of his great
predecessor St. Hugh, in whose honoured memory
he wrote an appreciative epitaph to be engraved on
his restored shrine.

William Barlow (1675–92) was not an active
Diocesan. It is said that he never entered his
Cathedral after his consecration. His preference
for a quiet life at his episcopal residence in Hun-
tingdonshire gained for him the sobriquet of " The
Bishop of Bugden." He and Bishop Compton of
London saw the failure of the plot for the assassina-
tion of ".The Merry Monarch."

Both Barlow and Compton outlived the restored
monarch. Of Compton, we shall have more to say
when we consider the period of the Revolution.
The general opinion of Barlow is that he was an
episcopal " Vicar of Bray," now railing against the
Pope; now inducing six hundred of his clergy to
sign an address of congratulation to James, on
his first Declaration of Liberty of Conscience, and
afterwards welcoming the Prince of Orange with
open arms.

The feeling of churchmen during the earlier part
of the period was one of exuberant triumph, but
the old Protestant feeling was by no means crushed.
In spite of the various methods of attempted
repression, the Puritan spirit was still vigorous.
The " Acta " of the Archdeacons' courts, right up
to the end of the period, exhibit this fact. Many

entries like the following formed the subject of
" Presentations " in both counties :—

. . . "for sitting at the saying of the Beliefe when all
the rest stand up, and using the same posture in all
the prayers ;" . . . " for teaching school without a license ; "
. . . " for inscribing texts of scripture in the Chancel
over the Communion table, 'Ye worship ye know not
what,' and over the door, 'in vain do ye worship me ;'" . . .
" for not christening his child being three years old."

The zeal for religious persecution, which had
possessed the land for 150 years, was soon to
give place to another phase of the Church's
trial. She had now to choose between liberty
and the tyranny of a despotic King in his attempt
by a side wind, to reinstate the power of Rome
as a factor in the religious life of the nation.
The Church and the nation had something to
say about this attempt, and they said it with no
uncertain voice.

CHAPTER XXV

REVOLUTION AND REST—ESSEX AND HERT-FORDSHIRE

" A voice from long-expecting thousands sent,
Shatters the air and troubles tower and spire,
For Justice hath absolved the innocent
And Tyranny is baulked of her desire."

WORDSWORTH.

THE three years of the misrule and duplicity of James II. were years of sore trial for the Church. His fair promise "to preserve the government of the Church as it is now established" evoked the popular response, "We have the word of a King." The word was soon to be broken. Behind the promise lay a fixed purpose to restore the Roman ascendency in Church and State. The King's defiance of the *Test Act*, his autocratic publication of a new *Declaration of Indulgence*, and his command that all clergy should read it from their pulpits, were signals of the coming storm. The clergy, almost without exception, refused to obey. The trial and acquittal of the seven Bishops are subjects too well known to need recital. Compton, still

Bishop of London, though not sharing the honour
of imprisonment, was suspended, and was the one
Bishop who boldly signed the invitation to the
Prince of Orange and promised him support, for
he saw what lay behind the monarch's fair words
of charity.

With the landing of William at Torbay in 1688,
and the flight of James, on December 23rd, of the
same year, the Revolution was complete. A *Toleration Act* marked a new era for Nonconformity, but
within the Church the Revolution was the occasion
of new trouble. English churchmen were willing
enough, by accepting the *Act of Toleration*, to
reward the dissenters who had stood by them in
their battle against the threatened revival of
Roman tyranny ; but when it came to the question
of taking the *Oath of Allegiance* in 1689, the
Primate, and six Bishops, four hundred clergy, and
a large body of laymen refused. This, as is well
known, was the origin of the term *Non-Juror*.

It is not certain how many of the clergy of
our two counties were expelled from their benefices.
The names of some of them are recorded in—

"A list of clergy, and others in the Universities of
Oxford and Cambridge, who were thought not to qualify
themselves upon the Revolution, viz.—Mr. Arthur Battel,
Curate and Usher at Hertford ;[1] Mr. Aaron Hodgson,

[1] In 1645, Ralph Battle was appointed to the Vicarage of Newen-
ham. In 1676, Ralph Battle was instituted to the Rectory of Letch-
worth. On June 25th, 1685, Affabel Battle was inducted to the Rectory
of Digswell.

Curate and Usher to the School of Stanstead ; Mr. Polford, of —— ; Mr. Alexander Horton, Rector of Kelshill, brother-in-law to Bishop Turner of Ely ; Mr. Davenport, Rector of West Raising in Hertfordshire (?), and Mr. Jeremiah Donne, who had been for some time Non-Jurors, afterwards complied on further consideration ; Mr. Richard Mills, Vicar of Ridge (described as of Middlesex), who afterwards qualified ; Mr. Charles Banks, Curate of St. Christopher, and Vicar of Cheshunt ; Dr. Charles Trumball, Rector of Stystead in Essex and Hadley in Suffolk, Chaplain to Dr. Sancroft, Archbishop of Canterbury ; Mr. Samuel Dodd, Vicar of Chiswell (? Chishall or Chigwell) ; Mr. Woodroffe, Vicar of Fealstead." [1]

The state to which these clergy were reduced may be gathered from the fact, that the deprived Bishops issued a letter of charitable recommendation, dated July 22nd, 1693, representing that—

"Many of our *Deprived* Brethren of the Clergy, with their Wives, Children and Families are reduced to extreme want . . . recommending their Necessitous Condition to all Pious good People," etc.[2]

The influence of the Non-Jurors on the life of the Church has been too frequently underestimated. For years these men, some of them the most devoted, though possibly mistaken sons of the Church, lived in isolation, and alas ! laid the foundation of a new, though happily a short-lived schism. The greater number either suffered in silence, or, like Sherlock among the clergy, and

---

[1] Complete Collection of the Works of John Kettlewell, vol. ii. appendix vi. London, 1719.

[2] *Vide* also Kettlewell's Collections.

Nelson among the laity, returned to the fold. Some of those who remained in isolation, together with their immediate successors, were soon to become the precursors of the dawn of a new religious revival. During the years which succeeded the Revolution, the Church had become tainted with the spirit of political expediency, and what was worse, she had fallen into a state of religious indifference. The extent of that indifference may be judged by a further consideration of some of the marks of the times, about to be indicated.

Compton (1675–1714), of whom we have already spoken, was Bishop of London throughout the time to which we are now referring. He did his best to evoke a more active interest in the affairs of the Church, but the political excitement of the day was against pastoral activity. Still, we find him promoting the work of *Queen Anne's Bounty*, founded in 1704 for the purpose of augmenting smaller benefices, not for the encumbrance of either the richer or the poorer by encouraging heavy loans. The statute was entitled "*An act for making more effectual Her Majesty's Gracious Intentions for the augmentation of the Poor Clergy*." The more or less immediate effect of it was to encourage private benefactions, and within the next forty years eleven benefices in Hertfordshire and thirty-four in Essex were so augmented.[1] Bishop Compton is said to

---

[1] For a complete list to 1754, *vide* Ecton Thesaurus, "R̄m. Eccm," pp. xviii.–xx.

have himself purchased a parsonage house, together with thirty-five acres of land and some tithes, for Marks Tey, and to have presented the patronage to Balliol College, Oxford. This work of augmentation has been going on quietly ever since, though the use of the powers of granting loans has not always been wisely exercised by the Governors.

In January, 1689, the Bishop wrote to his clergy, bidding them lay before the people the blessings of the Revolution. In September, 1699, he confirmed about two hundred men, women, and children at Purleigh, and on July 31st, 1700, held an ordination there.

Compton's contemporary, Thomas Tenison (1692–95), did nothing to distinguish himself as Bishop of Lincoln. Swift's estimate of him is amusing. He describes him as "a very dull man, who had a horror of anything like levity in the clergy, especially of whist."

Thomas James Gardiner (1695–1705), a Whig and a Low churchman, ruled a portion of Hertford-shire for eleven years, during the depths of the despair. He was fully alive to the deadly character of the abuses which were gaining ground. He attacked with no unsparing hand the general negligence, simony, and too common immorality of the general rank and file of the clergy. Samuel Wesley (writing of the clergy of this date), in the *Athenian Oracle*, said that out of fifty or sixty clergy that he knew, he could not think of above three or four who disgraced their office. The Bishop's view ranged over a wider field. Doubtless, as he looked round his still immense diocese, he had only too cogent reasons for alarm at the numbers of incompetent clergy whom Samuel Wesley could not know. He complains of the lack of regular services on Sunday, of the neglect of the fasts and feasts of the Church. The observance of Good Friday and Ascension Day had fallen into almost entire neglect. His special burden of complaint was the scandalous slovenliness in the administration of the Holy Communion. There seems to have been at least a partial revulsion from the order of Laud as to the position of the Altar, and a return to the nave for the celebration of the Divine Mystery ; for he says, in a tract to his clergy, on the eve of his first visitation—

"There is great inconvenience in consecrating in so strait a place as an alley of the Church, and delivering the Bread and Wine in narrow seats, over the heads and treading upon the feet of those who kneel."

He exhorts the clergy and lay-people "to take more care to fit their chancels" for the proper performance of the Office, and says—

"that some lie wholly disused in more nasty manner than any cottager of the parish would keep his own house ; others are employed for keeping school, by reason of which the seats, pavements and windows are commonly broken and defaced, not to mention other rudenesses and indecencies which are not fit to be permitted in a place set apart for God's worship." [1]

The performance of the other offices of the Church was also a subject of scandal. Private baptisms and clandestine marriages were rife. These abuses were the fruit of years of lax episcopal rule, and were not easily eradicated. The following extract shows that Bishop Gardiner was strict in the matter of unlicensed preachers :—

"I, Daniel Skingle, of the Parish of Munden Magna in the County of Hertford, do acknowledge and confess to have committed a great fault, by taking upon me to preach contrary to the law, in the Chapel of Minsden, within the Parish of Hitchin, and do beg the Right Rev. Father in God, James, Lord Bishop of Lincoln, his pardon, and all others offended thereat ; and do promise that I will not commit or do the like for the future, witness my hand this 20 day of Dec., 1700. Daniel Skingle. *Concordat cum orig. Testibus nobis, Fr. Bragge, Vicar de Hitchin,* Thomas Harris." [2]

Another submission was made in Hitchin church on Sunday, November 23rd, 1701, by John Heath, chapel warden of Minsden, that he "permitted and suffered Daniel Skingle, a mere layman, and in a lay habit, to preach, and did invite and encourage him."

The next Bishop, William Wake (1705–1716),

---

[1] *Advice to the Clergy of the Diocese of Lincoln in order for his Primary Visitation :* quoted in Perry's "History of Lincoln," p. 319, *et seq.*

[2] Urwick, "Nonconformity in Herts," p. 642.

attacked the prevailing corruption in a more systematic manner, requiring returns from every parish in the deanery. He was in every way careful about details. An evidence of this may be noted in his foundation of a library at Buckden (1716), for use of the neighbouring clergy. He laid down a rule that every clerk presented by him to any preferment should make a gift of books to the library; this rule remained in force till the time of Bishop Kaye, when, in 1837, the episcopal residence was transferred to Riseholme. The library was left under the care of the Vicar of Buckden till 1870, when, on the sale of the Buckden estates, the books were removed to the Grammar School at Huntingdon. Finally, in 1890, the Archdeacon of Huntingdon erected a new building for the library.

The establishment of clerical libraries was a special feature of this date. Doubtless a good many existing libraries in country towns could be traced to this period.

The pages of *The Spectator* were enlivened by satires at the expense of the clergy and laity of the time. The clergy were lampooned for the character of their prayers before the sermon, and their use in them of titles and epithets applied to great men. It seems to have been a common custom to conclude a long prayer with the words, "O let not the Lord be angry, and I will speak but this once." "There is another pretty fancy,"

says Steele, " when a young man has a mind to
let us know who gave him his scarf, he speaks in
a parenthesis to the Almighty, ' Bless, as I am in
duty bound to pray, the right honourable the
Countess,' as much as to say, ' Bless her, for thou
knowest I am her Chaplain.' "

The Rector of St. James, Garlick-Hithe, afterwards Archdeacon of St. Albans, affected his
hearers by his reading; " the Confession was read
with such a resigned humility, the Absolution with
such a comfortable authority, the Thanksgiving
with such a religious joy," etc.

Even in those days, the clergy were not without
eccentric members of their congregation; one
writes—

" A widow lady, who straggled this summer from
London into my parish for the benefit of the air, as she says,
appears every Sunday at Church with many fashionable
extravagances. . . . She introduces above fifty Italian airs
into the hundredth psalm; and whilst we begin ' All
people,' in the old solemn tune of our forefathers, she in
quite a different key runs divisions in the vowels, and
adorns them with the graces of Nicolini; if she meets
with an ' eke ' or an ' aye,' which are frequent in the
metre of Hopkins and Sternhold, we are certain to hear
her quavering them half a minute after us to some sprightly
airs of the opera. . . . I am apprehensive that the infection
may spread, for ' Squire Squeekum,' who by his voice
seems (if I may use the expression) to be cut out for an
Italian singer, was last Sunday practising the same airs."

The question of behaviour in church is a frequent subject of remark in *The Spectator*, in the

days of good Queen Anne. Among other customs,
attention is called to the repetition of the prayers
after the minister, especially the Absolution. "The
Commandments fare no better." The repetition is
described as being "done in so audible a manner"
that sometimes the voices of the congregation were
as loud as that of the clergyman. The conduct of
the famous "Sir Roger de Coverley" is too well
known to need more than a reference. We do not
forget "that, being a good Churchman, he beautified
the inside of his Church with several texts of his
own choosing;" that he gave "a handsome pulpit
cloth and railed in the Communion Table at his
own expense," and provided "his (*sic*) parishioners
with a hassock, to induce them to kneel, with a
Book of Common Prayer, to excite them to response, and employed an itinerant 'singing-master'
to instruct them in the tunes of the Psalms." A
delightful picture is presented of his personal devotion in his occasional threefold "Amen," and we
read of his kindly inquiries after the well-being of
his dependents, as he passed through their ranks at
the close of the service.

The letter of "Jenny Simper" is probably not
so well known. It is so charmingly naïve, that we
cannot resist the temptation of quoting it at length.

"I am a young woman, and have my fortune to make,
for which reason I come constantly to church to hear
divine service and make conquests; but one great hindrance in this my design is that our clerk, who was once

a gardener, has this Christmas so over-decked the Church with greens, that he has quite spoiled my prospect ; insomuch that I have scarce seen the young baronet I dress at these three weeks, though we have both been very constant at our devotions, and do not sit above three pews off.   The church, as it is now equipped, looks more like a greenhouse than a place of worship.   The middle aisle is a very pretty shady walk, and the pews look like so many arbours on each side of it.   The pulpit itself has such clusters of ivy, holly, and rosemary about it, that a light fellow in our pew took occasion to say that the congregation heard the Word out of a bush like Moses.   Sir Anthony Love's pew in particular is so well hedged that all my batteries have no effect.   I am obliged to shoot at random among the boughs, without taking any manner of aim.   Mr. Spectator, unless you will give orders for removing these greens, I shall grow a very awkward creature at church, and soon have little else to do there but to say my prayers." [1]

Complaint is made that many persons come late to the service.   An acquaintance of " Will Honeycomb "—

" seldom comes in till the prayers are half over, and when he has entered his seat (instead of joining with the congregation) he devoutly holds his hat before his face for three or four moments, then bows to all his acquaintance, sits down, takes a pinch of snuff (if it be the evening service, perhaps takes a nap), and spends the remaining time in surveying the congregation."

Further complaint is made of—

" a certain enormity which is chiefly in use among the politer and better bred part of mankind; I mean the ceremonies, bows, courtesies, whisperings, smiles, winks,

[1] *Spectator*, Jan. 23, 1711–12, No. 282.

nods, with other familiar arts of salutation, which take up so much time in our churches."

These playful pictures indicate the tone of the new phase of respectable orthodoxy which was beginning to settle on the Church, when her affairs ceased to stir, as they had done in the past, the zeal of the rank and file of the nation, misguided as it oftentimes had been. Doubtless, many of our readers could furnish, from their parishes in the two counties, proofs that the pictures are no exaggeration of the growing laxity of the times, in spite of the brief period of revival which was fostered by a few devout churchmen of the day. Notably, of course, we think with gratitude of the founders of the Society for Promoting Christian Knowledge, the Society for the Propagation of the Gospel, and of the Corporation of the Sons of the Clergy.

The high aims and the consistent practice of a few men in this reign were, it is much to be feared, the exception rather than the rule, and the death of Queen Anne stifled their bright hopes and lofty ambitions, and then the Church became "the tool and the plaything of party spirit; and as the bells rang out, in 1714, to welcome the accession of George I., they sounded the death-knell of her high ideals and her vigorous life for more than half a century." [1]

[1] Wakeman, "History of the Church of England," p. 420. 3rd ed. 1896.

X

CHAPTER XXVI

THE HANOVERIAN SLUMBER—ESSEX

> "*Ye shall find the key of the church under the threshold*
> *Ye may go in and drive away the daws.*
> *My surplice with one sleeve ye shall find there,*
> *And the old cut-work cope that hangs by geometry.*
> *Pray ye turn them carefully they are very tender,*
> *The remnant of the books lie where they did*
> *Half puffed away with the churchwardens pipings.*"
> BEAUMONT AND FLETCHER, "*Spanish Curate,*" iii. 2.

> "*Lord, ere our trembling lamps sink down and die,*
> *Touch us with chastening hand, and make us feel Thee nigh.*"
> KEBLE.

IT is said that the Bishop of a great midland see, on coming to his episcopal throne a few years after the death of George IV., was accosted with the remark, "Your see, my lord, is called ' *Mare Mortuum.*'" He retorted, "' *Mare Pacificum,*' you mean." These terms might be indiscriminately applied to most sees, during the days of the earlier Georges.

The rest that followed all the religious storms and struggles of centuries was succeeded by slumber; slumber gave place to indifference, and indifference to paralysis. The days of George I.

may be truly described as a time of dismal desolation. Parish churches had come to be regarded as the almost exclusive possession of the few. In the churches the squirearchy, the yeoman, the tenant farmer, the successful tradesman, as the representatives of "respectability," were wont to ensconce themselves in the glory of private pews, lined with baize and carpet, while the despised labourer and the small shopkeeper were relegated to the back seats under the gallery, or shivered on the deal benches in the cold paved aisles. The Bishops, with few exceptions, were mere tools in the hands of statesmen, and the few who troubled themselves about church matters were chiefly concerned with speculative theology, the production of Erastian theses and counter blasts to Deism and enthusiasm. The voice of Convocation was silent, and the clergy were left to themselves without any effective oversight. Lax and careless as they were, they had huge difficulties to contend with. The whole tone of society, and of fashionable literature, was against them; drunkenness and immorality of all sorts were the order of the day. The prevailing indifference and ungodliness presented a formidable problem to solve.

When John Robinson (1714–23) was translated from Bristol to the see of London, in the first year of the reign of George I., he made no real effort to stem the tide. Little is known of him, beyond the facts that he was "a little brown man of grave and venerable appearance," of Swedish origin ; and that he wrote a *Circular Letter* to the clergy of his diocese warning them not to adopt an Arian innovation in the Doxology. He was the last Bishop who held the office as Lord Privy Seal. He was evidently a generous man, as we find he augmented seven benefices in Essex to the extent of £200 each.

He was succeeded by Edmund Gibson (1723–48), who was translated from Lincoln, where he had made a good record. He was a man of considerable power, and with a high sense of duty. He made a vigorous attempt, though without much success, to draw the attention of the Church to her surrounding difficulties and duties, and defended those clergy who were struggling against the tide, from the attacks and slanders to which they were subjected. We shall speak later on of his attitude towards the Wesleyan revival.

On the death of Bishop Gibson, Thomas Sherlock (1748–61) was translated from Salisbury. His previous appointments as Dean of Chichester and Bishop of Bangor, together with his great ability as a controversialist, made him a prominent man. We must leave our readers to decide whether it was his power in swimming (at which he was an adept), or his love of plunging into controversy, which brought upon him the satire in the *Dunciad* as the " Plunging Bishop." He does not appear to have made any marked impression on the habits of the people. It

will always be in his favour, that, though not very
friendly to the Wesleys, he was ever true to his old
friend, William Law, the Non-Juror. Two years
after he became Bishop of London, a shock of
earthquake threw the city into a state of alarm.
He seized the occasion by issuing a Pastoral on the
subject, a hundred thousand copies of which are
said to have been distributed. Law followed it by
an impassioned appeal, which is worth quoting, not
only for its historical interest, but also for its lofty
eloquence and its evident piety of purpose.

"O Britain, Britain," he exclaims, "think that the Son
of God saith unto thee, as He said to Jerusalem, 'O Jerusalem, Jerusalem, how often would I have gathered thy
children, as a hen gathereth her chickens under her wings,
and ye would not ! Behold, your house is left unto you
desolate.'" And now let me say, "What aileth thee, O
British earth, that thou quakest, and the foundations of
thy churches that they totter ? Just that same aileth thee
as ailed Judah's earth, when the Divine Saviour of the
world, dying on the Cross, was reviled, scorned, and
mocked by the inhabitants of Jerusalem ; then the earth
quaked, the rocks rent, and the sun refused to give its
light. Nature again declares for God ; the earth and the
elements can no longer bear our sins ; Jerusalem's doom
for Jerusalem's sin may well be feared by us. O ye
miserable pens dipt in Satan's ink, that dare to publish
the folly of believing in Jesus Christ ; when will you hide
your guilty heads, when Nature dissolved shall show you
the Rainbow, on which the crucified Saviour shall sit in
judgment, and every work receive its reward ? O tremble !
ye apostate sons that come out of the schools of Christ
to fight Lucifer's battles, and do that for him which

neither he nor his legions can do for themselves. Their inward pride, spite, wrath, malice, and rage against God and Christ, and human nature, have no pens but yours, no apostles but you. They must be found to work in the dark, to steal privately into impure hearts ; could they not beguile you into a fond belief that you are Lovers of Truth, Friends of Reason, Detectors of Fraud, Great Geniuses, and Moral Philosophers, merely and solely because you blaspheme Christ and the Gospel of God. Poor deluded souls, rescued from Hell by the Blood of Christ, called by God to possess the thrones of fallen Angels, permitted to live only by the mercy of God, that ye may be born again from above ; my heart bleeds for you. Think, I beseech you, in time, what mercies you are trampling under your feet. Say not that reason and your intellectual faculties stand in your way ; that these are the best gifts that God has given you, and that these suffer you not to come to Christ. For all this is as vain a pretence, and as gross a mistake, as if ye were to say that you had nothing but your feet to carry you to Heaven." [1]

The short episcopate of Thomas Hayter (1761–62) adds nothing to the interest of our story, though he had a reputation in the diocese of Norwich for integrity of purpose.

At the close of Hayter's rule, Richard Osbaldeston (1762–64) was translated from Carlisle. He held the see for two years only. His career may be summed up in the description given of him that "he was a Whig in politics, liberal in his church views, rich, indolent, and chiefly non-resident." [2] Both he and his immediate successors had

---

[1] From the "Spirit of Prayer," Law's Works, vii. (2) 160–62.
[2] "Dictionary of Nat. Biog."

much controversy over the question of dilapidations [1] of his episcopal residence.

He was succeeded by Richard Terrick (1764–77), who ruled over Essex for thirteen years, being translated from Peterborough. Horace Walpole describes him as a man without any special characteristics, save "a sonorous delivery and an assiduity of back-stairs address." [2] At the close of 1765 he began to prosecute " Mass Houses" in his diocese. On March 17th, 1777, he addressed a letter to his clergy on the need of the better observance of Good Friday, lamenting at the same time the general " decay of religious principles in this age of licentiousness and profligacy ; " he also enforced the duty of attendance at public worship. During his episcopate a return was made of the number of churches and chapels in the county of Essex, with the following result:—Archdeaconry of Essex, 175 ; of Colchester, 161 ; of Middlesex, 83. Rural Deans had not been appointed for many years.

Robert Lowth (1777–87) passed quickly through the sees of St. Davids and Oxford to the throne of London. We shall speak in another chapter of his relation to the Revival movement, then in its flood-tide.

He made some attempt, in the midst of his scholarly occupations, to effect some reform in

---

[1] " Notes and Queries," 3rd Series, iv. 149.
[2] *Gentleman's Magazine*, 1704, vol. lxiv. pp. 208–210.

church discipline. We find him protesting against
the growing custom of incumbents acting as "warm-
ing-pans" and giving *Bonds of Resignation*. In
1780 the patron of the benefice of Woodham
Walters brought an action against the Bishop in the
Court of Common Pleas for refusing to institute his
nominee, the Rev. John Eyre, on the ground that
the latter had given a bond of resignation, under
a large penalty, to resign the living on request. In
a final appeal to the House of Lords, judgment
was given in favour of the Bishop upon a division
of nineteen against eighteen.[1] The decision is
noteworthy, not only as an important test case,
but from the fact that Bishops have never since
spoken and voted as judges in the House of
Lords.

Not much can be told of Bishop Porteus (1787–
1809), beyond the fact of his special interest in
the abolition of slavery, and his support of the
Society for the Propagation of the Gospel. In
this respect he carried on the tradition of Lowth,
for whom he appeared to have acted for some
time. He was generally benevolent in his public
and private life, and a strong supporter of Sunday
schools. Like his predecessor, he took up the
question of *Resignation Bonds*. He was also active
in attempting to induce a better observance of
Holy Days, and especially of Good Friday. In a

[1] Phillimore's Edition of Burns, under "Simony." Phillimore,
"Ecclesiastical Law," vol. ii. pp. 1121, *et seq.*

series of sermons preached in London, he described benevolence as "the favourite, the fashionable virtue of the age." "It is," he said, "universally cried up by infidels and libertines as the first and only duty of man, and even many who pretend to the name of Christians are too apt to rest upon it as the most essential part of their religion." He was not lavish in the number of special sermons. Once, when asked by a clergyman to preach a charity sermon, he replied, "I give one in a year and next year is promised." [1]

The episcopates of John Randolph (1809–13), and of William Howley (1813–28) (an Erastian, who adopted the axiom that "the King can do no wrong"), left no special mark on the diocese. During the episcopate of Howley we come across an illustration of the spirit of the times in relation to the custom of school-treats. It is related that at the "Anniversary" of the National schools in the rural deanery of Tendring, which was held in a meadow near Thorpe Hall, on August 9th, 1816, nearly two thousand children were present, together with a great multitude of friends and spectators, estimated at from eight to ten thousand. The Bishop of London preached at Thorpe Church, inspected the children, and was, according to the chronicler of the event, "highly gratified by their decency of deportment, as well as by their healthy

---

[1] *Vide* "Memoirs of Bishop Blomfield," 2nd ed. London, 1864, p. 44.

appearance and dress." Amongst other refreshments, it is mentioned that the children were supplied with *half a pint of beer each.* No remark is made on their deportment afterwards. The day's festivities closed with a dance at the Hall.[1] Against this narrative should be set the extension of the work of elementary education, fostered by the church under the auspices of the National Society, founded in 1811, and of the gradual establishment, here and there in the county, of the system of Sunday schools.

Before going on to speak of the rule of the last of the Hanoverian Bishops, it will be well to make some reference to another aspect of church matters. The decay of church fabrics was lamentable, and what was worse, right on through this period and into the reign of Queen Victoria, there was a wholesale destruction of many of the ancient churches of the county. The story is indeed a sad one, and though it is easy in these days of a revived and enlightened reverence for antiquity to cast stones at our predecessors, we must not forget that the appalling desolation of ruin, in many cases, together with the lack of the knowledge of gothic architecture, which had almost died out, placed the guardians of our old churches in a state of bewildering helplessness. We must give them the credit of a desire, according to their lights, to make things at least respectable. In those days of plurality and absenteeism, it is little

[1] *Colchester Gazette*, August 16, 1816.

wonder that the local magnates, the village church-wardens, and the estate carpenters and masons, made sorry havoc. Nor indeed is it at all likely, had the Rector or Vicar been present at the vestry-meetings, when these matters were usually decided on, that he would have had a much more appreciative knowledge than they of the architectural history of the parish church, or have exercised much restraining influence on the subject of its repair. However this may be, a woeful record has to be made of old churches in the county, which have been totally destroyed, with the exception in some few cases of the towers, which survived the wreck. The following is the list :—

Aldham, Arkesden, Birch, Bowers Gifford,* St. Runwald (Colchester), Cold Norton, Cricksea, Downham,* Dunton, South Fambridge, Farnham, Foulness, Great Hallingbury,* Hanningfield, Havering-atte-Bower, Hutton, Latchingdon, Loughton, Markshall, Mayland, Myland, Mucking, Little Parndon, Pitsea,* Quendon, Ramsden Bellhouse, Ramsden Crays, Rawreth,* Rayne, Romford, Steeple, St. Lawrence (Newland), Stapleford Abbots, Theydon Bois, Thorpe-le-Soken, West Tilbury, Upminster,* Weeley, Walton, Wickford, Wickham Bishops, Widford.

New chancels, mostly taking the place of the old, have been erected at Ardleigh, Ashen, North Benfleet, Little Canfield, Canvey Island, Great Clacton, Frinton, Littlebury, Radwinter, Great Saling, Salcott, Stock, Ulting, North Weald, Wimbish.[1]

* The towers were left.

This unhappy panic of destruction took place

[1] This list was compiled by the late Rev. J. A. Sparvel-Bayley, and published in the *Essex Review.*

chiefly in the period of which we are speaking, though it is to be feared that, even in later days, the spirit of destruction had not been exorcised. We must charitably suppose that grim necessity prompted the action of those responsible. We must be content with summing up the story by saying that it speaks of great zeal and little knowledge.

Side by side with this sad tale, there is a brighter story of attempts to meet decay and ruin by the wiser method of repair, though here again the repairs were often executed with a lack of that reverence for antiquity which we could have wished. We quote one or two instances of the methods occasionally adopted for restoration.

On January 18th, 1800, a great part of the parish church of Chelmsford [1] was wrecked through the prevalent custom of intra-mural burials, and the carelessness of workmen in digging a vault. A *Brief* was issued for its repair in 41 George III. which recites—

"that the parish church of Chelmsford is in a very ruinous condition, the roof and south isle thereof and part of the north isle having fallen down, whereby it is considered incapable of having Divine Service performed therein, and the gallery and many of the pews are destroyed."

The repairs were estimated by John Johnson, Esq., "an able and experienced architect," at £3600, exclusive of old materials, "which sum the inhabitants are not able to raise among themselves, being mostly tenants at rack rents, and greatly burdened

[1] See *Gent. Mag.*, 1800, Pt. I. pp. 79, 432, 433.

with poor." A *Brief*, to run for one year, was granted from house to house throughout the country. Another instance of a *Brief* being resorted to occurs much later (56 George III.). The *Brief* recites—

"that on the 29th day of March last, a considerable portion of the roof of the parish church of Brightlingsea and two of the arches of the said church standing between the centre of the said church and the south aisle thereof fell down, whereby the south aisle of the said church was very much injured, and the church in general so much dilapidated, that the roof thereof must be entirely rebuilt, and a very considerable sum laid out in the general reparation of the said church to make it safe for the parishioners of the said parish to assemble therein to attend Divine Service."

It was to run for a year, from Lady-day to Lady-day. Mr. Thompson, of Dedham, "an experienced architect," estimated the cost at £919 10s. or thereabouts.

Writers in the *Ecclesiologist* give the following examples of the state of the churches in the latter part of the Hanoverian period, *e.g.*, at Wicken Bonant, a pew existed which divided the chancel from the nave, and there was no access to the altar without passing through one door and out of the other. At Rickling, a very fine decorated church had most of its windows gutted ; two of them were defiled by the protrusion of two chimneys. In the parish church of St. Michael, Mile End, Colchester (according to the statement of a visitor), a large chest, painted yellow, served as the Holy Altar.

The font at Pentlow was hidden among pews, and contained at this period (1) an old cotton umbrella ; (2) a common hand-basin ; (3) a smaller ditto ; (4) a brown stone jug ; (5) a dust broom.

Among other signs of the times, we may note the increase of Faculty pews, or as the late Archbishop Magee used to call them " enclosures on the common of God's poor." The church records of the period abound in evidences of this new method of ejection.

Charles James Blomfield (1828–46) was the last Bishop of London to exercise episcopal jurisdiction over the whole county of Essex. He had been Rector of Chesterford, and for a short time held the Archdeaconry of Colchester. As Archdeacon he showed some of the qualities which indicated his future career as a distinguished prelate. He made his first visitation, as Archdeacon of Colchester, in 1822, and remarks in one of his letters (dated April 16th, 1822), "of the churchwardens of 154 parishes, not one was absent, except in two cases of illness." It is to be feared that the churchwardens of to-day, while not lacking in respect for the persons of the venerable holders of the archidiaconal office, are not so careful about their duty in attendance at these ancient and useful courts of the Church. He did much to revive ruridecanal life generally, preferring the regular and organized action of the clergy to the irresponsible gatherings of clerical societies, which had then begun to be popular. This energetic Archdeacon was raised to the see of Chester in 1824, which he held for about four years. Though he is sometimes styled a "Greek Play Bishop," he soon proved his sterling qualities as a ruler of the Church.

His translation to the see of London was well received, and he lived to see the Church rise to her responsibilities. He soon set himself to try to improve the state of diocesan matters, while the great national questions of education and the like, took up much of his time. In his primary visitation he advocated the substitution of " early prayer or Matins on all weekdays, for morning service on Wednesdays and Fridays." He recommended the use of the surplice instead of "the gown" for morning sermons, though he did not approve of flowers as a decoration for the Holy Table, at least when they were "symbolically and fancifully arranged." The following anecdote of Blomfield is an indication of the gradual change which was springing up in relation to various matters of externals. On one occasion, being asked whether he had any message to send to the King (William IV.), he said—

"You may present my duty to His Majesty, and say that at this tropical season I find my episcopal wig a serious encumbrance, and that I hope he will not consider me guilty of a breach of court etiquette if I am induced to lay it aside."

The King took the message gravely, and replied—

"Tell the Bishop that he is not to wear his wig on my account; I dislike it as much as he does, and shall be glad to see the whole Bench wear their own hair." [1]

[1] "Memoir of Bishop Blomfield." London, 1864, p. 97.

From that time the episcopal wig gradually fell into disuse.

This Bishop was strict, for the times, in the matter of non-residence. He was once at an informal gathering of Essex incumbents, many of whom had license of non-residence on account of the alleged unhealthiness of their districts, and had left curates in charge. He proceeded to remind the incumbents that curates were flesh, and that the residence which was possible for the one was not impossible for the other.

"Besides," he added, "there are two well-known preservatives against ague ; the one is a good deal of care and a little port wine ; the other, a little care and a good deal of port wine. I prefer the former, but if any of the clergy prefer the latter, it is at all events a remedy which incumbents can afford better than curates." [1]

A matter of special interest to churchmen in the diocese has now to be recorded, and though it falls more properly in the Victorian days, yet the Bishop was concerned, and it may be treated of here. This was the proposed new re-arrangement of the dioceses of London and Rochester. The ever-increasing population of London proper, the wide area of Essex, together with a considerable part of the county of Hertford, must have made large demands on the good Bishop's time. It must have been an intense relief to him when the negotiations for the transference of the outlying

[1] "Memoirs of Bishop Blomfield." London, 1864, pp. 61–118.

members of his great diocese were brought to a climax, and the prospect of a lighter burden for his successor was assured. The change was effected by an Order in Council, dated August 8th, 1845, in pursuance of 6 and 7 William IV. c. 77, when the whole county of Essex (except the parishes of Barking, East Ham, West Ham, Little Ilford, Low Leyton, Walthamstow, Wanstead, Woodford, and Chingford, which were to continue a part of the Diocese of London)[1] and the whole county of Hertford were to be transferred to the Diocese of Rochester. The actual transfer came into effect on January 1st, 1846.

Thus, on the death of Bishop Blomfield, "the old order changed, yielding place to new." The change satisfied nobody. The vicissitudes of Essex, that diocesan Cinderella, now the poor relation of the family of London, now of Rochester, must have meant much spiritual starvation. She met her isolation bravely, and gave strong evidence of vigorous life. Her faithfulness under the rule of three successive Bishops of Rochester, George Murray (1846-60), Joseph Cotton Wigram (1860-67), Thomas Legh Claughton (1867-77), was to receive its reward when the last-named Bishop was raised to the see of St. Albans. This happy event brought, as we shall see, to the churchmen of the two counties, new hopes and possibilities of a brighter future.

[1] *Vide infra*, p. 352.

Y

CHAPTER XXVII

HANOVERIAN SLUMBER—HERTFORDSHIRE

"Thrice blest is he to whom is given
The instinct that can tell
That God is on the field, when He
Is most invisible."

FABER.

WE must now turn to Hertfordshire, in Hanoverian days, and give some notes of the state of Church matters in that county. We have spoken, in a previous chapter, of William Wake, who ruled the see of Lincoln from 1705 to 1716.

Bishop Wake had an able successor in the person of Edmund Gibson (1716–23). He made the clergy feel that he was a real overseer of the flock. He was distressed by the social disorders and general neglect of religion, but he did not approve of Wesley's methods of correcting them.

Richard Reynolds (1723–44) was translated from Bangor to Lincoln. His rule was long, but we are unable to present any special records of his doings in the portion of the county under his charge. He appears to have held visitations in his diocese on five occasions. In an address, preparatory to his fifth visitation, he proposed to himself, first, "to receive complaints and make redress of such disorders in and amongst the members of my diocese as are grown or growing up to notoriety;" secondly, "to collect a full and true state of the Churches, their edifices, and endowments for their effectual preservation from diminution and dilapidation." He regrets the customs of non-residence and plurality, and the consequent "temerarious entertainment of adventitious, unapproved, unqualified assistance," and declares his intention "to extirpate these roots of disorder."[1] How far he was successful we cannot say.

John Thomas (1744–61), who followed Bishop Reynolds, owed his advancement to the fact that he spoke German fluently, and was travelling companion and tutor to George III. He was popularly termed "Honest Tom," and his personal appearance and not uncommon name gave rise to some amusement. There were two bishops of that name at this date,—John of Lincoln, and John of Peterborough (and a little later a third, John of Rochester). Each had held city livings, and Lincoln and Rochester had been royal chaplains. The story is told that, some one having referred to Dr. Thomas, the following conversation took place:—

"'Which Dr. Thomas do you mean?' 'Dr. John Thomas.' 'They are both named John.' 'Dr. Thomas who

[1] "Diocesan History of Lincoln," S.P.C.K. 1897, pp. 331, 332.

has a living in the city.' 'They both have livings in the city.' 'Dr. Thomas who is chaplain to the King.' 'They are both chaplains to the King.' 'Dr. Thomas who is a very good preacher.' 'They are both very good preachers.' 'Dr. Thomas who squints.' 'They both squint.'"[1]

In addition to his "squint," he was deaf, but, in spite of these defects, he was married four times. He has left behind him an interesting letter, dated from "Bugden, 4th June, 1744." In it he describes how he had been occupied for some days—

"Ordaining a young sett of 'clergy,' and that he had found them all very well qualified, on a thorough examination, except one. . . . I kept the young sparks there three days strictly to their duty ; made them attend twice a day at prayers in the Chappell, when I tried the voices of those to be ordained Deacons, by making them read the lessons. None of them were suffered to gallop to and from Cambridge every day, as has been the practice. I made Ordination a little more solemn than usual at Bugden, and I had a smaller number of candidates than usual, taking all imaginable care not to be imposed on by False Titles."[2]

He distinguished himself in Hertfordshire by granting (December 8th, 1750) a Faculty for pulling down the old parish church of Chisfield, and ordered the materials to be used for the parish church of Gravely, as need should require. In 1753 the tower of Shenley church was pulled down, and the chancel, and nave arches were removed.

[1] Quoted from Chalmer's "Biography of John Thomas of Rochester," by C. J. Abbey ; "English Church and its Bishops, 18th cent.," vol. ii. p. 74.

[2] Historical MSS. Comm., pub. 1889, p. 489.

In 1757 the stained glass of the fourteenth century was removed from the churches of Stanstead Abbots and Eastwick, to admit modern windows.

Doubtless many like records could be found during his episcopate. He was translated to Salisbury in 1761, and was succeeded by John Green (1761–79), Dean of St. Paul's. In the Lincoln Registry a full account is given of one of Green's Confirmation tours (June 9th to 27th, 1771). The number of persons confirmed was about five thousand. The cost of the tour was considerable. The items for gratuities to parish clerks and sextons amounted to £1 2s. 6d.; to servants, £4 3s. 8d. The items for officials' fees amounted to £10 3s. 6d. The hotel bills; "for looking after and feeding six horses, and for greasing the carriage, £19 3s. 2d." These and sundry other amounts brought the expenses up to £64 3s. 3d. This was met by a contribution from the Bishop of £20, Procurations £30, the Chancellor and two friends, who travelled part of the way, gave £2 8s., the Deputy-Registrar £1 3s. At the end of the tour the Bishop paid the balance of £10 12s. 3d. This did not exhaust the charges on his lordship, which cost him an additional sum of £19 7s. 1d., for butler's bill, shaving, wig-dressing, turnpikes, shoeing, and board wages of coachman and butler and postillion.

At one place " the Churchwardens, as usual, treated my lord to a supper;" at another it is recorded that he " was met here as usual, about two miles out of town, by the wardens, assistants, etc., and treated afterwards by them with an elegant, cold collation." "It being rainy, the Bishop did not alight from his carriage, as customary, on meeting the cortège." At another place one of the officials "lent to the Bishop, to give to some poor people at the gate, 2s." [1]

In these days of special Confirmation classes, one is apt to charge the clergy of that period with neglect of preparation for the holy rite. The charge may be true, but, in one respect, they were more loyal to the spirit of the Prayer-book in this matter than we have been in the present day. The visitation returns of the period show the widespread use of public catechising both on Sundays and weekdays, especially during Lent. It was thus that the candidates were prepared. The Church Catechism was the basis of the instruction. We find that the returns as to catechising are varied in their character, *e.g.* "till all are instructed"; "till the whole is thoroughly explained"; "as often as there is occasion"; "frequently"; "constantly"; "greatest part of the year"; "Easter to Michaelmas"; "Lent to Whitsuntide"; "in summer"; "every Sunday"; "every other Sunday"; "once a month"; "every Wednesday and Friday"; "Catechising and expounding every Sunday in the afternoon"; "now and then"; "but seldom"; "duly." A noteworthy

---

[1] For fuller details, see *Lincoln Dioc. Mag.*, vol. v. No. 37, pp. 73, 74.

feature about the Confirmations of the period is that usually a local clergyman was appointed to preach. There were nine such preachers in the Confirmation tour, to which we have just referred. It would be interesting to trace whether this was in substitution of the Preface " to be read by the Bishop, or by some other minister appointed by him," or of the address by the Bishop; or whether "the preacher" refers to the reader of the Preface.

Thomas Thurlow (1779–87) does not add lustre to the Hanoverian age. He lived at a time when the clergy revelled in plurality, and himself held the deanery of St. Paul's concurrently with his bishopric, but he showed himself to be no iconoclast, for Cussans [1] tells us that in the valuable collection of *Hertfordshire Notes and Sketches*, belonging to Baron Dimsdale, appended to the sketch of the old church of Ayot St. Lawrence, is this note—

" Sir Lionel Lyde, thinking it stood in his way, . . . intended to take the church down, but tho' the new building (a neat erection of the Grecian style) was consecrated and appropriated for parochial use, yet when the Baronet began to demolish the old structure, the Bishop interfered and made him desist, leaving the walls without a roof and the tower standing, in which are two bells, which ring for service in the other church, that fabrick being without those usual appendages." [2]

[1] Cussans, " History of Hertfordshire," vol. ii. p. 238.
[2] Drawings of the old and present church, made in the year 1791, are to be found in the British Museum. Add. MSS., No. 9063, fo. 37.

The day for the consecration of the neat Grecian edifice having arrived (July 28th, 1779)—

"The Bishop was preceded by a band of music, and upwards of twenty men and women, dressed in neat uniforms at the expense of Sir Lionel. When they arrived at the church, the doors were thrown open (each of the populace eager to enter first), when the usual service was performed, after which the company was regaled under tents, fixed for the purpose, with wine, cakes, etc. They then returned to the mansion-house, where an elegant dinner was provided, after which the company dispersed in the adjoining fields, where they diverted themselves in innocent rural games, till the close of the day, and at last parted, highly delighted with the pleasure they had received. A wedding was the only thing wanting to complete the festivity, which was intended, but the consecration of the church was not over until past twelve." [1]

George Pretyman Tomline (1787–1820), like Bishop Thurlow, at one time held both his Bishopric, and the Deanery of St. Paul's. He set to work to secure a real reformation in the lax habits of the clergy, and made his power felt in his diocese.

This Bishop held eleven general visitations of his diocese during his episcopate. In 1799 a return was made of one district in his see, from which we learn something of the state of the church life of the period. This return is preserved in the British Museum, and indicates the neglect of public

---

[1] *Gentleman's Magazine*, vol. xlix. p. 374.

worship, of family prayer, and of Bible reading ; the fewness of Sunday schools, and the prevalence of drunkenness, wakes, feasts, dancings, cock-fightings, petty races, and ale-houses which were opened on Sundays. The same return throws some interesting light on the development of the Wesleyan movement. Many still attended the altar of the Parish church, and held their meetings at different hours from the Church services. Some had begun to " set up their own altars." A third party had been infected with wild enthusiasm, and vigorously opposed the Church as a dying institution. We shall refer to this movement in another chapter.

In 1820 Bishop Tomline was promoted to Winchester, and the see of Lincoln had to submit to the rule of the Hon. George Pelham (1820–27). His own conspicuous example of plurality did not tend to discourage the practice, which had become notoriously rife among the rank and file of the Clergy.

He was succeeded by John Kaye (1827), who effected gradual but lasting changes for good. He was instrumental in reducing the scandals which had grown up in connection with non-residence and plurality, and wrought many improvements in the diocese. His burden of care was greatly diminished when, in 1846, he handed over to the care of the Bishop of Rochester such part of the county of Hertford as still remained in his diocese.

Thus the last connecting link of Hertfordshire with
the see of Lincoln was broken. The names of the
Bishops of Rochester who ruled over the whole
county from this date have already been referred to.[1]

Having recorded the diocesan succession, a few
sidelights on the general tone of the Church during
this period may be interesting. The following
advertisement of 1753 throws some light on the
spirit of those times in relation to assistant curates.
It appeared amongst some quaint extracts given in
the *Reading Mercury* of a few years ago.

"A clergyman to assist in the Care of a Church in a
large town, with easy Duty and a Salary of above £50
per annum, besides many valuable Perquisites. Signing
formal Testimoniums being the Aversion of the Conscientious, none will be required or given, but Time will
be allowed for him for Trial, and no Pains will be spared
for his Improvement. He must be zealously affected to
the present Government, and never forsake his Principles ;
singular in his Morals, sober and abstemious, grave in
his Dress and Deportment, choice in his Company and
exemplary in his Conversation. He must be of superior
Abilities, studious and careful in the employment of Time,
a lover of Fiddling, but no dancer. He shall be kindly
entertained, introduced to the best of company, calmly
admonished, and upon all Occasions treated with
Humanity and Respect."

The "perquisites" were probably *honorariums*
for funeral sermons, the composition of Latin
epitaphs, baptisms in private houses, tuition, etc.

[1] *Vide supra*, p. 321.

The required "gravity of dress" seems to point to the fact that the canonical dress had been falling into disuse.

The lack of a due sense of order and reverence, coupled with the general low tone, must sorely have tried the better type of churchmen. Our county of Hertford was not without its sad witness to the prevalent laxity. The Rev. —— was a striking example of the pluralist. At one time he was vicar of Hemel Hempsted, of Great Gaddesden, perpetual curate of Bovingdon-cum-Flaunden, and minister of Quebec Chapel, and only had one curate to assist him. He lived at Gaddesden. Cussans gives the following account of this remarkable state of things :—

"On the appointed fourth Sunday, if the weather were fine, a man was stationed at the top of the tower of Bovingdon church, whence he commanded a view of the road leading from Hemel Hempsted. If he saw the parson or his curate approaching, he would descend and ring the bell to summon the parishioners to church. If it rained or snowed, it was quite unnecessary to place a man on the look out. It sometimes happened that for three consecutive months there was no divine service held either at Flaunden or Bovingdon. A labourer, not fifty years old, told me that he had often known a corpse, when it could no longer be kept in the house, to remain for three, four, or five days in the church, before a clergyman from the mother church could be procured to perform the burial service."

Cussans relates another story in reference to Flaunden (where service appears to have been said once a month), but with some hesitation, as he heard it applied to another parish. He evidently believes the truth of it, however, and gives it on the authority of a gentleman living in the neighbourhood, in whose time it is said to have occurred. A party of ladies and gentlemen were on a visit to a neighbouring squire,

" and walked down to old Flaunden church. At that time there were three or four families, not living exactly in the church, but under its roof, which had been extended so as to cover their cottages built against the walls. ' How very interesting,' remarked one of the party. ' I should so like to attend service here.' ' Well, to-morrow is the regular day,' replied the woman who was showing them over the church, ' but I do hope and trust it will rain, and then the parson won't come, for I've got one of my best hens a-sitting on thirteen eggs in the pulpit, and she don't come off till Tuesday.' "

No wonder that such parishes were a stronghold of much pious, if impatient, Nonconformity, and that the faithful services of their parish priests to-day are rendered a thousandfold more arduous, though if proof were needed of the divine mission of the church, it may be illustrated by the fact that she has been guided by God through all these and like times of trial.

As a further evidence of the state of things in reference to the churches, we may notice that in 1809 the old Norman and Early English church of Northaw was destroyed by the then lord of the manor, and a building of brick and stucco erected in its site. This has happily been burnt down, and a new and splendidly appointed church has taken its place.

The west end of the south aisle of Pelham Furneaux church was blocked off and used as a rubbish hole, and a staircase ran through the west window. The condition of the parish church of Anstey was not much better.

As an example of "restoration" we may quote the case of Digswell church, a thirteenth-century building, which "was repaired and beautified" in 1830. An Early English arch in the chancel was bricked up, two arches in the north arcade of the nave were removed, and the west window was carefully "boarded up." High pews, and the regulation "three-decker" were erected. String-courses, corbels, mouldings, etc., were ruthlessly sacrificed, and stucco and whitewash reigned supreme. All this has since been altered.

It is asserted that, at an early alteration of one church in the county, many tombstones and memorial slabs were recklessly dispersed. A Purbeck marble slab was laid before the entrance of a public house, the taproom being paved with gravestones. It is also said that a baker of a neighbouring town used some grave-slabs on the floor of his oven with the inscription upwards. Gruesome results appeared on the loaves. This church has since been restored in a reverent and conservative way, and is a pattern of what a restoration should be.

The Hanoverian spirit shows itself in many ways besides in an utter disregard for ecclesiastical architecture, as the inscriptions on bells and tombstones show. On the treble bell at Watford was to be found—

> "At proper times my voice ile raise,
> And sound to my subscribers praise."

The bell at Welwyn (which, in 1747, was substituted for the five ancient bells) was rather hard on the Wesleyan movement—

> "Prosperity to the Established Church of England,
> No encouragement to *entusiam*."

During this period bells were sold at Flaunden, Pelham Stocking, and Wigginton, to pay for repairs. Inscriptions on tombstones gave evidence in the same direction. The negligence of the day is further illustrated by the fate of the Registers of Broxbourne, of which it is alleged that those earlier than 1688 are missing, through the carelessness of an eighteenth-century Vicar, who committed them to the care of the parish clerk, a tailor, who is reported to have cut the earlier Register into slips for measures. Happily, all this is altered by the great care and attention which is now bestowed on such priceless records.

We might go on *ad nauseam*, but enough has been said to show the state of things which existed until the flood-tide of revival brought new life.

There is much to be said (as Abbey and Overton

remind us) on the other side, but unfortunately our dioceses did not largely illustrate advancing church life in those days of deadness and decay. It is hardly to be wondered at that so little is to be said for the progress of the Church generally. When we remember that the nation had been passing through a century of unrest and war, men's minds were turned from the progress of the Church to the safety of the State. Although "Church and State" was never more emphasized as a doctrine of national faith, the Church was little more than a sleeping-partner, so far as the real purpose of her mission was concerned.

It is only fair to admit, however, that a good deal of the sad discredit which attaches to the Church in the Hanoverian age is due to the following facts. The fabrics of the churches themselves were in a disgraceful condition when the period began. It was an age in which there was a lack of appreciation, and but little knowledge of ecclesiastical architecture. The fabrics in many cases were so ruinous and mutilated, that large sums would have been required to reinstate them, and this at a period when the nation was being heavily taxed for war. In spite of this, there are evidences of a desire among the better sort of the laity to do their best (according to the taste of the time) to remedy the scandal. Even our own counties are not wanting in examples of an effort, architecturally misguided as it was, to "restore the waste places."

The wealthier classes were largely concerned in rebuilding and repairing their mansions, which had shared in the general decay, attributable to a long period of national unrest and insecurity.

Churchmen of the day were more given to polemical strife than to practical work. At the same time, the days of the Georges are not wanting in evidences of an earnest spirit of piety and practical devotion. Some of the best sons of the Church, from the accession of Queen Anne onwards, greatly lamented the slackness of the times, and were striving their utmost to rouse men to a more vigorous and active spiritual life. We shall see the effect of this desire and effort as we trace the outline of the great Hanoverian revival, fostered by the *Society* life of John Wesley and his precursors in the movement.

CHAPTER XXVIII

HANOVERIAN REVIVAL—ESSEX AND HERT-FORDSHIRE

"The heart dies down—O mightiest, then,
Come ever true, come ever near,
And wake their slumbering love again,
Spirit of God's most holy fear."

KEBLE.

"We thank Thee, O Lord, for these and all Thy mercies; Bless the Church and King, and grant us truth and peace through Jesus Christ our Lord."—
JOHN WESLEY'S *"Grace."*[1]

A REVIEW of the history of the Church during the Hanoverian period would be incomplete without special reference to the Revival which centred round John Wesley, and others. The reasons for this will be obvious to thoughtful observers of the times, and to faithful recorders of facts.

In the opening days of George I., some signs of life were not wanting, but they were of a flickering character.

The Non-Jurors had not yet lost their fervour, nor, in spite of their schismatic tendencies, had they forfeited their claim to respect. The influence of

---

[1] Hampton's "Life of Wesley," vol. iii. p. 216.

Archbishop Sancroft, Bishop Ken[1] (born at Little Berkhampsted), Lloyd, and others, lived on, and bore its fruit in the lives of men like Brett, Nelson, and Law, who were the salt of the Church in their day. Nelson was amongst the earliest supporters of the Society for the Propagation of the Gospel, and the Society for Promoting Christian Knowledge, and scarcely any religious book had so great a sale during the Hanoverian period as his " Fasts and Festivals."

Nicholas Ferrar, of Little Gidding, in the adjoining diocese of Ely, and Jones, of Nayland, on the borders of Essex, both exercised a powerful influence for good. Both were great admirers of Law in his earlier days, before he developed his doctrines of mysticism. The life fostered by men like these was, it is true, confined to a comparatively small circle, composed chiefly of laymen. There was still left, however, some witness of the abiding strength of the Non-Jurors, both amongst clergy and laity. Essex seems to have been the more prominent of our two counties. Some sixty Essex men and women, together with six from Herts (including Romanists), were fined, on the accession of George I., to the extent of £10,610, for refusing to take oath. This, of course, meant strong religious conviction on the part of a few. Other marks of a growing shame at the state of spiritual indifference have been indicated in previous chapters, such as the increasing care about ordinations, bonds of

[1] For a time Rector of Little Easton, Essex.

resignation, catechisings, and the support of religious societies, etc. In spite of all this, a lamentable apathy was still prevalent when Wesley appeared on the scene.

Wesley's standpoint was that of a churchman. This is the reason of some reference to his work in the two counties. The character and position of the men who stood by him in the beginning of the movement, his repeated declarations, of his intentions and objects, abundantly testify to his desire to strengthen the position of the Church, however much we may question some of his methods, and regret his errors of judgment. His declaration in 1744, "at the first meeting of all our preachers in Conference," was, "I exhorted them to keep to the Church."[1] In 1746 he put his position more strongly—

"I dare not renounce Communion with the Church of England. As a minister, I teach her doctrines; I use her offices; I conform to her rubrics; I suffer reproach for my attachment to her."[2]

Again, on October 24th, 1786, he says—

"I met the Classes at Deptford, and was vehemently importuned to order the Sunday Service in our room at the same time with that of the Church. It is easy to see that this *would be a formal separation from the Church*. We fixed both our Morning and Evening service, *all over England*, at such times as not to interfere with the Church."[3]

[1] "Works of John Wesley, M.A.," vol. xiii. p. 239. 3rd edition, with last correction of the author. London, 1829.
[2] Ibid., vol. iii. p. 444. Same edition.
[3] Ibid., vol. iv. p. 353. Same edition.

These deliberate statements received additional emphasis on December 11th, 1791, a little over a year before he died : "I declare once more that I live and die a member of the Church of England ; and that *none who regard my judgment or advice will ever separate from it.*" [1] In the face of these facts, whatever we may think of the members of Conference, we claim Wesley, the great Hanoverian Revivalist, as a Churchman. To say that other Churchmen, prior to, or contemporary with him, had no credit for that Revival, would be unjust to their memory, and untrue in fact. Our devotion to-day is quickened as we read, for instance, the "Meditations" of Hervey, "The Serious Call" of Law, "The Fasts and Festivals" of Nelson. Our souls are lifted up as we sing the morning and evening hymns of Bishop Ken, himself a Hertfordshire man. John Byrom inspires us in his "Christians, awake ;" and other hymns and writings of the time are instinct with the spirit of life which had begun to stir the deadness of stagnation. The Wesleys caught the fervour of these good men, and the Church to-day thanks God that His Spirit, through the two brothers, "breathed on the slain," and that He moved the one to pour out his devotion in "Author of Life Divine," and the other in "Hark ! the herald Angels sing."

Let us give these great evangelists their place, but let it be the right one. Others before them

---

[1] "Works of John Wesley, M.A.," vol. xiii. p. 241. 3rd edition, with last correction of the author. London, 1829.

had begun to clear the rough ground and to till
the barren wilderness ; they stepped in to share the
work, and reaped a rich harvest of slumbering souls
awakened to new life.

Before tracing the course of the revival in the
area covered by our diocese to-day, it will be well
to point out a very common error as to the origin
of the *Society* system of Wesleyanism. Every one
admits the evangelizing genius and the spiritual
fervour of Whitefield and of the Wesleys. It must
not be supposed, however, that the *Society* movement had its origin at the meeting of the two
Wesleys, Whitefield, Hervey, and a few others, at
Oxford in 1726, for the purpose of forming " a little
society among themselves for mutual edification in
religious learning and holy living."

Similar *Societies* had already been founded, and
though lacking the leading of men of the peculiar
force and special power such as John Wesley had
gathered round him, they had already begun to
leaven the Church with their quiet work. Wesley's
revival resulted in a more directly evangelistic
application of the method which had already begun
gradually to fructify the wilderness of neglect. It
was, in fact, an expansion of an existing method,
and not a newly-created force.

For instance, as early as 1678 (possibly in
imitation of St. Vincent de Paul, who flourished
on the Continent about sixty years before), Dr.
Horneck, of the Chapel Royal, Savoy, and Lecturer

at St. Michael's, Cornhill, had constituted a society for weekly religious conference, prayer, and Bible reading. In the time of James II. similar societies had sprung up to encourage attendance at daily prayer, more frequent Communions, and for the establishment of works of mercy. Thirty-nine such *Societies*, more or less on the same model, were in existence in London alone, in the reign of William and Mary, and they had begun to spread gradually in the more populous centres throughout the country. The general object of these *Societies* was embraced in the most common definition : " A Society for the encouragement of Piety and Religion." The revival of daily prayer was very remarkable. It was intended to counteract the daily *Mass* which was celebrated in the Chapel Royal at the direction of James II. Pepys, Steele, and others make note of it in and around London. A contemporary writer observes—

" Prayers were set up in so many places and hours, that devout persons might have that comfort every hour of the day, and there were greater numbers and greater appearances of devotion at prayers and sacraments than had been observed in the memory of man."

As an instance a little later on, of the survival of the custom, we may mention that Young (the author of " Night Thoughts "), Rector of Welwyn (1730–65), like John Wesley, always religiously observed Wednesdays and Fridays by prayers in his parish church. Cowper's lines point to the general custom—

> " Yon ancient prude, whose withered features show
> She might be young some forty years ago,
> Who sails with lappet head and mincing airs
> Daily at clink of bell to morning prayers."

Services on Saints' days, and on Wednesdays and Fridays lingered on, long after the daily offices were gradually falling into disuse.

The efforts of men like those of whom we have spoken had not ceased, but there was a general decay of religious habits, and with it the consequent social corruption and laxity. The day of a great opportunity had dawned, and the Church, in the person of Wesley, seized it, though many of her rulers were either opposed or indifferent to the movement. It needed a spiritual earthquake to arouse the Church from her slumber. The forces of convulsion were slowly gathering. The writings and practice of the best men of the Non-juring school were among the chief factors of the up-heaval. The great religious revival owed more to Law's " Serious Call " than to any other book. John Wesley, in his early days, was much under the personal influence of the author, and consulted him on various matters. Law himself says, " I was at one time a kind of oracle with Mr. Wesley ; " and on one occasion wrote thus to him—

" My dear friend, you reverse matters from their proper order. You are to follow the Divine Light wherever it leads you, in all your conduct. It is God alone gives the blessing. I pray you calmly mind your own work, and go on with cheerfulness, and God, you may depend on it, will take care of His. Besides, Sir, I see you would fain convert the whole world; but you must wait God's own time. Nay, if after all, He is pleased to use you only as a hewer of wood and drawer of water, you should submit, yea, be thankful to Him that He has honoured you so far." [1]

Byrom, like John Wesley, was devoted to William Law. With warm heart and ready wit he wrote of him—

> " O how much better he from whom I draw,
> Though deep yet clear, his system—' Master Law,'
> *Master* I call him; not that I incline
> To put my faith on any one divine.
> But man or woman, whosoe'er he be
> That speaks true doctrine, is a Pope to me." [2]

Before the death of George II. the Revival had spread far and wide, and English churchmen looked on amazed and puzzled by the impassioned eloquence of Whitefield and the fervid enthusiasm of the Wesleys.

We will now briefly illustrate the attitude of two of the Bishops towards the movement, and refer to its course in the two counties. In spite of the sneers of the day at enthusiasm, and of Lavington's depreciation of its effects, it proved to be a marvellous shaking of the dry bones.

Very early in the movement, Gibson, Bishop

---

[1] "Life of William Law," by Canon Overton, p. 80. London, 1881.
[2] Epistle to a Gentleman of the Temple.

of London, met the Wesleys. Complaints had been made to him that they preached the doctrine of assurance and justification by faith only, and re-baptism of those who had received lay-baptism. At an interview with the Bishop in 1738, John Wesley put the following questions to him : "Did he think his reading in a religious society made it a conventicle?" and, "Are religious societies conventicles?" The Bishop gave a wary answer : "I think not, but I determine nothing." Moreover, he promised the brothers to receive no accusation but from two or three witnesses, and added, "you may have free access to me at all times."[1]

It is pleasant to find this desire on the part of the Hanoverian Bishop to grant at least a fair hearing. Bishop Gibson, however, seems to have mistrusted Wesley from the first, for when he was consulted, three years previously, as to the latter's appointment to succeed his father at Epworth, he spoke "some disadvantageous things" of him, referring to his misrepresented strictness of life.

The Bishop's real attitude could not long be concealed, and the storm broke. He published, on August 1st, 1739, "A Pastoral Letter," of great length, addressed to the people of his diocese, "by way of caution against lukewarmness on the one hand, and enthusiasm on the other." This settled the question of his opinion of the movement. It is alleged that, five years later, he again took up

[1] "Wesley's Works," vol. viii. p. 365.

his pen, anonymously, to make "Observations on the conduct and behaviour of a certain sect, usually designated by the name of Methodists." Much as he disapproved of what he regarded as Wesley's extravagance of doctrine and breach of ecclesiastical discipline, he could not be brought to inhibit him.

In 1747, in reply to the churchwardens of St. Bartholomew the Great, who complained that their Rector allowed Wesley to preach, he says, "What would you have me do? I have no right to hinder him. Mr. Wesley is a clergyman, regularly ordained, and under no ecclesiastical censure." The four succeeding Bishops of London apparently made no protest. When Wesley dined with Bishop Lowth at Lewisham, the latter refused to sit above his guest at table, remarking, "Mr. Wesley, may I be found at your feet in another world." Wesley, in his journal, says of this Bishop, that "his whole behaviour was worthy of a Christian Bishop." In 1758 Wesley visited Colchester, on his way to Norwich, and found a decrease in the Society which had been established there. Next year he visited it again, and says, "The word of God has free course, only no house will contain the congregation." He preached on one Sunday on St. John's Green. The number of the *Society* was then about a hundred and sixty, but Tyerman says that many of them "were either expelled or seceding Dissenters. . . . During the visit Wesley baptized seven of them, all adults, and two of

them by dipping." He visited the town again on
his return from Norwich, and yet a third time,
at the end of the year, to open the new chapel.

How far the movement affected the county
generally is not clear, but it did not fall under his
remarkable influence, to the same extent as many
other districts. Thus, in the return made to Conference in 1767, while prosperous circuits were
noted in Yorkshire, Cornwall, and Bristol, only
one was recorded as existing in the whole county
of Essex (at Colchester, numbering a hundred and
forty-five members). The cause dwindled much
during the next twenty-three years. In October,
1790, Wesley visited this circuit for the last time,
four months before his death, when he was eighty-
eight years of age; he says of his people there, "the
Society was lessened and cold enough, preaching
was discontinued, and the spirit of methodism
quite gone from the preachers and the people."
One who heard him, writes—

" He preached in the Great Round Meeting House.
He stood in a wide pulpit, and on each side of him stood a
minister, and the two held him up, having their hands
under his armpits. His feeble voice was barely audible;
but his reverend countenance, especially his long white
locks, formed a picture never to be forgotten. There was
a vast crowd of lovers and admirers. It was for the most
part a pantomime, but the performance went to the heart."

The attitude of the Bishops of Lincoln to this
movement must also be noted as affecting Hertfordshire. Bishop Reynolds and Bishop Thomas

do not seem to have troubled themselves much about the matter. Bishop Green, their successor, spoke his mind very freely in a pamphlet addressed to Whitefield, which was a bantering attack on his methods. It came strangely from the only Bishop who voted for the *Protestant Relief Bill*. He does not seem to have laid the leaders under inhibition, but merely to have regarded them as "playing the droll."

Amongst the clergy of Hertfordshire who opposed the Revivalists in their early career was the Rev. Charles Wheatley (Vicar of Pelham Furneaux, and author of "A Rational Illustration of the Book of Common Prayer"), who, as early as 1739, preached a sermon in St. Paul's against the "new enthusiasts."

There are several mentions in Wesley's journals of preaching tours through Hertfordshire, which he seems generally to have combined with Bedfordshire and Northants. He visited Barnet, and Hertford, amongst other places, but no circuit appears to have been formed in the county as late as 1767, when the first complete list of members was reported to conference. A beautifully sculptured figure of John Wesley has been placed in one of the niches of the new pulpit in the parish church of Chipping Barnet, as a reminder of his power as a preacher, and of his position as a churchman.

Tyerman says, " In this year (1767) one-seventh of the Methodist circuits in the United Kingdom,

and one-fourth of the members, were in Yorkshire." [1]
It is clear, therefore, that after the movement had
been in progress for more than a quarter of a
century, it had not as yet deeply affected the life
of the diocese of which we are speaking. Most
of the Wesleyan chapels in Hertfordshire have
been erected during the present century.

One effect of the movement, doubtless regretted
by Wesley himself, as a successor of the earlier
revivalists, was the almost entire substitution of
irregular prayer meetings for the canonical daily
services. So much had this become the case by
the end of the eighteenth century, that Thomas
Scott, a pronounced leader of the early Evangelicals,
spoke of the mischief wrought by prayer meetings
as "bad bills indorsed by good men." Even Charles
Simeon, an evangelical leader, who had instituted them in his parish, said of those attending,
"instead of retaining their original simplicity,
many of them were filled with a high conceit of
their own attainments, and with a contempt of
their authorized instructors."

Later on, Bishops Howley and Blomfield of
London raised their voices against the "anomalous
assemblies called prayer meetings," as tending to
weaken the sense and utility of public worship.
Richard Mant, the well-known vicar of Great
Coggeshall, declined to go to extemporaneous
prayer meetings for the same reason.

[1] Tyerman's "Life and Times of Wesley," vol. ii. p. 609.

If the noble work of Wesley has not, in many ways, developed in the directions which he himself intended, we must be content with saying that "an enemy came and sowed tares in the field." Let us not at the same time forget to pray that, in God's good time, those who call themselves Wesleyans, whose devotion and piety we acknowledge, but whose separation we deplore, may return to the fold of their founder, and so promote the nearer dawn of that day when our Lord's prayer for unity shall be fulfilled.

We must be content with a general reference to the Evangelical and Tractarian movements. Each contributed in its own direction to the revival of vital religion. Though our counties produced no great leaders in the movements, their influence was felt far and wide in revived piety and the restoration of reverent worship, and in a more thorough realization of the mission of the church. It is more or less directly due to the influence of the latter movement that we owe the measures which prompted the earlier steps, at least, which led to the restoration of the ruins of the Abbey Church, and finally to the foundation of the new see of St. Albans, of which we shall now proceed to give some account.

CHAPTER XXIX

THE FIRST BISHOP OF ST. ALBANS—UNITY

> *" Now shall the Sanctuary*
> *And the House of the Most High be newly built ;*
> *The ancient honours due unto the Church*
> *Buried within the ruined Monasteries,*
> *Shall lift their stately heads, and rise again*
> *To astonish the destroyers' wondering eyes.*
> *Zeal shall be decked in gold ; Religion,*
> *Not like a virgin robbed of all her pomp,*
> *But bravely shining in her gems of state,*
> *Like a fair Bride be offered to the Lord."*
> WEBSTER, " Fam. Hist.," ed. Dyce, 173.

> *" We hail renowned Alban*
> *With joy thy festal day,*
> *For thou to England's children*
> *Hast op'd a blessed day."*
> *" Legenda Monastica."*

LET me, at the risk of the charge of repetition, and for the sake of clearness, recapitulate the changes in diocesan rule, indicated in the preceding pages, before telling the tale of accomplished diocesan unity, and the progress of Church life in the two counties under one bishop.

The story of Essex is easily summarized. The days of the rule of the Roman Mellitus were brief, probably only about twelve years. Then followed the Celtic missionary rule for about thirteen years, which gave place to the settled rule under ninety-nine successive Bishops of London till 1846. In 1846 the county (with the exception of the Barking Deanery) was transferred to Rochester, under Bishop George Murray. He died February 16th, 1860, and was succeeded by Joseph Cotton Wigram. In 1867 the whole county, including the Barking Deanery, by the operation of the *London Diocese Act* of 1863, owned allegiance to Thomas Legh Claughton, who had been raised to the vacant see of Rochester.

The diocesan story of Hertfordshire is more complex. Like Essex, it fell under the direct influence of the Celtic missionary bishops for about twenty years (656–679), after which, for nearly two centuries (680–870) it was ruled by the Bishops of Leicester. For two centuries more (870–1073) the pastoral charge of the county was committed to the Bishops of Dorchester. The county was next transferred, with the exception of some thirty parishes in the Deanery of Braughing (which from the days of Cedd had been under London), to the Diocese of Lincoln, the jurisdiction of St. Albans Abbey being as yet exempt from diocesan control. This arrangement remained intact for nearly five hundred years, when, on the translation of Bishop Holbech from Rochester to Lincoln, the allegiance of twenty-two parishes under the authority of the Abbey was transferred to London. These parishes, together with the Deanery[1] of Braughing, brought about half the county under common rule with Essex. The next change, three centuries later, brought the climax of complete union nearer, for in 1846 the whole of Hertfordshire was transferred to the Diocese of Rochester.

In 1877 the new see (phœnix-like) rose out of the ruins of St. Albans, and its Abbey became the Cathedral Church. Then (*Laus Deo*) the Diocese of St. Albans was an accomplished fact, testifying to the marvellous vitality of the Church. Thus the wooing of 1550 resulted in the engagement of 1846, and the marriage of rich Hertfordshire and poor Essex was celebrated in 1877. It seemed, however, as if a divorce were impending, for twelve years of happy wedlock had scarcely passed when a Committee of the House of Laymen recommended the following scheme of diocesan re-distribution, viz.— Norwich for the county of Norfolk, Bury St. Edmunds for Suffolk, Chelmsford for Essex, St. Albans for Hertfordshire and Bedfordshire, and Ely for Cambridgeshire.

The children of the Rochester union took up the cry, and in a family gathering of the Diocesan Committee of Conference, 1889, not without some misgivings, resolved that any arrangement with regard to the counties of Essex, Hertford, and Bedford, be conditional upon the Barking Deanery (which until 1867 formed an integral portion of

---

[1] Browne Willis so speaks of it.

the Diocese of London) being dealt with in a scheme affecting London as a whole. Provided this arrangement could be effected, the Conference was of opinion that the county of Essex should be constituted a separate diocese, and that Bedfordshire united to Hertfordshire should form the Diocese of St. Albans.

There is much to be said for the proposal. Why should not " Cinderella " have a coach of her own ? and where is the kind, rich fairy who will provide it ? This is a playful digression, and we must proceed to deal with facts, not with fancies, possibilities, and hopes.

We come now to the more immediate steps which resulted in the climax of 1877.

To put the matter briefly, funds had to be raised, and powers to be acquired, before application could be made for the consummation of a long dreamed-of unity which should centre round the shrine of St. Alban.

An appeal was issued for the furtherance of the scheme, which resulted in the transfer to the Ecclesiastical Commissioners of £11,500 Railway Stock, in which the subscriptions of the public had been invested. The endowment was further augmented by the investment of £42,400, the net proceeds of the sale of Winchester House in St. James's Square. The transfers from the see of Rochester of an annual sum of £500, and of a [like annual sum of £500 from the see of Winchester, were further additions. A sum of £3815 14s. 4d., part of the proceeds of the sale of Danbury Palace, has since been partially appropriated towards the provision of a site for a future house of residence for the see.

The ultimate result of the years of prayer, work, and self-sacrifice, was the foundation of the see of St. Albans, by order in Council at the Court of Windsor, April 30th, 1877, in pursuance of 38 and 39 Victoria, c. 34, which became effective on May 4th, 1877. Another Order of July 11th, 1877, set forth a scheme prepared by the Ecclesiastical Commissioners with respect to the bishopric. The order is too long to quote here, but as it is a document of great interest and importance to the diocese, a copy of it is set forth in an appendix.

The Right Reverend Thomas Legh Claughton, formerly of Trinity College, Oxford, Vicar of Kidderminster, and Canon of Worcester, was translated to the new see from the bishopric of Rochester.

He was solemnly enthroned on June 12th, 1877, by the Lord Archbishop of Canterbury, who preached on the occasion from Ezekiel xxxvii. 3, " Can these bones live ? " A vast congregation assembled to share in the celebration of this great event, and there were no less than 270 clergy in the procession. Amongst the notabilities present were the Earls of Dudley, Essex, Selborne, Lords Verulam, Brownlow, Grimthorpe.

A year after Bishop Claughton had been appointed to the new see, he delivered his primary charge. After much difficulty, a copy has been obtained. Lest, in the necessarily fleeting form of its publication, it should be lost, a considerable portion of it is now reproduced. The reasons for this are obvious, for, apart from its general interest, it has an historic as well as a diocesan character. A hundred years hence, if this book survives, some searcher in diocesan lore may find it a helpful illustration of the diocesan life of the period. It refers also to tasks as yet undone, and to possibilities and developments yet to be accomplished, but which are now engaging serious attention throughout the diocese.

Those portions of it pertinent to the erection of the see are here quoted, together with a few statistics, the rest being of general, rather than of diocesan interest.

The Bishop said—

"I did not think when I held my last Visitation that within five years we should be assembled together in this Abbey Church of St. Albans, as the Cathedral of a new diocese, called by its name ; that the earnest desire of good men, of whom we may say in the Psalmist's words, 'It pitied them to see her in the dust,' would be so soon accomplished, and that these two conterminous counties, Herts and Essex, would be united under ecclesiastical rule and administration. We are so swayed in England by the territorial divisions to which we have been long accustomed, that it is difficult to get men to embrace the idea of a new conjunction. These two counties have now been in the same diocese for more than thirty years. For that space of time one man has been their Bishop, and I am inclined to hope that the title he now bears, linked as it is with the most venerated traditions of the Church and our country, will help somewhat towards that unity of feeling which is the strength of the episcopate as a system ; that neither of these two counties will say they can do without the other, but will unite heartily for all Church purposes, for Church extension in its largest sense, to promote every one of those objects for which we have express sanction and authority in Holy Scripture-Divine worship and service, the training up of children in the Faith, holy discipline, the pastoral charge, and superintendence. Under these heads I think the whole work of the Church may be classed ; and I see no reason why in two conterminous counties, united together for the promotion of this work under one head, and bearing the name of England's Proto-martyr, we may not make a cheerful, hopeful united effort to set forth to the utmost of our strength and ability the glory of the Redeemer.

"I trust that round this Cathedral of St. Albans, the seat of the Bishop, all to whom the work of the Church is precious, and who know the necessity of its due organiza-tion, will gather willingly to do all that in them lies to make it a praise and an excellency, the joy of faithful hearts through the generations. That there is much to be done is undeniable. The condition of the building itself is such that grudging, envious eyes would regard its re-newal as a hopeless task. But surely what has been done is an earnest of what may be done. The beautiful Lady Chapel was a school ten years back. The process of ruin and decay had gone on for three centuries ; earth lay piled against its walls, many feet thick. No man that entered it could have felt the slightest hope that it could ever be restored. Its beauty was a thing of the past. Look at it now; can any man look at it with any other feeling than that of thankfulness and hope? Between this and the eastern end of the church a public footway ran, a token that at one time all hope of the restoration of the Abbey Church had faded out of the very imagination of the people. That, with consent of the citizens of St. Albans, has now been carried round instead of through the sacred building. One day an alarm was given, only too well founded, that the great tower was in danger of falling. Nothing but the promptness of those on the spot could have saved it from ruin. But saved it has been—is it too much to say by God's mercy?—for its fall would have entailed the loss of all we are now rejoicing in. If the establishment of the see of St. Albans be a benefit and a blessing, as we all hope it may be, the fall of that tower, which was imminent, would have rendered it almost impossible. When all this had been done, and the work of centuries had been preserved by vigorous effort and great liberality, the ruinous condition of the nave, at its western end, called for no less prompt and vigorous effort than the threatened fall of the tower. That, too, has been accomplished. I mean its safety has been secured ; and in the course of the operations it was discovered that what remained of the three western porches, the great ornament of the western end of the Cathedral, was a sufficient guide to their perfect restoration, if ever the means should be forthcoming. I think I am justified in saying that the great things that have been done, are an earnest of yet greater things which must be done before this ancient Abbey church ever fulfil her destiny. She is now the mother church of this diocese. Everything that is done within these walls should be done in the best way. Nothing that tends to make God's worship and service solemn, holy and beautiful, should be wanting here. Whatever can best set forth God's glory to the eye and ear, as well as to the souls of men, within them, was sought, you may depend on it, and formed part of the purpose and design of the builders of this church. These were their thoughts : ' How shall we ourselves best realize, how shall we best help them who worship with us to realize, the glories of heaven, the employments of the blessed, but by building houses for worship exceeding magnifical' (that was the expression of David's sanctified experience. 'The house that is to be builded for the Lord must be exceeding magnifical'), 'by furnishing them with such means of extolling His Name and His praise, as he Himself prescribed under the former dispensation?' 'He set singers also before the altar, that by their voices they might make sweet melody and sing daily praises in their songs.' These thoughts were in the hearts of the founders of these churches, and we who have entered into their labours and enjoy the benefit of their precious work, should surely endeavour to realize, as far as we can, the ends they had in view, and give effect to their designs.

"The Cathedral of the diocese of St. Albans has no endowment as such. Even when it shall have been restored as perfectly as I hope some here shall see it, it must depend for its needful reparation on voluntary offerings, unless before that need arises some of those to whom God has given wealth and power shall have been moved to provide for the Lord's house, as their own forefathers provided for it, and were blessed in their deed.

"But meanwhile we must remember His will of whom the wise man spake, 'He beautified their feasts and set in order the solemn times until the end, that they might praise His Holy Name, and that the Temple might sound from morning.' Though these walls are bare of ornament, albeit grand in their plainness—though the furniture of the house be of the meanest, albeit God meets His praying people here—there is no reason why, with such means as we can command, we should not try to set forth the praises of God here with the best members that we have.

"And I deem a suggestion that has been made to me reasonable and wise, that though we cannot do all that is in our hearts to do—though we cannot in our generation altogether build up the waste places of many generations—though we cannot all at once establish a new see, restore and furnish a church larger than most of our

Cathedral churches, and likewise provide such endowments as hitherto have been judged necessary—yet we may, by giving annually for a few years as we can afford, raise a sufficient sum to ensure what is called Cathedral service in this Cathedral, more or less effectually, as we give more or less.

"Let us consider what might be done to promote divine worship in this Cathedral. In the city itself, and in the immediate neighbourhood, men can be found who take pleasure in choral service, who have cultivated a taste for sacred music, who, though they earn their livelihood by trade or labour, could, if they were remunerated for their time, attend in their courses as the Levites did, to take part in the service of song. Of course, there are difficulties, especially as concerning practice and instruction, to be overcome ; but I know not how without great difficulty any work like this can be carried on. If we yield to difficulties, we had best fold our hands and give up God's cause.

"There are many who will hear that I proposed that every parish should contribute to the Cathedral, and who will ask almost flippantly, 'What is St. Albans Cathedral to me?' It is for the hope of what it may be to the county in which it is situate, and to the adjoining county ; it is because we trust it may be, by the beauty and order of its ministrations, a pattern in some sort to the diocese ; it is because we thankfully remember what it has been of old, when it was said of the church of St. Albans under Paul the fourteenth Abbot, exactly 800 years ago, 'Et facta est Ecclesia S. Albani quasi schola religionis et disciplinaris observantiœ per totam Angliam ;' and hope that like ex- cellent things may be said of her again.

"It would greatly help towards this end if, until other provision be made, a house in the city of St. Albans were either bought or even hired, simply furnished as prebendal houses in our Cathedral precincts commonly are, and pro- vided with service and maintenance in which always or generally one of our honorary canons, by agreement

among themselves, might reside in turn for a fortnight, or
three weeks, or a month, and during that residence assist the
Rector in so far as the Cathedral service is concerned ;
take especial charge, if he were so willing, of the choir ;
preach in their residence by agreement with him, help
him, if he desired it, in certain of his parochial ministrations. (I see nothing impossible in this arrangement ;
nothing which, if those who undertook it said in their
hearts, as one of old did, in whatever he took in hand,
'Ad majorem Dei gloriam,' might not be blessed and
greatly prospered.) The Act of 1840, which was passed
when there was a jealousy of Cathedral endowments, on
account of prevailing abuses, simply deprived the Cathedrals
of a portion of their revenue, without either providing for
their reform, as they then existed, or so much as con-
templating the possibility of future foundations. Of
what inestimable value would those suppressed canonries
have been to Truro or St. Albans, to Liverpool or Newcastle.

"There is enough of the nobility of heart in the
members of the Church of England to found, if conviction
and sentiment unite that way, at least the beginnings of a
Chapter for St. Albans. I need not say that if I was
permitted to see even one canonry founded I should
greatly rejoice. But my ambition for the see of St.
Albans goes beyond the foundation of a single canonry.
It is surely of vast importance that these new dioceses,
though they be less richly endowed in the first instance
than the older sees, should not lack the help which the
capitular system affords to the diocesan. I have no means
of securing the assistance, otherwise than voluntary, of any
man skilled in theology, for the education of students ; in
music, for the conduct of divine service in the Cathedral.
Miserably endowed as this Abbey Church is for the
purposes unto which it was saved out of the wreck of
the monastery, viz., to be one of the parish churches for
the town, it is far worse endowed as the mother church of

a diocese not being furnished with one instrument or auxiliary of any kind.

"The conditions under which the Cathedral may be the centre of the spiritual life of a diocese, are exactly the same as those under which the church and the parsonage are, or ought to be, the centre of the spiritual life of the parish.

"The history of this ancient Abbey furnishes an abundant illustration of what I now say, in the character of its most illustrious Abbots. Of William de Trumpington, who died in the year 1235, it is related that he never returned from a journey but he gave largely to the poor ; never missed a service, and always took part in the service, standing in his place in the choir, both on festival and ordinary days ; preached in the order of his course, studied much, inquired diligently into every cause, was honoured alike by the mighty and by the lowly. Of John de Cella, his predecessor, we read that having been, soon after his election to the abbacy, harsh and imperious, his character afterwards softened : he became as another man, and before the end he ordered himself to be carried into the choir, stripped of his robes and upper garments, when now in extreme old age, and then expressed his willingness to make reparation to any whom he had injured or offended, almost in old Samuel's words. Such were the men who, with others like-minded, though of less note, made the Abbey of St. Albans what it was before the days of the decadence. We have traces even in their time of the existence of the worldly element, which probably afterwards gained strength ; though I would never believe, except on far less questionable evidence than that on which the last Abbot and his monks were condemned, that, though some were corrupted, the whole body had so fallen from the glory of their prime. I cite those instances to show that this Abbey Church might yet be as a Cathedral Church, if such men as those I have described held place in it, with what I may call the halo of a double glory around it ; that it is a parish church also, and that with the blessing of God, it may be a centre of light to both diocese and parish. With these hopes for its usefulness and greatness, you cannot wonder that I should be especially anxious that the building itself should be both restored and set in order. And with a view to this being effected speedily, I think we should not be continually devolving the burden of its restoration on others, but each try what we can do ourselves. Some are always saying, 'It is a national, an historical monument; it should be restored at the cost of the nation.' Others say, 'It is a Hertfordshire Church; let the county of Herts do it.'

"What is needed is, that the whole diocese should count it their duty to see that their Cathedral is restored: till this is done, and done worthily, men will take up their parable against us.

"These are the chief and most prominent wants of the diocese of St. Albans: the restoration of its Cathedral: the sustentation at once of its holy services: such endowment, in the course of time, as shall place it on a level with other Cathedrals. . . ."

The Bishop then passed on to consider diocesan statistics—

"I see from the answers to my Visitation questions, that the Lord's Supper is administered weekly in more than one hundred parishes; twice in the month in about eighty; once a month in nearly four hundred; less than once a month in not more than twenty. The frequency of celebration increases at each visitation; there is service on Ascension Day in five hundred and sixty churches, as many in the diminished diocese as there were over the whole area, including Kent, in 1873. . . .

"I find that in by far the largest number of churches the custom of catechising in the church has entirely gone out of use; that in many churches where it is used, it is only at certain seasons of the year; and the most general reason given for its disuse, is that the children are now carefully taught in the day school. This, of course, does not apply to many parishes where there are Board schools.

" These affect eighty-five parishes in Essex, in Hertford-shire only sixteen. The returns from between three and four hundred parishes in Essex show that where more than thirty thousand children in the day school were examined by the Diocesan Inspector in religious knowledge, there were twenty-five thousand Sunday scholars, and upwards of two thousand Sunday school teachers. Catechising in Church has fallen into disuse, but I trust teaching in Sunday schools is not neglected. There is every reason why we should strive with all our might to sustain it. Already, in the experience of us all, the observance of the Lord's Day has become so lax and irregular, as to excite the serious apprehension of all religious people.

" The words of the Abbot, John de Cella, when he was addressing the community over which he had presided for many years, almost for the last time, may best express the feelings with which I have entered upon the third visitation (the first of St. Albans) of my diocese : 'Vobis per aliquod interfui præfui ; et minus quam decuit profui.' " [1]

[1] Primary charge of Thomas Legh Claughton, First Bishop of St. Albans.

CHAPTER XXX

THE FIRST BISHOP OF ST. ALBANS—TOIL AND REST

" With reverent feet the earth he trod,
Nor banished nature from his plan,
But studied still with deep research,
To build the Universal Church,
Lofty as is the love of God,
And ample as the wants of man."
> LONGFELLOW.

ONE of the first works of Bishop Claughton was the establishment of " The Bishop of St. Albans Fund," so energetically fostered by his successor, for the purpose of aiding, practically of providing for, the spiritual needs of " London over the border," [1] or the district of the south-west corner of Essex, lying between the Thames and the Lea. This district, in 1801, had a population of 20,441, with a clergyman to every 1572 ; on the accession of the late Queen it still consisted, more or less, of separate villages and small towns, with a total population of not more than 40,000. In

---

[1] The name given to it by Charles Dickens in *Household Words*, September 12th, 1857.

course of time the Victoria Dock was begun (1855). Then followed the opening of the Thames iron-works, and the indiarubber works at Silvertown, which resulted in a great increase in the population. To meet the spiritual needs of the ever-growing multitude, the "Plaistow and Victoria Dock Mission" was founded, with Sir Antonio Brady as its leading spirit. In 1863 the "Bishop of London's Fund" was instituted with a special view of aiding, among others, this district, which was then still within the diocese of London. By the operation of the "London Diocese Act," on the death of Bishop Wigram of Rochester, 1867, the whole district, including the Deanery of Barking in Essex, and the Deaneries of Greenwich and Woolwich in Kent, were, as we have seen, transferred to the see of Rochester, to which Thomas Legh Claughton had been appointed as bishop. The population by this time had grown to 100,000. "The Bishop of Rochester's Fund," most liberally aided by the Marquis of Salisbury, successfully met the growing needs of the district for the next ten years, till 1877, during which period the number of inhabitants had reached 200,000. Bishop Claughton being translated to the newly erected see of St. Albans as its first Bishop in 1877, had still to face this seething mass of humanity with the mission of the Church. How, under the altered diocesan conditions, was it to be done?

A meeting was summoned for March 14th,

1878, at 28, Great George Street, Westminster, under the presidency of Bishop Claughton, and the " Bishop of St. Albans Fund " was founded, with rules and bye-laws formed on the main lines of the two funds of which we have already spoken.

The need was urgent, but its urgency soon became intensified by the formation of the Albert Docks (1880), the creation of the Beckton Gasworks (the largest in the world), and the inclusion of the Tilbury Docks, the population increasing by leaps and bounds. On the resignation of Bishop Claughton in 1899, the population had grown to 380,000, with fifty-six clergy and thirty-five lay-workers, as living agents of the Fund.

Another of the early acts of Bishop Claughton was the revival of the office of the Suffragan Bishop of Colchester,[1] to which, in 1882, the Venerable Alfred Blomfield, Archdeacon of Essex, was appointed. Bishop Blomfield was consecrated at St. Albans Cathedral on the Feast of the Nativity of St. John Baptist.

The help thus given to the over-worked Diocesan greatly strengthened his hands. With the united energies of the Bishop and his Suffragan, assisted by the zeal of an attached body of clergy and laymen, the work went on steadily.

At the same time the great movement for the

---

[1] For an account of the former Bishops of Colchester, *vide* Appendices.

thorough restoration of the Abbey (now the Cathedral Church) was in progress.

It would be out of place here to trace the history of the many previous attempts at restoration from the year 1612 onwards. It will be sufficient for our purpose to record that on March 27th, 1877, a faculty was granted to an Executive Committee of Restoration, consisting of the Earl of Verulam; Sir Edmund Beckett; the Venerable Anthony Grant, Archdeacon of Rochester and St. Albans; the Reverend Walter John Lawrance, Rector of St. Albans; the Rev. Owen Davys, Rector of Wheathamstead; Henry J. Toulmin, John Evans, Robert Pryor, Esquires; Dr. Lipscomb, Benjamin Agutter, and Thomas Kent, the three Churchwardens of the Abbey Church, and to future Rectors and Churchwardens. This faculty authorized them, as an Executive Committee, "to restore, repair, and refit the said Abbey Church as a Cathedral or Collegiate, and Parish Church, subject to such rules and conditions as had been or might thereafter be framed." A further faculty was granted to Lord Grimthorpe to continue the work of restoration. The story of the Abbey itself would fill a large volume, and we must be content with saying that the result of the long series of restorations has been to save the venerable pile from falling into hopeless ruin, and however deeply the disappearance of some of its ancient features must be regretted, it stands to-day firm for ages to come, a witness to the devotion of the sons and daughters of our Church in past and present days, a monument to the generosity, largely of one man, in the present generation, and, above all, the pride and glory of our diocese as its Cathedral Church.

Thus while other good works were proceeding in the diocese, the vision of the restored Abbey, so vividly depicted in the first visitation charge of the Bishop, became a living reality, and gave new impetus to diocesan life.

The opening service, at which the long series of restorations and gifts were dedicated to God, was held on October 21st, 1885. The *Guardian* gives the account which has been summarized above, and adds, together with a *verbatim* report of the sermon of the Archbishop of York—

"On Wednesday the nave was re-opened with a very stately service. The procession included the Mayor and Corporation in their gowns, a vast array of clergy in their surplices, the Bishop of Nova Scotia, the Archbishop of York, and the Bishop of St. Albans, who was preceded by his chaplain, bearing his pastoral staff. Mr. Chapple, to whom so much of the success of the restoration is owing, was present in the two-fold capacity of Alderman and Churchwarden. The vast throng also included the Earl of Verulam (Lord Lieutenant) and Lady Jane Grimston, the Earl and Countess of Essex, the Danish Minister and Madame de Falbe, the Countess Dowager of Caledon, Lady Jane Alexander, Lord Denman, Lord Crewe, Lady Paston-Cooper, Mr. Coope, M.P., Mr. and Mrs. R. Pryor, Mrs. Holland Hibbert, Mr. R. Smith (Goldings), Mr. Archer Houblon (Essex), Mr. W. Winckley, F. S. A., etc. Probably two thousand persons were present. Matins was intoned by the Rev. T. G. Gibbons ; the first lesson (Isa. lx.) was read by Sir Edmund Beckett, and the second (Rev. xxi. v. 10 to end) by Archdeacon Lawrance, Rector of St. Albans. The *Te Deum* was Smart in F ; the *Jubilate*, Bennett in G ; and the anthem was ' In that day' (Elvey). The Litany was said by the Bishop of the diocese ; and at its close the Archbishop of York preached from Psa. lxxviii. 4 ; ' Showing to the generations to come the praises of the Lord, and His strength, and the wonderful works that He hath done.' " [1]

As some further indication of the activity of the Church during Bishop Claughton's thirteen years' episcopate of the newly-founded see, it should be mentioned that sixteen new ecclesiastical districts were formed, fourteen in Essex, and two in Herts, and thirty-seven new churches and chapels were consecrated. He also introduced the order of Lay Readers, and set apart ten for the work. In the last eleven years of his rule, there were 76,994 persons confirmed. The number of clergy also largely increased.

After twelve years of continuous labour and over-sight, the great age and failing health of the Bishop had begun to prepare the mind of the diocese for the announcement which he made at the Diocesan Conference on October 23rd, 1889, at Colchester, that he could no longer remain at the helm.

" I am convinced," he said, " that it has become my duty to you, and myself, to retire from my office ; " and with a voice trembling with emotion he

---

[1] *Guardian*, October 25th, 1885.

thanked the diocese "for all the kind support which never failed him, and for the joy and comfort, friendship and affection, which cannot end with this life." Later on, during the Conference, an address was presented to the venerable father in God, expressive of the sorrow and sympathy with which the announcement of his retirement had been received, and of the assurance of deep and lasting affection, of gratitude for the love which had marked his whole life in the diocese, and adding a prayer that he might spend in peace and comfort the remaining years of his life.

Thus, most appropriately, the official career of the first Bishop of St. Albans closed.

His increasing weakness resulted in a paralytic seizure at Danbury Palace, and he passed away at 11 a.m. on July 25th, the Feast of St. James, 1892. His body lay in state in the Palace Chapel at Danbury, where clergy and others kept watch over it night and day till Friday morning the 29th, when there was a final celebration of the Holy Eucharist. It was then removed for interment at the Cathedral Church of his diocese, where it arrived at 3.30. After a solemn service, attended by the chief dignitaries of the diocese and 140 clergy in surplices, and many others unrobed, and a crowd of leading laymen and representatives of guilds, congregations, and civic bodies, the second Bishop of St. Albans laid its first Bishop to rest in an earthen grave on the north side of the Abbey

Churchyard, and, with pastoral staff in hand, gave the Church's benediction of peace.

On his coffin was a raised brass Latin cross and Calvary, extending nearly its full length, with an inscription at the foot—

"THOMAS LEGH CLAUGHTON,
Bishop,
Born 6th November, 1808,
Died 25th July, 1892."

"While the obsequies" (writes one who was present) "were as unostentatious as possible, in accordance with the Bishop's wish, they were deeply impressive and touching, and the crowded scene in the Abbey and around the grave, lit up and shadowed, too, by the glorious summer sun, will not easily be forgotten." [1]

A memorial has been erected in the north transept of the Cathedral, consisting of a cenotaph, on which rests the effigy of the good Bishop. The following is the inscription :—

"Thomas . Legh . Claughton . S.T.P. Primus . Albanensis . Episcopus . Roffensis . prius.
"Natus . VI° . DIE . Novembris . A.S. MDCCCVIII : obdormivit . in . Xto . XXV° . DIE . IVLII . A.S. MDCCCXCII. R.I.P."

The life and work of the first Bishop cannot be summed up better than in the eloquent tribute of Bishop Festing, spoken on the occasion of the unveiling of the monument, based on the words—

"'*Remember them that have the rule over you which spake unto you the word of God, and considering the issue of*

[1] *Guardian*, August 3rd, 1892.

their life, imitate their faith.' 'That,' his lordship observed, 'was an injunction which they had assembled to observe that day. In the monument before them, which would stand for ages in that great Church, there would be a record for future generations of the remembrance which they in their time had of one who, by God's providence, had ruled over them so wisely, so tenderly, so faithfully, and so well. The late Bishop Claughton would no doubt have been very unwilling to have allowed mere personal thoughts of him to be in their minds on such an occasion as that. That unselfishness, that quiet holiness which was his, would have shrunk from anything like laudation in the House of God. But while it was impossible to think of him without strong personal feelings, they might on that occasion turn their particular attention to one or two points of a public character connected with him. He who was taken from them was a striking example of certain great things which had come to pass within the last few years in the history of the Church and country. Claughton of Kidderminster was a name very familiar indeed throughout the whole Church. He was one of those men who by their wisdom, by their energy, by their devotion, and by their piety, had enabled the Church to grapple with the great difficulties of the day. He was a true example of the parish priest of his time, and he was also an instance of the extension of the Church's life in various directions. As a Bishop of Rochester he spoke to them of the long continuity of the English Church.

"'As the first Bishop of St. Albans he spoke to them of the Church extending her work as the demands upon her increased, and so historically, it was right, it was a necessity, that there should be a memorial to him who was the first Bishop of the see, in that the Cathedral Church of the see.

"'There were other thoughts associated with him as a Bishop. All who were acquainted with him knew how he realized in himself that tender title "A Father in God." Those who had anything to do with him, whether they were his clergy or whether they went to him as candidates for confirmation and heard his addresses, knew how he spoke and dealt with them with the full love of a tender heart, and as one really devoted to God and his people. His memory was with them, and it was for them to thank God earnestly and heartily for what He gave to them in him, and to endeavour to show that same devotion, that same zeal for God which Bishop Claughton showed, so that when the time of their work was over it might be said of them, as it was said of him, " He giveth His beloved sleep." ' "

The inscription on the stone which marks the site of the good Bishop's burial place in the Cathedral grave-yard runs thus—

"Sacred to the memory of Thomas Legh Claughton, D.D., born Nov. 6th, 1808. Entered into rest July 25th, 1892. Vicar of Kidderminster 1841 to 1867 ; 97th Bishop of Rochester 1867 to 1877 ; 1st Bishop of St. Albans 1877 to 1890. R.I.P.

" I sleep but my heart waketh."

CHAPTER XXXI

THE SECOND BISHOP OF ST. ALBANS

" Sun never sets but 'tis to rise again."
Inscription in King's Langley Church, Herts.

ON the resignation of Bishop Claughton, the Hand of God singled out another parish priest to rule over the diocese, in the person of Bishop Festing, formerly Prebendary of St. Paul's, and Vicar of Christchurch, Albany Street, London. We may confidently and respectfully say that the diocese has been fortunate in having Bishops eminent in the parochial pastorate of the Church as its first two rulers.

The second Bishop was consecrated in St. Paul's Cathedral on the Feast of the Nativity of St. John Baptist, June 24th, 1890. His consecrators were the Archbishop of Canterbury, the Bishops of London, Carlisle, Lichfield, Llandaff, St. David's, Madras, Colchester, Bedford, Marlborough, and the Bishops Campbell, Barry, and Marsden.

The enthronement took place on October 7th

in the same year, in his Cathedral Church. An event of such significance to the diocese is worthy of record. The following is an account of the proceedings—

" The ceremony was witnessed by about four hundred clergymen, and as many of the laity as could be accommodated in the spacious Abbey Church of St. Albans. Flags and banners were displayed in various parts of the city, and peals were rung on the Cathedral bells, and also on the bells of St. Peter's church. It rained steadily all day, to the great discomfort of visitors. At one o'clock there was a luncheon at the rooms of the County Club, lent for the occasion. Invitations had been issued to the clergy, beneficed and unbeneficed, of the diocese; the guests including several ladies. . . . The procession included the Mayors of Luton, Dunstable, Maldon, Harwich, Colchester, Chelmsford, and St. Albans, and the Deputy-Mayor of Hertford, accompanied by the Corporation officials, the choir, a large number of the clergy of the diocese, the Archdeacons, and Archdeacon Eden (Canterbury), the officials of the diocese, Lord Grimthorpe, and the Bishop, who was preceded by the bearer of his pastoral staff, which has been handed over to him in trust for the diocese by Bishop Claughton.

" Evensong was proceeded with to the end of the First Lesson (the special psalms being cxxii., cxxxii., and cxxxiv.). Then followed the ceremony of enthronization.

" The new Bishop, addressing the Archdeacon of Canterbury, requested to be inducted into the Bishopric, and the Archdeacon expressed the great willingness of the Cathedral body to accede to this request. The Bishop then took the oath of fidelity to the Cathedral Church of St. Albans, promising to defend its rights, liberties, and dignities; the Chancellor of the diocese, Mr. Jeune, Q.C., attending the Bishop during this part of the ceremony.

The Bishop was then conducted to the episcopal throne, and Archdeacon Eden addressed to him the words of formal installation. Then the Bishop recited the Lord's Prayer to the words 'deliver us from evil,' the congregation taking up the closing doxology. This custom, not being very common in English churches, was a new experience to many of those present. The Bishop then 'passed his hand' to several dignitaries of the diocese who presented themselves at the throne for the purpose of this paternal greeting, the choir meanwhile singing Psalm cxxxiii. Archdeacon Eden read the collect, 'Prevent us O Lord,' after which Evensong was continued. The *Magnificat* and *Nunc Dimittis* were sung to Stainer in B flat, and the anthem was Beethoven's 'Hallelujah.' The First Lesson (Isaiah lxii.) was read by Archdeacon Johnson, the second (Eph. iii.) by the Bishop of Colchester. On entering the pulpit the Bishop read the 'Bidding Prayer.' Taking for his text, 1 Kings iii. 9, his lordship spoke of the promise Solomon had given of ruling in righteousness at the beginning, and how far he fell off later, from the standard of this earlier period. In thinking of the lives of individuals and the history of institutions like those recalled by that Abbey Church in which they were now assembled, they had to bear in mind both original purposes proposed and later failures from the standard set up. Certainly the monastic orders were not to be judged by the condition of some of their houses at the time of the Reformation. Having referred to the significance of the proceedings in which they had been taking part, the Bishop said he entered into the inheritance which his predecessor had won for the Bishop of this diocese by his loving labour. Both Bishop and clergy had still the help of his prayers. His predecessor was still leading them now as he had led them in the years that were past. In conclusion, he asked in all humility, that they would pray to God to give him in his new work a wise and understanding heart. During the offertory (for the Cathedral Trust Fund and the Bishop of St. Albans

Fund) the hymn, 'Glorious things of Thee are spoken,' was sung. After the presentation of the alms, the Bishop pronounced the *Benediction*, and the service was closed, having lasted two and a half hours." [1]

The most fitting way of bringing the story of the life of the diocese up to the present time will be to quote some of the salient points in the two charges which the Bishop has delivered. In the first charge (1892), after a touching reference to the first Bishop, he began by enunciating the principle which was to guide him, "it is in the faithful exercise of the pastoral office that the life of the Church really consists, and her true strength is exhibited and maintained." Like his predecessor, he enforced the need of a Cathedral Chapter, and the establishment of a daily choral service. After a statistical reference to the growth of the popula-tion, which is again noted in his second charge, he passed on to emphasize the claims of the " Bishop of St. Albans Fund " and the support of diocesan institutions generally, on which points he added some interesting facts. In 1891, " there was raised in the diocese itself (including about £10,000 for the Bishop of St. Albans Fund) for general maintenance of Church work about £140,000, for Church building and extensions about £79,000."

He next reverted to Missions, and again gave facts. " From the returns that have been made I find that out of the 624 parishes in the diocese in

[1] *Guardian*, October 8th, 1890.

1891,—422 contributed to Foreign Missions, 315 to Home Missions, 377 to Diocesan Institutions."

Confirmation statistics were next dealt with, and the increase was noted. He then went on to speak of the training and work of the Diaconate, strangers officiating, preacher's books, the duties of church-wardens, faculties, parish terriers, presentments, Church trusts, daily prayer, visiting, difficulties in work. He insisted with great earnestness on the necessity and duty of maintaining Church schools, and added these striking words—

"While it is very important that we should put our schools in good order, and that the general teaching and training in them should be as good as they possibly can be, the matter of chief importance with us is the maintenance of the religious teaching and training. *Without this a Church school is a fraud.* Its reason for existence is taken away. It has ceased to be the power in the religious life of the place which it should be, *and it is not too much to say that it makes for irreligion rather than religion.*"

The charge closed with an announcement of great importance, "We have now been able," he said, "to secure the services of a Diocesan Missioner, and have founded a Diocesan Mission Society."

Between the interval of the first and second Visitation a sad loss befell the diocese in the death of the first Suffragan Bishop of the new see, who had endeared himself to all who knew his work and worth. He entered into rest, at his residence at Brentwood, November 5th, 1894. One who had excellent opportunities of estimating his character described him thus—

"A ripe scholar and a courteous gentleman, a zealous churchman, a sagacious judge of men, a singularly open and straightforward character, who knew his own mind and was not afraid to express it, a warm-hearted friend, a kindly host, a cheery companion of genuine and ready wit, and withal of untiring industry and devotion to duty, Bishop Blomfield was a worthy son of Dr. C. J. Blomfield, Bishop of London. . . . He has done his life's work, and done it well, and he leaves behind him the memory of a true and genial friend, and a good servant of Christ and his Church, by whose departure this life is poorer." [1]

His body was laid to rest on November 9th in the little churchyard of Shenfield, near Brentwood, in the presence of a large concourse of genuine mourners, clerical and lay, from all parts of the diocese. In the Cathedral of St. Albans a fitting memorial has been erected, with the inscription—

" In loving memory of
ALFRED BLOMFIELD, D.D., Bishop of Colchester,
First Suffragan of St. Albans.
Born, August 31, 1833. Died November 5, 1894." [2]

The accuracy of the expression " first Suffragan of St. Albans " has been contested. The description is surely correct, for though he was not the first Bishop of Colchester historically, he was in reality the first Suffragan of the see of St. Albans.

The vacancy caused by his death was filled by

---

[1] T. L. P., *Guardian*, November, 1894.   [2] *Ibid.*

the promotion of the Venerable Henry Frank Johnson, Archdeacon of Colchester, and Rector of Chelmsford, formerly Curate of Richmond, Surrey, Vicar of High Wych, Hertfordshire. He was consecrated Bishop Suffragan in St. Paul's Cathedral on December 28th, 1894. It would be presumptuous on the part of the writer to do more than to echo the prayer, " Long may he live."

It may at this point be properly recorded that the dawn of the new century has gladly witnessed a further welcome addition to the episcopal force of the diocese by the elevation of Archdeacon Stevens to be a second Suffragan.[1] This event has the double significance of being the last episcopal arrangement sanctioned by our late beloved Queen, and the first appointment made by His Majesty King Edward VII. It is thus referred to in the *Guardian*—

" The new Bishop Suffragan was a Scholar and Exhibitioner of Magdalen College, Cambridge, and graduated in 1863. In the same year he took the post of assistant-master at the Charter-house School, and was ordained in 1865. His first curacies were at St. Mary's, Charter-house, and Woodford, Northamptonshire. In 1868 he went to St. Mark's, Victoria Docks, and spent four years there, two as curate and two as vicar. Work as curate of St. Botolph's, Bishopsgate, and at Holy Trinity, Brompton, followed, and in 1875 Mr. Stevens was again attracted to the Victoria Docks, this time filling the vicarage of St. Luke's. Here he remained seven years, proceeding thence to Saffron

---

[1] By Letters Patent under date Feb. 11th, 1901, in pursuance of Henry VIII. c. 14.

Walden, where he served as vicar for a like term. He was appointed an Honorary Canon of St. Albans in 1891, and three years later was appointed Archdeacon of Essex. In 1889 he became Vicar of St. John's, with Holy Trinity, Stratford, Essex, and he recently succeeded Canon Henson as incumbent of the Hospital Chapel of St. Mary, and St. Thomas of Canterbury, at Ilford. He is a Past Grand Chaplain of the Masonic body." [1]

His consecration, as Bishop Suffragan of Barking, in the Diocese of St. Albans, took place at St. Margaret's, Westminster, on Quinquagesima Sunday, February 17th, 1901.

Prior to the last-named appointment, a new dignity and advantage had fallen on the diocese in the constitution by Royal Prerogative,[2] of the Deanery of St. Albans, and the promotion of the Very Reverend Walter John Lawrance, Archdeacon of St. Albans, and Rector of the Abbey Church, to be the first Dean of the Cathedral Church. Thus another dream of those who desire to see the capitular organization shaping itself, has been happily fulfilled. The Dean was installed by the Bishop of the Diocese on July 18th, 1900, and active steps are being taken to provide an adequate endowment for the Deanery, and to promote the establishment of a capitular body.

After this necessary digression, we proceed with the story of other marks of progress during the present episcopate. Again, we cannot do better

---

[1] *Guardian*, February 6, 1901.
[2] Letters Patent bear date May 10th, 1900.

than record some of our Bishop's words. His statement of facts will be much better than any speculative generalities which the writer might present from his own imperfect observations.

Five years of ever-increasing work and responsibility had passed by since the Bishop made his first visitation. In 1897 he again reviewed the affairs of the diocese in his second charge, which, like the first, is full of information as to facts which make up the history of a diocese. After references to the celebration of the Queen's Jubilee, to the fifteen-hundredth anniversary of the coming of St. Augustine, and to the Roman attack on the English Ordinal, he gave some diocesan statistics, the following of which are most relevant to our purpose :—

"In 1878, the first year of the episcopate of my predecessor as Bishop of St. Albans, there were 5516 persons confirmed; last year there were 9671.

"At the present time the incumbents in this diocese are receiving £57,409 a year less, from tithes alone, than they did fourteen years ago, when tithes were at par. Out of the 610 benefices in the diocese, there were last year 250 with a net income below £200. There were 56 with a net income below £100, the average income of these 56 being £64 a year."

He then went on to say—

"I now place before you some statements, compiled from the returns which have been made, which I think of particular interest and value.[1] In 1891 (and I take this

---

[1] There are 630 benefices in this diocese.

year because it was the one the returns for which I quoted at my former visitation) there were 422 parishes which contributed to Foreign Missions ; last year there were 479. In 1891, 315 contributed to Home Missions ; last year 379. In 1891, 377 contributed to Diocesan Institutions ; last year 444.

"I am glad to notice an advance in some other points. The number of churches in which, in obedience to the order of the Church, there is daily prayer, has increased from 111 in 1891 to 177 last year. The churches open for private prayer have increased in number from 178 in 1891 to 262 last year. The number of churches opened during the day might well be increased.

"The number of celebrations of Holy Communion each month are as follows :—in 1891, early, 906 ; midday, 839 ; after midday, 44 ; in 1896, early, 1253 ; midday, 994 ; after midday, 59."

In the course of the charge he unfolded what is the great anxiety of his heart, and what must be, of necessity, the burden of any Bishop who has to cope with it, the care of the vast and rapidly increasing population in the Barking deaneries, which more than ever presses itself on the attention of the Church.

The subject is of such vital importance, that although reference has been made to the history of the foundation of the fund for meeting the spiritual needs of the seething multitudes in the district referred to, these needs are so urgent, and the supply of them so vital, that any chronicler of the history of the diocese would be lacking in his sense of responsibility if he did not make them clear. We cannot do this more forcibly than by quoting the words of the good and devoted secretary of the fund. In writing at the close of the century, he says of the population: " It has increased during the last three years at an annual rate of at least 43,000, and there is now only room in consecrated churches for one-eighteenth of the population." What this means will be better understood by a striking comparison which he made, when he added that this increase represented a population " equal to that of Oxford, with its eighteen churches; or that of Cambridge, with its sixteen churches; and half as much again as that of Colchester, with seventeen churches."

Churchmen, nay, Christian men and women everywhere, ought to know and take to heart what has been, and what is being done, unostentatiously, and yet with holy persistence, in carrying the cross of Christ into the midst of these dense multitudes, who, without the agency of which we are speaking, would lapse into the spiritual desolation of the days before the saintly Cedd went forth to preach the Faith. Could his feet tread again where once they trod of old, and could he see what our eyes behold to-day, he would tremble at the appalling need, and rejoice at the effort to meet it, and he would plead with the eloquence of a life inspired with a knowledge of the love and the power of the Cross that the Church of to-day might rise in all her might to meet the needs of this vast population.

What is being done is of good omen. The fund,

2 C

quoting the report of 1899, supports in the district 151 living agents, at a cost of nearly £10,500 a year, inclusive of twenty rents for mission buildings. It has established thirty-two mission districts, fifteen of which have since become separate parishes with consecrated churches. Sixteen parsonages and two clergy houses have been built, fifty-four mission churches or rooms have been aided or built, eighteen sites have been given, and forty-two purchased by its efforts at a cost of nearly £20,000, besides supporting Day and Sunday schools, and other cognate undertakings. A fresh effort is now being made to build at least twenty new churches, and sixteen new mission buildings. The sites are all ready, but only three are in process of erection. It has been considered necessary to set forth these statistics to show the startling needs of the case.

The clergy and workers of the Church in our quiet country towns and villages can scarcely realize what the self-denying life of their brethren is in this vast wilderness of brick and mortar, amongst these "multitudes in the valley of decision." We respect a man who can suffer imprisonment for conscience sake, and we often speak of him as a martyr, but what shall we say of these men and women who are giving their days and nights, nay, their very lives, in self-sacrifice in the midst of all their dismal surroundings? God has blessed, is blessing, and will reward their noble witness to the Faith. The following extracts from a recent report of the work will serve to illustrate some of its difficulties and encouragements. A mission clergyman writes—

"There are two men now accompanying the organ with violins, who had not been into any place of worship for twenty years, and only a short time since used to lecture in front of the parish church on Disestablishment and Socialism. They have now abandoned all this, and are most loyal and devoted to the Church. They are seldom absent, and have asked permission to become communicants."

Another clergyman writes—

"We very much need *lady* visitors, who will not be afraid of breaking up new ground. We find that local female visitors cannot obtain an entrance, but the clergy and the vicar's mother are welcomed everywhere, both by the indifferent and dissenters, as well as by regular Church people. I have appealed for this help to one or two more favoured districts, and I hope it may in time be arranged. It would be at least as valuable for the lady visitors as for our people. We experience less difficulty in getting Sunday school teachers, as a good many London School Board teachers are ready to help us, and are very efficient teachers."

A clergyman writes—

"The most gratifying feature of the work this year has been the reaching of several men who appeared to be outside all Church influence. One of our most regular communicants now is a man, formerly a choir-boy in a neighbouring parish, who had utterly fallen away. Last Christmas Day a young married woman, who had forsaken the Lord's table since her marriage, made her communion, as we believe, in answer to the intercessions which were offered on her behalf."

A mission clergyman writes—

" This parish helps to show that the working classes can take a great interest in Church work and can show great love for their Church. The whole of the Church officers are working men, and no more efficient men could be found. There is a representative Church Council, which is of the greatest value to the clergyman. A very large proportion of the congregation are Church workers, over seventy working in the Sunday schools alone. A special feature here is the work among the young. The number on the books in the Sunday schools and bible classes is three times as large as the total Church accommodation. The Young Men's Institute is answering well, and an institute has been started for young women. In several cases entire families are Church workers. That so many working people can be found who are willing to give up their only chance of rest, and throw themselves heartily into Church work, is a wonderful tribute to the power of the Church among the poor."

A clergyman near the docks writes—

" The people are very loyal and responsive. A good deal is done with the factory boys and girls at Silver's rubber works and Tate's sugar works. We get many of our confirmation candidates from them. The people come well to special week-night services. On All Saints' Day the church was more than full, and every Wednesday in Advent and Lent good congregations attend. The people are very generous in giving towards the new Church Fund. Many subscribe a penny weekly, and working men have given as much as £1 and 10s. at a time. One working girl sent 6s., with a letter, saying that she was sorry it was no more, but so much had gone to pay the doctor's bill."

A clergyman writes—

" I had a letter the other day from a man now living in Queensland, who, when living here, used with his wife and children to be a most devout and regular worshipper and communicant. In this letter he speaks of 'the old happy times at St. Mark's,' where he 'learnt of eternal life and of the blessed Saviour from everlasting death.' When here, he was only a clerk in a city warehouse, and his earnings were not large, but he once told me that he always put by a tenth of his income for God's work. He took a very keen interest in the building of St. Mark's, and one day he sent me £10 towards the Building Fund. This was, I know, an act of real self-sacrifice, as, at the time, he was far from being well off."

The Rev. E. B. Bhose, the clergyman in charge of the Lascar Mission at the Victoria and Royal Albert Docks, writes as follows :—

"From small beginnings the Lascar Mission has steadily grown year by year, and, at the present time, it is in close touch with thousands of Indian sailors, who come in British vessels to the Victoria and Royal Albert Docks. It would be difficult to speak too highly of their good conduct during their stay here ; instances of insobriety or disturbance of the public peace being very rare indeed amongst them. They are peaceable, industrious, and loyal to those placed over them. The Mission Room, which I look upon as the most important part of our organization, and where much useful work is carried on, has been well attended during the year, and if a little more interest were taken in these poor fellows, and the good work among them more liberally supported, it could be made to look more inviting. It will only accommodate a limited number, but, such as it is, they are very thankful to us for it, and I am informed that on their return home, they tell all their friends that some kind English people have provided for them, at their own expense, a place where they may spend their evenings in recreation and reading."

Well has it been declared that, in a work like

this, unique not only in the history of the nation, but in the history of the Church, she cannot, "without forfeiting her high position, ignore the call that comes from this great isolated district of London, a call that appeals to all the patriotism, Church feeling, and Christianity of England."

Bishop Claughton, in his farewell appeal to the diocese (dated September 27th, 1889), says, "It is the cause of religion and charity, and, I might truly say, of social order in the land."

Burning words like these lay before us the duty of to-day.

Of the future, who shall dare to speak? Shall we not rather say, with the inspiring memory of the great things God has done in our counties in the past, who shall dare to be faint-hearted?

We have looked back to the day when Alban gave his life for the Faith; we have thought of the humble chapel which marked the place of his burial; we have traced its growth into a noble Abbey, sheltering his shrine, once resplendent with the homage of devotion to his memory; we have seen that shrine a desecrated ruin, and the Abbey a pile wasting with decay; we have asked with an anxiety, born of despair, "Can these bones live?" The answer came of faith, "O Lord God, Thou knowest." We look round, and lo! the breath has come into them, and they live.

Yet once again we look where ruin reigned, and chaos fell, and lo! the ancient Abbey has become the Cathedral Church, a joy to thousands who cluster in devotion round its Bishop's throne ; the living stones of the temple are being built up, and with grateful hearts we cry, " The Lord hath done great things for us already, whereof we rejoice."

Once more, " What of the future ? "

With new hopes, chastened by the trials, elated by the joys, hallowed by the memories of the past, we nerve ourselves to face the problems, and to do the duty of to-day. If we firmly hold the Apostolic Faith, speak it clearly, teach it lovingly, live it truly, we need not fear the future.

Dark days may loom, and the spirit quail as we near the problems yet unsolved, and meet the duties yet undone, but the promise still holds sure, " He that now goeth on his way weeping and beareth good seed, shall doubtless come again with joy and bring his sheaves with him."

The blood of the martyr has proved to be " the seed of the Church."

The Lord of the Harvest is on the field.

APPENDIX A

BISHOPRIC OF SAINT ALBANS ACT, 1875.

(38 & 39 Vict. Cap. 34.)

"An Act to amend the Acts relating to the Ecclesiastical Commissioners, and enable them to carry into effect a certain proposal for the re-arrangement of the Dioceses of London, Winchester, and Rochester, and the erection of a new Bishopric of Saint Albans. [29th June 1875.]

A.D. 1875.

"WHEREAS, having regard to the great increase of population in the counties adjoining the metropolis both north and south of the Thames, and in particular in the county of Surrey, it is expedient to provide increased episcopal supervision in such counties, and with a view thereto an arrangement is proposed whereby a new bishopric, to be called the Bishopric of Saint Albans, will be formed to the north of the Thames, to consist of the counties of Hertford and Essex (which will be taken away from the diocese of Rochester), and more complete episcopal supervision will be secured to South London and the district situate to the south of the Thames, including a large part of the county of Surrey, by adding to the diocese of Rochester, in exchange for the counties to the north of the Thames so taken away as aforesaid, the several parishes in this Act hereafter specified, of which the greater portion form at the present time part of the diocese of Winchester :

"And whereas the Bishop of Winchester, with a view to further such arrangement as aforesaid, and in particular to provide more complete episcopal supervision as aforesaid in South London and

A.D. 1875. the district situated to the south of the Thames, has assented to the sale of the episcopal residence in London attached to the bishopric of Winchester, and to the application of the proceeds of such sale as a basis for an endowment of the bishopric of Saint Albans, and it is intended to make such further provision for the endowment of the said bishopric as is herein-after mentioned :

"Be it therefore enacted by the Queen's most Excellent Majesty, by and with the advice and consent of the Lords Spiritual and Temporal, and Commons, in this present Parliament assembled, and by the authority of the same, as follows :—

Short title of Act.   "1. This Act may be cited for all purposes as the Bishopric of Saint Albans Act, 1875.

"*Bishopric of Saint Albans.*

London house of Bishop of Winchester to be sold, and proceeds carried to Bishopric Endowment Fund.   "2. The Ecclesiastical Commissioners for England (in this Act referred to as 'the Commissioners') shall, as soon as may be after the passing of this Act, sell the episcopal residence attached to the bishopric of Winchester, and situate in the liberties of the city of Westminster, and shall carry over the proceeds of such sale, after deducting the expenses thereof, to a fund to be called the Saint Albans Bishopric Endowment Fund.

Public contributions to be carried to Bishopric Endowment Fund.   "3. The Commissioners shall receive all contributions which may be made by the public for the purposes of the endowment of the bishopric of Saint Albans, and carry the amount of such contributions to the said Saint Albans Bishopric Endowment Fund.

Bishopric to be established on sufficient endowment being provided.   "4. Whenever the Commissioners certify to Her Majesty under their seal that the Saint Albans Bishopric Endowment Fund amounts to a sum which (exclusive of the value of any episcopal residence which may have been provided, or any sum appropriated for the purpose of providing such episcopal residence), produces a net income of not less than two thousand pounds a year, Her Majesty, by Order in Council, may found a new bishopric of Saint Albans, with a diocese consisting of the counties of Hertford and Essex, and of that part of the county of Kent which lies north of the River Thames, or of such parts thereof as to Her Majesty may seem meet, and may assign to such bishopric as a cathedral church the abbey church of Saint

Albans, in the county of Hertford, but subject to the rights of A.D. 1875. the incumbent of such church, and may declare the time at which such Order founding such new bishopric is to come into operation.

" Her Majesty, by the same or any other Order in Council, may constitute the Bishop of Saint Albans a body corporate, and may invest such bishop with all such rights, privileges, and jurisdictions as are now possessed by any other bishop in England, or such of them as to Her Majesty may seem meet, and may subject such bishop to the metropolitan jurisdiction of the Archbishop of Canterbury.

" 5. Her Majesty may by the Order in Council founding the New constitution of bishopric of Saint Albans, or by any other Order in Council, to diocese of take effect at or after the time at which such first-mentioned Rochester, and alteration of the residue of the diocese dioceses of of Rochester remaining after such constitution as aforesaid of the London and bishopric of Saint Albans out of the counties of Hertford and Winchester. Essex, all such parishes situate wholly or partly in the parlia mentary divisions of East Surrey and Mid Surrey as now form part of the diocese of Winchester, also all such parishes situate in the county of Surrey as now form part of the diocese of London.

" Her Majesty may in any such Order in Council as is mentioned in this section make such modifications in the provisions herein contained respecting the transfer of parishes as to Her Majesty may seem meet.

" 6. Subject to the rights of the persons who are at the time Additional endowment of the passing of this Act Bishops of Winchester and Rochester, of bishopric there shall be transferred to the Saint Albans Bishopric Endow- of Saint ment Fund such portion of the endowment or income of the bishopric of Winchester as will yield a net annual sum of five hundred pounds, and such portion of the endowment or income of the bishopric of Rochester as will yield a net annual sum of five hundred pounds.

" 7. The number of Lords Spiritual sitting and voting as The number of bishops Lords of Parliament shall not be increased by the foundation of sitting in the bishopric of Saint Albans, and whenever there is a vacancy not to be among such Lords Spiritual by the avoidance of any of the sees increased. of Canterbury, York, London, Durham, or Winchester, such vacancy shall be supplied by the issue of a writ of summons to the bishop acceding to the see so avoided, and if such vacancy

A.D. 1875. is caused by the avoidance of any see other than the five sees aforesaid, such vacancy shall be supplied by the issue of a writ of summons to that bishop of a see in England who having been longest appointed bishop of a see in England had not previously become entitled to such writ.

" Provided, that where a bishop is translated from one see to another, and was at the date of his translation actually sitting as a Lord of Parliament, he shall not thereupon lose his right to receive a writ of summons to Parliament.

" *Supplemental Provisions.*

Appointment of Bishop of Saint Albans.

" 8. So long as there is not a Dean and Chapter of Saint Albans, Her Majesty may appoint the Bishop of Saint Albans by letters patent, and such letters patent shall be made in the like manner, so far as circumstances admit, and have the same effect as letters patent of Her Majesty nominating a bishop in the case of a bishopric where a dean and chapter have not proceeded to elect a bishop in accordance with the license and letters missive of Her Majesty.

" From and after the foundation of such dean and chapter a vacancy in the bishopric of Saint Albans shall be filled in the same manner as a vacancy in any other bishopric in England.

Courts, officers, archdeaconries, and other incidental arrangements constituting the bishopric of Saint Albans to be provided by a scheme of the Ecclesiastical Commissioners, approved by Order in Council.

" 9. Whenever such certificate as is in this Act mentioned has been given by the Commissioners with respect to the net income produced by the Saint Albans Bishopric Endowment Fund, the Commissioners shall lay before Her Majesty a scheme—

" (1.) For assigning to the Bishop of Saint Albans all or any such courts, officers, and jurisdiction belonging to any bishop in England, and not otherwise assigned by this Act, or any Order in Council made thereunder, as it may be thought expedient to assign, and for making provisions for dispensing with the confirmation or other agency of a dean and chapter in relation to any matters in which such confirmation or agency would otherwise be required, and for the custody of the spiritualities by the Archbishop of Canterbury during a vacancy in the see ; and

" (2.) For making such arrangements as may be thought expedient, by the creation of new archdeaconries or otherwise, for the archidiaconal supervision of the parishes affected by the foundation of the bishopric of Saint Albans, and by the alteration of the boundaries of the bishoprics of London, Winchester, and Rochester, with power on the next avoidance of the archdeaconry of Rochester and Saint Albans, and before such avoidance with the consent of the person who is now Archdeacon of Rochester and Saint Albans, to divide the archdeaconry of Rochester and Saint Albans; provided, that from and after such division the canonry in the cathedral church of Rochester now annexed to the archdeaconry of Rochester and Saint Albans shall be permanently annexed to the archdeaconry of Rochester; and

" (3.) For giving the bishop of each of the dioceses of London, Winchester, Rochester, and Saint Albans the patronage of every ecclesiastical dignity and benefice situate in his diocese, the patronage of which ecclesiastical dignity or benefice is, at the date of the scheme being made, vested in the bishop of the diocese in which such dignity or benefice is then situate; and

" (4.) For transferring the portions of the endowments or income of the bishoprics of Winchester and Rochester directed by this Act to be transferred to the Saint Albans Bishopric Endowment Fund; and

" (5.) For enabling any existing archdeacon to reside in any place in which he is residing at the time of the passing of this Act, and for making such arrangements as to the officers of the said bishoprics as may seem to the Commissioners requisite to preclude any existing officer from being prejudiced by this Act or any Order in Council made thereunder; and

" (6.) For founding honorary canonries in the cathedral church of Saint Albans, with power to dispense with the consent of any dean and chapter so long as there is no such dean and chapter in existence at Saint Albans, and to provide that honorary canons in the cathedral church of Rochester who, upon the foundation of the bishopric of Saint Albans, may be holding benefices in the diocese of Saint Albans shall become honorary canons in the cathedral church of Saint Albans instead of being honorary canons in the cathedral church of Rochester ; and

" (7.) For providing for the transfer as soon as may be practicable to the registrar or other officer of the diocese of Saint Albans, from the registrars or officers of the dioceses of London, Winchester, and Rochester who may be respectively in possession of the same, of all terriers, tithe apportionments, maps, plans, and other documents relating to the several parishes which shall be situate in the diocese of Saint Albans ; and

" (8.) For making such other provisions and arrangements, whether similar or not to the foregoing, as may be necessary for carrying into complete effect this Act or any Order in Council made thereunder.

" Any scheme made in pursuance of this Act shall be of no effect until it has been approved by Order of Her Majesty in Council, but when so approved shall be published in the *London Gazette*.

" A copy of any scheme made in pursuance of this section, and approved by Order of Her Majesty in Council, shall be laid before both Houses of Parliament as soon as conveniently may be after such Order is made, if Parliament be then sitting, or if Parliament be not then sitting, within one week after the next meeting of Parliament.

Validity of Order in Council.

" 10. Any order made by Her Majesty in Council in pursuance of the provisions contained in this Act, shall be of the same effect as if such Order were enacted in this Act.

Sale by Commissioners of Danbury.

" 11. At any time after the passing of this Act, the Commissioners may, with the consent of the Bishop of Rochester, sell the episcopal residence attached to the bishopric of Rochester, and situate in the parishes of Danbury and Sandon, in the county of Essex, and after the person who is Bishop of Rochester at the time of the passing of this Act ceases to be entitled to reside therein, may sell the same without such consent ; the Commissioners shall in the first place out of the proceeds of such last-mentioned sale, after deducting the expenses thereof, provide, in the county of Surrey, a suitable episcopal residence for the Bishop of Rochester, and shall carry the surplus to the Saint Albans

Bishopric Endowment Fund, with a view to providing within the diocese of Saint Albans a suitable episcopal residence for the Bishop of Saint Albans.

" The expression ' episcopal residence situate in the parishes of Danbury and Sandon' shall include any gardens, pleasure grounds, farms, and lands usually held or occupied with the said residence.

" 12. The Commissioners may sell any episcopal residence or land by this Act authorized to be sold by them, with or without special conditions of title, or otherwise, as they may think fit, and they shall have power by any conveyance or instrument under their seal to vest in the purchaser all the estate and interest therein of the bishop of the bishopric to which it was attached and his successors, and any other estate and interest therein (if any) belonging to or held in trust for such bishopric. *Effect of conveyance of episcopal residences by Commissioners.*

" 13. The Saint Albans Bishopric Endowment Fund shall be held by the Commissioners upon trust to provide a net annual income not exceeding four thousand five hundred pounds a year, and a residence, for the Bishop of Saint Albans, and subject as aforesaid upon trust for the foundation of a dean and chapter for the bishopric of Saint Albans, in such manner as may be from time to time provided by Order of Her Majesty in Council. *Trusts of Bishopric Endowment Fund*

" All annual income arising from the Saint Albans Bishopric Endowment Fund shall, until the bishopric of Saint Albans is founded, as provided by this Act, be invested and accumulated as part of the fund ; but the Commissioners shall have full power to sell (discharged from all trusts), invest, manage, lease, and otherwise deal with the fund and the property in which it may for the time being be invested in such manner as they may deem most expedient for the purposes of their trust. The Commissioners may invest the whole or any part of the Saint Albans Bishopric Endowment Fund in the purchase of land, and may hold such land without any license in mortmain, and may from time to time, with the consent of the Bishop of Saint Albans for the time being, assign to such bishop and his successors, as an endowment for the see, the lands so purchased, if convenient to be held by such see : Provided that there shall not be assigned as an endowment to the said bishopric, exclusive of an episcopal residence, a greater extent of land than will, after deducting the costs of management, produce as nearly as may be a net annual income of four thousand five hundred pounds.

" The endowment of the bishopric of Saint Albans under this Act shall be deemed to be for all purposes subject to the same laws as the temporalities and endowment of any other bishopric in England.

" *Temporary Provisions.*

Provision as to existing Bishop of Rochester.

" 14. If the person who at the passing of this Act is the Bishop of Rochester is translated to the bishopric of Saint Albans, he shall be entitled, so long as he continues Bishop of Saint Albans, to a writ of summons to sit in Parliament, and to the same rank and precedence in Parliament and elsewhere as if he had continued to be Bishop of Rochester ; and he shall be entitled, so long as he continues Bishop of Saint Albans, to reside at the episcopal residence of Danbury (until sold with his consent), and to receive out of the revenue of the bishopric of Rochester such annual sum as will, together with the revenue of the bishopric of Saint Albans, make up his net annual income to the same amount as that which he received as Bishop of Rochester ; and if he resigns the bishopric

32 & 33 Vict. c. 111.

of Saint Albans, in pursuance of the Bishops Resignation Act, 1869, and thus becomes entitled under that Act to a retiring allowance of two thousand pounds, and at the date of such resignation was receiving any annual sum out of the revenues of the bishopric of Rochester, such retiring allowance shall be paid partly out of the revenue of the bishopric of Rochester and partly out of the revenue of the bishopric of Saint Albans, and the amount of the portion so to be paid out of the revenue of the bishopric of Rochester shall bear the same proportion to the amount payable out of the revenue of the bishopric of Saint Albans as the annual income which he was receiving at the time of his resignation out of the revenue of the bishopric of Rochester bore to the annual income which he was receiving out of the revenue of the bishopric of Saint Albans.

" Provided that if during the payment of any such retiring allowance as aforesaid to any bishop an augmentation is made in the revenue of the bishopric of Saint Albans, a proportionate increase shall be made in the quota payable towards such allowance out of the revenue of the bishopric of Saint Albans, and a corresponding reduction shall be made in the quota payable out of the revenue of the bishopric of Rochester.

" Provided, that if at any time after the passing of this Act the annual income of one of the said bishoprics of Saint Albans and A.D. 1875. Rochester is for the time being less than the income of the other of the said bishoprics, and less than four thousand five hundred pounds, then (subject and without prejudice to such provisions of this Act as are limited to take effect in the event of the translation to the bishopric of Saint Albans of the person who at the time of the passing of this Act is the Bishop of Rochester) the person for the time being holding such one of the said bishoprics as has the less income shall, in the event of his becoming entitled to a retiring allowance under the Bishops Resignation Act, 1869, be only entitled to be paid one third part of the income enjoyed by him before his retirement, and shall not be entitled to receive the annual sum of two thousand pounds in place of such third part.

" *Saving Clauses, and Repeal.*

" 15. The service of any person, either before or partly before Saving as to and partly after the foundation of the bishopric of Saint Albans, as service as incumbent or curate in any parish which, in pursuance of this Act, curate in transferred is constituted part of a different diocese from that of which it parishes. forms part at the passing of this Act, shall, for the purpose of qualifying such incumbent or curate to be presented or nominated to any benefice in the patronage of the chapter of any cathedral or collegiate church, be deemed to be service in the diocese in which such parish is situate at the time of the passing of this Act, or in the diocese in which such parish is situate at the date of the presentation or nomination.

" 16. Nothing in this Act shall authorize the Commissioners to Common apply any portion of their common fund towards the endowment fund of Commis- of the bishopric of Saint Albans, or of the dean and chapter of sioners not applicable to such bishopric, save in so far as relates to the net annual sums of endowment. five hundred pounds and five hundred pounds by this Act made payable out of the endowment or income of the bishoprics of Winchester and Rochester.

" 17. There shall be repealed, from and after the date of the Repeal of passing of this Act, any enactment of any Act of Parliament incon- certain Acts and parts of sistent therewith, and from and after the date at which any Order Acts. of Her Majesty in Council made in pursuance of or for the purposes of this Act comes into operation, any enactment of any Act of Parliament inconsistent with such Order in Council."

2 D

APPENDIX B.

COMPARATIVE TABLE.*

(Showing the method of raising funds for the foundation of six new bishoprics.)

New see.	Donations.a £ s. d.	Approximate No. of donors] published.	Legacies. £	Church offertories. £ s. d.	No. of offertories.	Dividends or Bank interest. £ s. d.	Other sources. £ s. d.	Total raised by voluntary effort. £ s. d.	Annuity from contributory see or sees. £	In gifts of £1000 or upwards. £	Cost or value of residence. £
St. Albans	**13,458 1 0**b	—	—	—	—	—	45,000 0 0c	**13,458 1 0**	**1,000**	**52,000**	d
Truro ...	73,604 3 3e	924	—	1,331 4 6	297	401 1 8	—	75,336 9 5	800	42,700	4,500f
Liverpool	93,084 10 7	457	—	2,103 10 0	158	2,279 9 2	—	97,467 9 9	300	61,000	7,007g
Newcastle	66,828 4 4h	—	16,200	1,871 2 11	—	2,767 5 6	—	87,666 12 9	1,000	35,500h	12,500
Southwell	69,557 4 11i	1,255	1,000	3,776 16 1	698	563 19 4	401 19 8j	75,300 0 0i	800	27,000	5,300k
Wakefield	85,460 8 11l	1,822	—	4,561 7 0	739	3,650 19 4	645 9 8j	94,318 4 11l	300	35,600	10,138m
Total	401,992 13 0		17,200	13,644 0 6		9,662 15 0	46,047 9 4	443,546 17 10	4,200	253,800	38,945

* Extracted from "The Wakefield Bishopric Movement," by Canon Straton. Pub. Elliott Stock, 1888.

(a) In this column the approximate amount of the contribution made by the Additional Home Bishoprics Society is included, but the analysis in the next six columns to the right has no reference to the details of this contribution, nor to the £10,138 raised for the residence of the Bishop of Wakefield.

(b) According to a statement of accounts, December 31st. 1881, published by the Home Bishoprics Society.

(c) Sale of Winchester House.

(d) Provision is made for the sale of Danbury Palace. The proceeds to be applied for providing a House for (i.) see of Rochester, (ii.) for see of St. Albans.

(e) Inclusive of two rent-charges given by Lords Devon and Clinton, and gift of £40,000 by Lady Rolle.

(f) Inclusive of a mortgage of £3000 provided by an annual payment, but exclusive of subsequent additions.

(g) Exclusive of subsequent additions.

(h) Inclusive of estimated value of Benwell Towers (£12,500) and £2000 from Executors of late Colonel Joicey, paid under the Newcastle Chapter Act.

(i) These figures are based, with one slight correction, on a statement, in round numbers, published by Sub-Dean Clements, in January, 1884, as to the full amount voluntarily raised. The legacy, offertories, dividends, and other details, are carefully gathered from the five county lists, and the remainder is given in the first of these columns as approximately correct.

(j) Chiefly collected in very small sums by district visitors and others,

(k) Estimated value of the old palace at Southwell, when offered by the Bishop of Nottingham, £9000 being further required for its completion as a see house. It is, however, now certain that the income of the see will be raised to £3500 a year without a house. For this purpose £11,000 already guaranteed, must be called up, towards which sum a legacy of £1000 has lately been received ; but this £11,000 is not included in the above Table.

(l) According to the lists of the Yorkshire Committee corrected to March 1st, 1888, and the returns of the Additional Home Bishoprics Society received in December, 1877, and inclusive of the £10,138 raised by the Ladies' Committee.

(m) Collected by the Yorkshire Ladies' Committee, and held in reserve for providing a bishop's residence.

APPENDIX C

At the Court at Windsor, the 30th day of April, 1877.

Present.—The Queen's Most Excellent Majesty in Council.

"WHEREAS in pursuance of the Bishopric of Saint Albans Act, 1875, the Ecclesiastical Commissioners for England on the 12th day of April, 1877, certified to Her Majesty under their common seal that the Saint Albans Bishopric Endowment Fund amounted to a sum which produces a net income of not less than £2000 a year.

"Now therefore in pursuance of the above-mentioned Act, Her Majesty is pleased by and with the advice of Her most Honourable Privy Council to order and declare as follows :—

"(1.) The bishopric of Saint Albans is hereby founded.

"(2.) The diocese of the said bishopric shall consist of the counties of Hertford and Essex, and of so much of the county of Kent as lies north of the River Thames.

"(3.) The Abbey church of Saint Albans in the county of Hertford, subject to the rights of the incumbent of such church, is assigned as a cathedral church to the said bishopric.

"(4.) The bishopric of Saint Albans is constituted a body corporate, and the Bishop of Saint Albans is hereby invested with all such rights, privileges, and jurisdictions as are now possessed by any other bishop in England, and is subjected to the metropolitan jurisdiction of the Archbishop of Canterbury.

"(5.) This order shall come into operation on the publication of the same in the *London Gazette.* [1]

"C. L. PEEL."

[1] The *London Gazette*, Friday, May 4th, 1877.

APPENDIX D

At the Court at Windsor, the 11th day of July, 1877.

Present.—The Queen's Most Excellent Majesty in Council.

"WHEREAS the Ecclesiastical Commissioners for England have, in pursuance of the Act of the thirty-eighth and thirty-ninth years of Her Majesty, Chapter thirty-four, duly prepared and laid before Her Majesty in Council a scheme, bearing date the twenty-eighth day of June, in the year one thousand eight hundred and seventy-seven, in the words and figures following, that is to say—

"We the Ecclesiastical Commissioners for England, in pursuance of the Act of the thirty-eighth and thirty-ninth years of your Majesty, Chapter thirty-four, have prepared and now humbly lay before your Majesty in Council the following scheme with respect to the bishoprick of Saint Albans :—

"Whereas the bishoprick of Saint Albans aforesaid was founded by an Order of your Majesty in Council bearing date the thirtieth day of April, one thousand eight hundred and seventy-seven, and published in the *London Gazette* on the fourth day of May next following; which Order was made in pursuance of the fourth section of the above-mentioned Act, and which Order, as appears by the terms thereof, came into operation on the said fourth day of May, one thousand eight hundred and seventy-seven.

"And whereas by the same Order it is ordered that the diocese of the bishoprick of Saint Albans shall consist of the counties of Hertford and Essex, and of so much of the county of Kent as lies north of the River Thames.

"And whereas by the same Order the Abbey church of Saint Albans in the town and borough of Saint Albans in the county of Hertford was assigned (subject to the rights of the incumbent of the same church) to the bishoprick of Saint Albans as a Cathedral Church.

" And whereas by the same Order the Bishop of the Bishoprick of Saint Albans was constituted a body corporate, and was invested with all such rights, privileges, and jurisdictions as are possessed by any other bishop in England, and was subjected to the metropolitan jurisdiction of the Archbishop of Canterbury.

" And whereas the Right Reverend Thomas Legh Claughton, being the person who at the passing of the said Act of the thirty-eighth and thirty-ninth years of your Majesty, Chapter thirty-four, was Bishop of Rochester, has by letters patent under your Majesty's great seal been translated to the bishoprick of Saint Albans, and was on the twelfth day of June, in the year one thousand eight hundred and seventy-seven, enthroned as Bishop of Saint Albans accordingly, and is now Bishop of Saint Albans.

" And whereas by the ninth section of the said Act of the thirty-eighth and thirty-ninth years of your Majesty, Chapter thirty-four, it is enacted that whenever a certain certificate therein mentioned shall have been given to your Majesty by us the said Ecclesiastical Commissioners for England, we shall lay before your Majesty a scheme for doing certain things which in the same section are specified and for otherwise carrying into complete effect the same Act or any Order in Council made thereunder.

" And whereas the said certificate has been given as by the said Order of your Majesty in Council of the thirtieth day of April one thousand eight hundred and seventy-seven appears.

" Now therefore, we, the said Ecclesiastical Commissioners for England, humbly recommend and propose that—

" (1.) The bishop for the time being of the diocese of Saint Albans shall have all such courts and officers and all such jurisdiction as were and was at the time of the passing of the said Order of your Majesty in Council possessed by the bishop of the diocese of Rochester, within the limits as defined by the same Order of the diocese of Saint Albans, and all terriers, tithe apportionments, maps, plans, and other documents relating exclusively to any parish or parishes situate in the said diocese of Saint Albans or otherwise relating exclusively to the same diocese (that is to say) to the area or any part of the area thereof shall be transferred from the custody of the registrar or other officer of the diocese of Rochester, in whose custody the same now are and shall become and be in the custody of such registrar or other officer or officers of the diocese of Saint Albans as the Bishop of Saint Albans shall appoint in that behalf.

" (2.) All parishes and places, churches and chapels, and all the clergy and others of your Majesty's subjects within the limits of the diocese of Saint Albans, as the same diocese is defined by the said order of your Majesty in Council of the thirtieth day of April, one thousand eight hundred and seventy-seven, shall be exempted and released from all jurisdiction, authority, and control of the Bishop of Rochester, and shall be under and subject to the episcopal jurisdiction, authority, and control of the Bishop of Saint Albans and his successors.

" (3.) Until a Dean and Chapter of and for the said Cathedral Church of Saint Albans shall have been created, the Bishop of the diocese of Saint Albans may, as to any and every matter with respect to which the confirmation or other agency of a Dean and Chapter is by law required for rendering effectual the action of a bishop take action in such matter without any such confirmation or agency, and his action so taken shall not be thereby made ineffectual or invalid.

" (4.) During every and any vacancy in the see of Saint Albans, whether such vacancy shall happen before or after the creation of a Dean and Chapter of and for the said Cathedral Church of Saint Albans, the Archbishop of Canterbury shall have the custody and be the guardian of the spiritualities of the see of Saint Albans.

" (5.) The archidiaconal supervision of the parishes and churches included within the diocese of Saint Albans shall for the present be provided for by the archdeacons of the existing archdeaconries of Rochester and Saint Albans, Colchester and Essex, respectively, as follows, that is to say—

" The archdeacon of the existing archdeaconry of Rochester and Saint Albans shall have archidiaconal jurisdiction over the whole of that part of the diocese of Saint Albans which is situate in the

county of Herts, and the archdeacons of the archdeaconries of Colchester and Essex respectively shall
continue to have the same jurisdiction within their
respective archdeaconries as they have heretofore
possessed and exercised; and the two archdeacons
lastly mentioned shall no longer be subject to the
episcopal jurisdiction of the Bishop of Rochester, but
shall be subject to the episcopal jurisdiction of the
Bishop of Saint Albans, and the archidiaconal dignities
of the same two archdeaconries shall be transferred
from the Cathedral Church of Rochester to the
Cathedral Church of Saint Albans; and the said
Archdeacon of Rochester and Saint Albans so far
as regards that portion of his archdeaconry, the
territory of which is co-extensive with the county
of Herts shall no longer be subject to the episcopal
jurisdiction of the Bishop of Rochester, but shall
be subject to the episcopal jurisdiction of the Bishop
of Saint Albans.

" (6.) The patronage of every ecclesiastical dignity and
benefice being within the diocese of Saint Albans, of
which dignity and benefice the patronage is now vested
for any estate or interest in the Bishop of Rochester,
shall to the extent of such estate or interest be,
without any conveyances or assurances in the law
other than this scheme and any Order of your Majesty
in Council ratifying the same, and upon and from the
day of the date of the publication of any such Order
in the *London Gazette* transferred from the Bishop
of Rochester and from his successors, and shall
become and be vested in the Bishop of Saint Albans
and his successors.

"And whereas by a certain deed bearing date
the 11th day of June, one thousand eight hundred
and seventy-seven, and made between the Right
Reverend Thomas Legh, then Bishop of Rochester,
of the one part, and the said Ecclesiastical Commissioners for England for the other part, the said
Thomas Legh, Bishop of Rochester (being the person
who was at the passing of the said Act Bishop of

Rochester), did surrender all rights and interests reserved to him by the sixth section of the same Act ; to the intent that the portion of the endowment or income of the bishoprick of Rochester which in the same section is mentioned (being such portion of the same or will yield a net annual sum of five hundred pounds) should form part of the Saint Albans Bishoprick Endowment Fund created by the second section of the said Act.

"Now therefore we further recommend and propose that—

"(7.) The said yearly sum of five hundred pounds shall be (as by virtue of the said deed the same already is) as from the date of the said deed of the eleventh day of June, one thousand eight hundred and seventy-seven, transferred from the bishop of the diocese of Rochester and become and be for ever thereafter payable and paid to or for the purposes of the Saint Albans Bishoprick Endowment Fund so as to become part of the annual income of the Bishop of Saint Albans for the time being.

"(8) And we further recommend and propose that, notwithstanding anything contained in the Act of the third and fourth years of your Majesty, Chapter one hundred and thirteen, it shall be lawful for the venerable Anthony Grant, who is and was at the time of the passing of the firstly herein-mentioned Act Archdeacon of the Archdeaconry of Rochester and Saint Albans, to continue to reside as heretofore at Aylesford in the county of Kent and diocese of Rochester.

"And we further recommend and propose with the consent of the Right Reverend Thomas Legh, Bishop of Saint Albans, in testimony whereof he has hereunto set his hand and seal, that—

"(9.) Every officer who at the date of the passing of the Bishoprick of Saint Albans Act, 1875, held and who still holds any office of emolument under the Bishop of Rochester, or under the Dean and Chapter of Rochester, or under the archdeacons of the archdeaconries of Rochester and Saint Albans, Colchester, and Essex, respectively, and who derived and still derives any portion of the emoluments of his office from sources arising within the diocese of Saint Albans, shall during his tenure of such office, perform such duties and receive such emoluments as an officer of or within the diocese of Saint Albans as he has hitherto performed and received as an officer of or within the diocese of Rochester: and he shall during his tenure of such his office be one of the officers mentioned in the first clause of this scheme.

" (10.) Twenty-four honorary canonries shall be founded by the authority of this scheme, and of any order of your Majesty in Council ratifying the same in the said Cathedral Church of Saint Albans and under the provisions of the Act of the third and fourth years of your Majesty, Chapter one hundred and thirteen, section twenty-three, it shall be lawful for the Bishop of Saint Albans to appoint as in that section is mentioned spiritual persons to such honorary canonries; and so long as there shall be no Dean and Chapter of the said Cathedral Church of Saint Albans, to make without the consent of any Dean and Chapter regulations respecting the honorary canons so appointed.

" Provided always, that any honorary canons in the Cathedral Church of Rochester, who upon the foundation of the Bishoprick of Saint Albans were holding benefices in the diocese of Saint Albans and who consent to such transfer shall (notwithstanding anything in the said last-mentioned Act and section contained) be transferred to and become honorary canons in the said Cathedral Church of Saint Albans, and shall therefrom (that is to say as to each of them upon his appointment to be an honorary canon of Saint Albans) cease *ipso facto* to be an honorary canon in the Cathedral Church of Rochester. Provided also that in the first year after the passing of any Order of your Majesty in Council ratifying this scheme, eight spiritual persons and no more (exclusive of any honorary canons who may be transferred from the Cathedral Church of Rochester as aforesaid) may be appointed to honorary canonries in the said Cathedral Church of Saint Albans.

" And whereas the said scheme has been approved by her Majesty in Council, now therefore Her Majesty, by and with the advice of her said Council, is pleased hereby to ratify the said scheme, and to order and direct the same and every part thereof, shall be effectual in law immediately from and after the time when this order shall have been duly published in the *London Gazette*, pursuant to the said Act of the thirty-eighth and thirty-ninth years of Her Majesty, Chapter thirty-four : and Her Majesty by and with the like advice, is pleased hereby to direct that this Order be forthwith registered by the Registrar of the said diocese of Rochester and by any Registrar of the said diocese of Saint Albans to be appointed in pursuance of the said scheme.[1]

" C. L. PEEL."

[1] The *London Gazette*, July 13, 1877, p. 4126.

APPENDIX E

"VICTORIA by the grace of God of the United Kingdom of Great
Britain and Ireland Queen Defender of the Faith, to the Right
Reverend Father in God, John Wogan, by Divine permission,
Lord Bishop of St. Albans, and to all others whom it may concern,
Greeting : Whereas We have by our Order in Council bearing
date the 30th day of April, 1877, made in pursuance of an Act of
the 38th and 39th years of our Reign, cap. 34, founded the
Bishopric of Saint Albans, and have assigned'the Abbey Church of
Saint Albans in the county of Hertford as a Cathedral Church to the
said Bishopric, which Order came into operation on the fourth day
of May, 1877, and whereas it has been represented to Us that it
would be expedient to found a Dean and Chapter for the said
Bishopric.   Now know ye that We of our certain knowledge
and mere motion have founded and created, and by these presents
do found and create a Dean and Chapter of the said Cathedral
Church of Saint Albans, and We do hereby constitute them a Body
Corporate with all such rights and powers usually enjoyed by all
Cathedral Chapters in England as we may from time to time
provide by any Order in Council made by us, and such Order in
Council may contain such provisions as may be necessary as to
the number of the said Chapter and the Revenues and Endowment thereof, and the enjoyment of Incomes and other Emoluments in relation thereto.   And we do further declare that the
said Deanery shall be in our direct patronage and every Canonry
in the said Chapter shall be in the Patronage of the Bishop of
Saint Albans for the time being.   In witness whereof we have
caused these Our Letters to be made Patent.   Witness ourself
at Westminster, the twenty-third day of February, in the sixty-
third year of Our Reign.

"By Warrant under the Queen's Sign Manual,
"MUIR MACKENZIE."

APPENDIX F

RE-ADJUSTMENT OF THE JURISDICTION OF THE ARCHDEACONRY OF SAINT ALBANS, 1846.

" WE therefore humbly recommend and propose, . . . that upon and after the first day of January, in the year one thousand eight hundred and forty-six, . . . So much and such parts of the said county of Hertford as now form part of the said Archdeaconry of Middlesex and all parishes and places in the same county over which the jurisdiction of the Archdeacon of Huntingdon at present extends shall be transferred to and included in and form part of the Archdeaconry of Saint Albans, and all parishes and places in the County of Buckingham over which the jurisdiction of the Archdeacon of Saint Albans at present extends shall be transferred to and included in and form part of the Archdeaconry of Buckingham." [1]

[1] Supplement to *London Gazette*, Wednesday, August 20th, 1845.

APPENDIX G

PECULIAR JURISDICTION OF CANTERBURY, IN THE COUNTY OF
ESSEX.[1]

Livings remaining in charge.

Rectories, etc., with their Patrons and Proprietors.

King's Books.					Yearly tenths.		
			Bocking R., St. Mary, Archbishop of				
35	10	00	Canterbury		03	11	00
			Lachingdon and Lawling R., St. Michael,				
37	00	00	Archbishop of Canterbury		03	14	00
			Stistede R., All Saints, Archbishop of				
22	00	00	Canterbury		02	04	00
			South Church R., Archbishop of Canter-				
27	00	10	bury		02	14	01

APPENDIX H

Peculiars of the Dean and Chapter of St. Paul's in Essex.[1]

In *Middlesex* [Archdeaconry], Belchamp St. Paul's, and Wickham St. Paul's.

In *Essex* [Archdeaconry], Barling, Navestock, Tillington,[2] West Lee.[3]

In *Colchester* [Archdeaconry], Heybridge.

[1] From "Thesaurus Rerum Ecclesiasticarum, Ecton." 2nd ed., by Browne Willis, LL.D. London, 1754.

[2] Tillingham.

[3] "Chapel to West Tilbury *destructa*."

Statement of Growth of Population of "London over the Border."*

Name of Civil Parish.	1801.	1811.	1821.	1831.	1841.	1851.	1861.	1871.	1881.	1891.	1901.
Barking Deanery, South { Barking	1,865	2,708	2,941	3,791	4,218	5,365	5,591	6,576	9,203	14,301	21,547
Great Ilford	2,041	2,835	3,433	4,245	4,500	4,523	5,409	5,947	7,645	10,913	41,240
Little Ilford	85	119	87	115	189	187	594	675	993	3,969	95,989†
East Ham	1,165	1,267	1,424	1,543	1,461	1,550	2,264	4,334	9,713	28,744‡	
Barking Deanery, West { West Ham	6,485	8,136	9,753	11,580	12,738	18,817	38,331	62,919	128,953	204,903	267,308
North Woolwich (Kent portion)	—	—	—	—	—	—	—	1,455	1,504	2,055	2,600†
Barking Deanery, North { Chingford	612	593	837	963	971	963	1,174	1,268	1,387	2,737	4,372
Leyton	2,519	3,162	3,374	3,323	3,274	3,901	4,794	10,794	23,016	43,906	98,899
Walthamstow	3,006	3,777	4,304	4,258	4,873	4,959	7,137	10,692	21,715	46,346	95,125
Wanstead (including Wanstead Slip	918	1,127	1,354	1,403	1,508	2,207	2,742	5,119	9,414	26,282	9,179§
Woodford	1,745	2,056	2,699	2,548	2,777	2,774	3,457	4,609	7,154	10,984	13,806
	20,441	25,880	30,266	33,769	36,609	45,246	71,489	114,388	220,697	395,140	650,056

* From 22nd Annual Report of Bishop of St. Albans Fund, 1899, from figures furnished by Rev. Canon Procter, by the courtesy of the Registrar-General, with the last census returns added.
† For 1901, East Ham and Little Ilford are returned as one.
‡ In the population of North Woolwich, Kent portion is estimated.
§ Wanstead Slip is included for 1901 under Leyton.

APPENDIX J

THE SEE OF COLCHESTER.

"Not long ago I chanced to be shown the draft of an inscription commemorative of late my Lord of Colchester, in which he was described as the first Bishop of that see. It so happened that a few months earlier I had been invited to look at some 16th century documents preserved in the church-chest at Canewdon, and, in making a cursory examination of them, had found a Suffragan Bishop of Colchester mentioned as forming, if my memory serves me, one of a Special Commission to inquire into matters of local interest. Clearly, then, Bishop Blomfield had had one predecessor. Time pressed, and the inscription placed him second in the order of succession. The kindly critic of a copy of it which was sent to the *Guardian*, soon afterwards pointed out that this was an error, and affirmed that Dr. Blomfield had had two predecessors. This set one wondering whether he might not have had more; but subsequent investigation has served to show that, apart from the more or less mythical bishops of Colchester referred to by Morant, the amended inscription in the Chigwell School Chapel now rightly assigns him the third place.[1] Of his two predecessors it is here proposed to give such account as from various sources we have been able to glean.[2]

[1] "In piam memoriam patris admodum reverendi Alfredi tertii episcopi Colcestriensis necnon huiusce scholæ fautoris benignissimi faciendum curaverunt R. et. M. amici maerentes. Requiescat in pace." (Abbreviated.)

[2] The D.Q. not being an antiquarian publication, it will suffice to note here in brief the authorities on which this account is based :— Newcourt's "Repertorium Eccl. Paroch. Londinense," 2 vols.; "Bibliotheca Topographica Britannica," vol. vi. Pt. XXVIII.; Codex MS.

Newcourt, as usual, furnishes much information, scattered up and down the pages of his monumental *Repertorium*, and, under Witham, refers to a list of Suffragans which, if compiled, was apparently never printed. The principal notice is found, as might be anticipated, under Colchester, where he speaks briefly of the occupants of that see, and of Suffragans in general. But among the MSS. preserved in the Archbishop's Library at Lambeth Palace is one compiled by the learned Henry Wharton, which contains a long list of these Suffragans. This list was printed in 1785, together with an interesting essay on the subject, written nearly fifty years earlier, by the Rev. J. Lewis, M.A., Minister of Margate, in Kent. Since that time, Dr. Stubbs, now Bishop of Oxford, but at that time Vicar of Navestock, Essex, has printed an annotated list of such Suffragans as he met with in the course of his laborious researches into the course of Episcopal succession in England.

The word "Suffragan" is used in two distinct senses; in the one it signifies a Diocesan Bishop—a beneficed Bishop, we may say, in relation to his Metropolitan, whose Suffragan he is said to be; in another sense it is used, roughly speaking, of Bishops conse-crated for special purposes, whose sacred orders validate any episcopal acts done by them. Two or more explanations of the origin of the term are given. So far as it applies to Diocesans, it may be that they, on being summoned by their Metropolitan to a synod, have the right to vote; or, less probably, it may be that his vote, or consent, was required for their consecra-tion; or, again, it may be that, just as the Suffragans of the diocesan Bishops were consecrated to aid them, so these latter were considered bound to assist the Metropolitan, who without them could not confer Episcopal orders. The Greek word, *chorepiscopus*, we may add in passing, is also sometimes used

Wharton (Lambeth), 582 ; Stubbs' " Registrum Sacrum Anglicanum " ; Statutes of the Realm : 26 Hen. VIII. cap. 14, s. 1. : 1 Eliz. s. 2 ; Patent Rolls (P.R.O.) : 28 Hen. VIII. Pt. II. m. 18 ; 24 Eliz., Pt. VIII. m. 12 ; Wood's " Athenæ Oxonienses," ed. 1813–20 ; Cooper's "Athenæ Cantabrigienses " ; " History of Audley End," by Lord Braybrooke ; Lyson's " Magna Britannia," II. i. p. 277 ; Strype's Whitgift, 399 ; Annals, iv. 398 ; Cranmer, p. 1049, ed. 1840 ; " Life of William Bedell," by Bishop Burnet, 8vo. Lond. 1685 ; Burnet's " Life of William Bedell," Camden Soc., 1872 ; Crockford's " Clerical Directory," p. lxvii. (1891).

(not, it would seem, quite accurately) as interchangeable with the Latin "Suffragan."

The earliest notice of the employment of a suffragan Bishop in England, as the representative of a diocesan one, occurs, according to Dr. Stubbs' list, in 1266, when Geoffrey or William, Archbishop of Edessa *alias* Rages, in Media, is mentioned. These bishops usually had foreign titles. From that time down to the Reformation they were very numerous, Wharton's list comprising no less than 276 bishops and over 150 sees; while that compiled by Dr. Stubbs, and stated by him to be by no means complete, furnishes more than ninety names and dates, exclusive of over sixty Irish bishops who had permanent duty in England. At a time when bishops were employed as high officers of state the pressure of secular duties led them to confide their more sacred ones to deputies; and the exempt monasteries, ever jealous of the intrusion of diocesan authority, gladly availed themselves of the good offices of a Suffragan when circumstances caused them to need the services of a consecrating bishop.

In 1534 the Papal authority in England was done away with, and in the same year an Act of Parliament was passed, the preamble of which sets forth that, after all that had been done towards ordering ecclesiastical affairs, no provision had been made for Suffragans, such as had been accustomed to be within the realm for the more speedy administration of the Sacraments, and other good, wholesome and devout things and laudable ceremonies, to the increase of God's honour and the commodity of good and devout people. It was accordingly enacted that twenty-six places should be accepted for sees of Bishops Suffragan to be made in England and Wales, the bishops of them to be called "Suffragans of this Realm." Any Archbishop or Bishop desiring a coadjutor, was to name two fit persons to the King, who might assign to one of them any see within the province to which the petitioner belonged, and issue Letters Patent to the Archbishop of the same directing consecration. The Suffragans were made subject to the Diocesans, under whose commission they acted, and, in default, were liable to the pains and penalties of the Statute 16 Ric. II. The costs of consecration are to be borne by the nominating Bishop, or by the Suffragan himself, but the latter may hold two benefices with cure, and yet live in his own house, provided that it be in the diocese for which he has his commission. The lack of any settled provision for their maintenance was, according to Dr. Brett, the probable cause of the disuse of Suffragans.

In pursuance of the provisions of this Act, bishops were consecrated in 1536 to the sees of Ipswich, Thetford, and Colchester. The Patent Rolls of that date doubtless give particulars as to the circumstances under which all the appointments were made; but it is of the last only that we have to treat here. The King's mandate, tested at Berechurch, on September 26th, 28 reg. [1536], required the Archbishop of Canterbury to consecrate William More, Clerk, Bachelor-in-Decrees, and a Master of the Court of Chancery, as Bishop Suffragan of the see of Colchester. The enrolment recites that the mandate issued at the instance of the Bishop of Ely, who had represented that his diocese stood in need of the help and solace of a Suffragan who might share his anxious labours "*qui suae sollicitudinis partem sustinere possit*," and had named William More, and Robert Wells, the Prior of S. Etheldred's, as suitable occupants of the see of Colchester, or of some other within the province of Canterbury. In pursuance of the Royal Order William More was consecrated on October 22nd, 1536, in the Lady Chapel of Blackfriars, by the Bishops of Rochester, St. Asaph, and Sidon, which last was himself Suffragan of London and Canterbury from 1535 to 1553. The Bishop of Rochester acted by virtue of the Archbishop's letters commissional.

Of More himself but little seems to be known, except with regard to the benefices he at one time or other held. Wood says of him that he " had part of his education among the Oxonians, but more at another University." Mr. Foster, in his *Alumni Oxonienses*, gives the following list of his preferments, from which I omit Willingale Doe, since, on reference to Newcourt, I find that William Mote, or Mott, S.T.B. (not W. More) was rector there in 1527. A note or two from Wood and Cooper is added :—

1510 (Aug. 12), Rector of Salcote Virley; being then a chaplain: resigned in 1525.

1534 (April 25), Rector of Bradwell-juxta-mare; vacated by his death.

1534 (Oct. 5), Rector of West Tilbury, being then B.D. ; vacated, by death of W. More, Suffragan Bishop of Colchester, in 1540.

1537, Vicar of Bradford, Yorks.

1537/8, Abbot of the Benedictine Convent of Walden.

1537/8, Canon of York. Wood says, " Prebendary of Geven-dale in the church of York, 1537 ; resigned, 1538."

1538, Vicar of Saffron Walden.

1539 (Sept. 14), Archdeacon of Leicester, in the place of Edmund Bonner, made Bishop of Hereford.

Newcourt tells us that More, as Abbot of Walden, which he held *in commendam*, presented to the Vicarage there in September, 1537. On March 22nd, in the following year, he surrendered the Abbey into the King's hands, having, it would seem, already as patron presented himself to the living, which he continued to hold until his death, and in which he was succeeded by another Suffragan, John Hodgkin, Bishop of Bedford, consecrated in 1537.

Lord Braybrooke, in his history of Audley End, quotes some letters of Lord Audley's in which More's name occurs. Between the years 1538 and 1540 Cromwell, as Vicegerent, was arranging the sale and apportionment of the Abbey lands, and to him Audley wrote, being anxious to secure Walden. He did so, but subject no doubt to certain annual charges by way of pension to the late holders. He himself estimated these at £64 for the eight monks, all in priest's orders, and £136 6s. 8d. for the Abbot. Later on, doubtless by way of lightening his own pecuniary burdens, he treats for the Archdeaconry of Leicester, to which More was to be elected in virtue of a letter from the King to the Bishop of Lincoln, supposing that Cromwell could get the then occupant to resign. In the event of the letter and the resignation being obtained, Audley agrees to send £20 to the Bishop of Hereford, and ends, Chancellor as he was, by heartily desiring Cromwell to put him to a quiet end in the matter, promising him for his labours in his suit £20 and his poor hearty good will during his life.

The first Bishop of Colchester, who was, as we have seen, a Suffragan of the Bishop of Ely, died in the summer-time of 1540, and on February 11th, in the following year, Letters of Adminis-tration were (says Cooper) granted to his brother, John More, of Waddon [Whaddon], co. Cambridge, esquire, the Bishop having died intestate. He came of an ancient race, for Whaddon had remained in the de Scalers family from the Conquest until 1467, when Sir John died, leaving three daughters, coheiresses, of whom one, Alice, married John Moore. From her, doubtless, the Bishop was descended.

But, in spite of the Administration already mentioned, it seems that the Bishop did not die intestate—a fact which would never have come to my knowledge, had it not been for Mr. J. Challenor Smith's recently-printed and invaluable list of early wills proved in the Prerogative Court, in which the testators' names are grouped in alphabetical order. For, having found that the brother administered in February, 1541, the most ardent searcher would hardly have looked for proof of a will in November, 1542. Strange as it may seem, this exists, and the will is, I think, sufficiently interesting to warrant my printing it almost *in extenso*. It is in English, and, as will be seen, was made by the testator himself :—

" In nomine patris et filij et spiritus sancti. Amen. The xixth. day of Aprele in the yere of our lorde God a Thousande fyve hundred and fourty, and in the yere of the Reigne of the most godlye and catholyck prince, our dreade soveraigne lorde the King, King Henry the VIIIth, the xxxii, I William More, by the sufferaunce of God, and of the gyft of my most drad Soveraigne lorde the King, bisshop Suffringham of Colchester, and vicar of Walden in Essex, make and ordeyn this my last wyll and testament. First, I give and bequeth my synfull soule unto my lorde the everlasting lyving God, Refusing his rightues Justes, and take me to his mercy, lyke as he hath redemyd me with so high a price as the redemption of his most glorious and precious blodde. And I desire the blessed virgyn Mary, his mother, and all the holy company of hevyn, to pray for me and with me, that I may offer up unto hym my synfull and Repentant Soule to be acceptabull unto his godhed to be amongest the hevynly company : my carcas and yerthly body I quieyt to the erthe to be layd among thother Christyans at the assignement and wyll of myn executour. I give and bequeth unto hym that shall bury my corpus, yf he be a bisshop, as I am, my cross with the caas, two of my best Rochetts, a gowne of skarlett, and xxs. for his costs. And in case that any other seculler priest bury my body, and no Suffringgam, then I give and bequethe unto hym that bury my body a gowne, a cappe, a typpet and vijs. vjd. And to other priests and clerks, as shal be servyng good by the discretion of my sayd executour, according to my substance that I leve unto hym, whiche ys in howsehold stuff ; for money have I none, nor never wyll have more than to paye every man his owne that I owe, or hereafter shall owe. I praye to God to send me grace to have so moche. *Item.* I give to fyve hundred poor people, to every one of theym, a King Henry penny whiche I have in a box redy for the same purpose. And I desire every good man may not to think that I kept them for that I coulde not fynde in my harte to distribute them myself, but that I wolde have alwayes something to be distrybuted at the daye of my buryall. And what I have done myself God is my Juge. I loke for no laude. *Item.* I give to every of my servauntes their beddes, that they ewssially ly in to be egally devyded amonge them, and one to by anothers parte. *Item.* I give unto William Spillman, my sister's sonne, and my godsone, twenty marks' worthe of my stuff that shal be thought fytt and necessary for hym in recompence of his father's bequest to whom I was executour."

The bishop further bequeaths :—To John Cotton, his steward and to his wife, and the longer liver of them, his bed ; to the former his best horse or gelding, and to the latter, his own gelding that he rides on. To his sister's son, John Yong, his bed and bedstead in the great chamber in the vicarage, the hangings, a ship chest, and a counter there. To Johan Cottum, the bedding and hangings in the buttery. To John More, of Bradwell, a gelding, with such stuff as the bishop has at Bradwell at the time. To William More, son and heir of Thomas More, of Whaddon, a gilt cup with a cover, when he is of age. To Francis More, his best trotting gelding or horse, a dozen silver spoons, and his velvet jacket. To Margaret Browne, a feather bed, two blankets, two pair of sheets, a coverlet, a bolster, a pillow with the pillowbere, and 40*s.* in money, or money's worth, on the day of her marriage. To William Belmer, other bedding and 20*s.* To each of the poor Bedemen of the Almyshowse, 4*d.* ; and to the four women, 4*d.* each. To his nephew, the son and heir of Thomas Spilman, a gilt pot with a cover, which the father is to take care of till his son come of age. To William Spilman the bishop leaves a bridle and saddle, his bows and arrows, and a doublet of satin and sarcenet. To the church of Walden a " coope of golde with the sewte of vestments thereto belonging." To Sir Thomas Webb, 40*s.*, to pray for his soul. To his servant, Robert Bradshaw, 13*s.* 4*d.* To John Stacy and his wife, 20*s.* To John Dyk, one of the plough horses called " the little baye." To Margaret Sorith, five quarters of barley and some bedding. To Agnes Browne, 5*s.* To his sister Doke, 40*s.*, to her daughter Joan, 20*s.* To Thomas Webb, a black gown in addition to his legacy. To his servant, John Bellowes, a horse with all manner of harness and 40*s*. To John Cotton and Anne his wife, the tenements called [*blank*] in Walden, lately purchased|of William [*blank*]. To the yomanry of my lord Chancellor's house, a goblet and cover, parcel gilt, to be sold and the proceeds divided among them. John Cotton, gent., the steward, is appointed executor and residuary legatee, to pay debts due to the King and others, and in recompence for his painful service, which the bishop cannot repay according to his deservings. " I have wrytten this with my owne hand . . . and the space left unwrytten to the entent that I may add and mynishe as I shall fell myself abule from tyme to tyme."

Proved in London, Nov. 15th, 1542.

(*P.C.C.* 12, *Spert*).

The original will appears to be no longer in existence, but there is a filed copy with a *Sententia* attached, from which it appears that it was contested by the Venerable John More, esquire, but without success. The alleged Administration I could not find, as the series of Act Books begin only in 1559, and the source of the reference to it in the *Athenae Cantabrigienses* is still therefore an unsolved mystery.

From the year 1540 onwards, the see of Colchester remained vacant, until, rather more than half a century later on, the Bishop of London, finding that he needed a Suffragan, presented to Queen Elizabeth John Sterne, S.T.B., and William Fisher, M.A., with a humble request that she would nominate one or other of them to that see, or to some other within the Southern Province. In compliance with this request a royal mandate directed the Archbishop to consecrate John Sterne in accordance with the statute already referred to, which had been abrogated by Mary, and revived in the first year of Elizabeth's reign. The writ was tested at Westminster on October 17th, 1592, and on November 12th, in the same year, the bishop was consecrated in Fulham Parish Church, by Archbishop Whitgift, assisted by the Bishops of London, Rochester, and Bristol. The event is noted by Strype, who says " the accustomed ceremonies were used, and oath by him taken of renouncing all Foreign Prelates, etc., and acknowledging the Queen's authority, in all ecclesiastical as well as temporal matters, according to the statute. He was vested by the Archbishop with episcopal robes."

" One of the last Suffragans, I think," adds the writer, " consecrated among us."

Of John Sterne's career something more is known. He matriculated as a pensioner of Trinity College, Cambridge, in December, 1560, but removed to Christ's College, Cambridge, whence he went out as Bachelor in 1564–5. His Master's degree he took in 1568, being then under-master at the Ely Grammar School, and, as is said, a member of St. John's College. In 1575 he was of Peterhouse, and thence took his B.D. degree, obtaining from the University in the following year a license to preach. According to Newcourt, he was Vicar of Rickmansworth from 1584 to 1587; and Vicar of Witham from 1588 until he died. He is said by Strype to have been suspended for not appearing in Convocation. This appears to have been in May, 1606; but Cooper states that he was suspended in 1603, and absolved in the year previously mentioned. The reason of his default remains to seek.

Another notice of Bishop Sterne occurs in Burnet's life of William Bedell, Bishop of Kilmore, who was himself born at Black Notley, and ordained by the Bishop of Colchester. In reference to this circumstance, Burnet writes : " Till I met with this passage,"—*i.e.* the statement as to the source of Bedell's orders —" I did not think that these Suffragans had been continued so long in England. How they came to be put down I do not know ; it is probable they did ordain all that desired Orders, so promiscuously, that the Bishops found it necessary to let them fall. For complaints were made of this Suffragan [of Colchester] upon which he was threatened with the taking his commission from him ; for though they could do nothing but by a Delegation from the Bishop, yet the Orders they gave were still valid, even when they transgressed in conferring them. Upon that the Suffragan said a thing that was as insolent in him, as it was honourable for Mr. Bedell, that he had ordained a better man than any the Bishop had ever ordained, naming Bedell." The light in which Bedell viewed Bishop Sterne and his officials was less favourable. Another version of his life, said to have been written by his brother, gives the following account :—" His entrance into Holy Orders was before he had left the University, concerning which he would complain of the greedy gaping for money by the officers and servants of the Bishop, without heeding so much the sufficiency or insufficiency of the man, as of money. Yet his orders he esteemed nevertheless religiously, though cumbered with some faults of the men that conferred them."

A few pages further on we find Bedell in conflict with Dr. Jegon, the Bishop of Norwich, as to the illegal exactions of his officials, which were, it seems, very high. In the final event the Bishop gave way, and left Bedell to pay " what he thought fit."

Wharton, in his edition of Strype's *Memoirs*, gives a curious, but as Mr. Lewis affirms, a misleading account of the manner in which Archbishop Cranmer treated the Suffragan Bishops. He says, " in those days, Suffragan Bishops, however usual, were treated with contempt enough, not wont to be admitted to dine at the Archbishop's own table," in the hall of his palace. There were generally three tables spread there and served at the same time; at one sat peers, privy counsellors, and gentlemen of the greatest quality; at the next (the Almoner's) sat the chaplains and all clergy below the rank of diocesans and abbots; at the third (the Steward's) sat all other gentlemen. " The Suffragan Bishops were wont to sit at the Almoner's table; and the Archbishop, in admitting his Suffragan, Thornden, to his own table, did him an unusual honour." On the whole, Wharton's phrase, " contempt enough," seems to lack justification; and Mr. Lewis states that he himself had dined even at the Steward's table, when one or two diocesan bishops had sat at the upper end of it. Though the Suffragans are not, like the older Diocesans, barons of the realm, they seem always to have been addressed and spoken of as such. In 1240, for instance, Lord John, Bishop Suffragan of Lord Eadmund, Archbishop of Canterbury, is so described in reference to an altar in the chapel of the infirmary of Rochester; and in a parish account book of the time of Philip and Mary, there is reference to a reward of 4*d.* given to " my Lord Suffragan's servant," when the chalice and corpus cloth were hallowed. Moreover, it is said that " my lord of Dover" is the usual description of Richard Yngworth (consecrated in 1537), when the mention of him is made in contemporary documents.

But to return in conclusion to Colchester. On February 18th, 1599, the Right Reverend Father in God, John Sterne, Suffragan Bishop of Colchester, and Mary Gee, of St. Martin's, Ludgate, London, widow of Thomas Gee, Merchant, had license to marry. (*Harl. Soc.*, *xxv.*) In the will of Thomas Sterne, Vicar of Feering, which was proved in the Consistory Court, on June 28th, 1605, the Bishop was named as one of three executors, but renounced probate, and his relationship to the testator is not mentioned in the Act ; nor could I find the will in the Register under the date mentioned. John Sterne, whose will I have not succeeded in finding, is said to have died in February, 1608. After him no other Suffragan was consecrated in England for well-nigh three hundred years.[1]

W. C. W.

[1] This account is re-printed from the *St. Albans Diocesan Magazine* (vol. ii., Nos. 14 and 15) by the kind permission of the writer, Mr. W. C. Waller, F.S.A., who has also revised the page-proof.

APPENDIX K

[An inventory of church goods referred to on page 102, where, for " Reformation," read " mediæval," and for " Therfield," read " Pelham Furneaux."

"The Church of Pelham Furneus is taxed to the full amount. The Vicarage house is within the churchyard and is worth ten marcs. The treasurer of St. Paul's has the patronage of the Vicarage. The churchyard is properly inclosed and in good order. A suitable bell-tower with two bells furnished with the necessary ropes. The church is consecrated in honour of the Blessed Virgin Mary. The nave of the church is very well roofed and the windows duly glazed. A wooden bowl for holy water at the entrance of the church, with asperses. Another bowl for holy water for the procession with asperses. A stone font lined with lead, and secured with a lock. The nave of the church is ornamented with ten images: viz. of the Holy Cross with the Blessed Mary and St. John on either side: of Angels, and St. John the Baptist; of St. Michael; Thomas Archbishop; Andrew, James, Mary Magdalene, Katherine, and Margaret. Four Altars. A sufficient lamp. One herse. A large staircase leading to the rood-loft is wanting in the body of the church. One pall of tapestry for the poor dead. Four frontals for the said Altars, torn and mutilated. Two hand-bells. One cross to be borne before corpses. Three sufficient banners. One super-altar to the Altar on the south side. The Altar on north side is dedicated. A chancel in good condition, well roofed. Windows glazed and barred. Separate sedilia with suitable seats and desks. A Sarum Ordinal. One Antiphone fully notated, with Psalter, Calendar, Capitulary, Collectarium, and notated Hymnal. One good Psalter without a Calendar, with the legends of the Saints and *Statutes of Fulk*. One Antiphone is wanting. A separate Tonal with the beginning of the Hymns "*de communi sanctorum.*" One *de temporali* legends of which the Martyrology is wanting. One Processional book. One Gradual with Sequence, which latter is wanting. One good notated Missal with Prefaces and Graduals. One good Manual fully notated with Calendars. Books sufficiently bound and covered. A linen pulpit-cloth of diaper. Another cloth of diaper embroidered with red. A suitable square curtain with curtains for the images. Two better surplices, and two smaller ones. Two Rochets. Two Manutergia. Two abstersoria (?) The curtain beyond the sacrarium in good condition. A stone Altar unconsecrated. A frontal to the Altar of linen cloth, and another frontal of diaper, embroidered with red and trimmed with tuaille. A suitable high Altar. Four consecrated Altar cloths of which one has an embroidered border of baudekyn, and another of lamb's wool, one principal vestment in good condition with border; and a cassock of baudekyn. Another Sunday vestment, with stole, maniple, and border of baudekyn. A third vestment for ordinary days with border, and a cassock of lamb's wool; stole and maniple of red samnite. Two pairs of corporals, with one case of red samnite. A dalmatic of lamb's wool, and a choir cope of baudekyn. Two cushions, of which one is covered with silk samnite and the other with diaper. The sponsalicus cloth is wanting. An ivory comb is sufficiently good. A silver gilt cup under the weight of two shillings. A tin cup, two saucers and one large wine-cruet and one basin of tin. A wooden box for offerings, a sufficient thurible, incense boat for incense, one spoon, and one small vessel for coals in winter. Two sconces, one of copper. One coffer, and a Paschal candlestick. A sufficient lamp and one light. A portable enamelled cross with banner of red silk (sindone). Another wooden portable cross. One image of the Blessed Virgin Mary with tabernacle. Two small hand bells. Two tin candlesticks. Two osculatoria, and one wooden case for holding the book of the Gospels (*textus*). A monstrance. A strong chest well bound and locked. An ivory Pix for the Eucharist furnished with a lock, in which is contained the Host, oil, and cup for anointing the sick. A tin chrismatorium with lock, with the Chrism and holy oil. Another wooden chrismatorium with lock. A tin water pitcher. Two wooden candlesticks." [1]

---

[1] This return was made by Inquisition in 1297 A.D., and is translated by Mr. Cussans from the original in the library of St. Paul's Cathedral, lib. i. ff. 108 *et seq.* *Vide* Cussans' " Hertfordshire," vol. i. p. 153. Hundred, Edwinstree.

APPENDIX L

The Division of the County of Essex into Classes, certified by the Committee for the County, March 3rd, 1646 (*vide* chap. xxii. p. 26).

1st Classis [1]	Becontree Hundred	14 Ministers
	28 parishes	32 Elders
2nd Classis	Barstaple Hundred	7 Ministers
	34 parishes	14 Elders
3rd Classis	Chelmsford	18 Ministers
	30 parishes	44 Elders
4th Classis	Rotchford	14 Ministers
	24 parishes	29 Elders
5th Classis	Dengle	11 Ministers
	20 parishes	24 Elders
6th Classis	Ongar Hundred	19 Ministers
	26 parishes	57 Elders
7th Classis	Harlow Hundred	8 Ministers
	11 parishes	24 Elders
	Waltham Hundred	4 Ministers
	4 parishes	10 Elders
8th Classis	Dunmow and Freshwell Classis	16 Ministers
		28 Elders
	Dunmow Hundred 25 parishes	} 8 Ministers
	Freshwell Hundred 10 parishes	8 Elders

---

[1] Board or Committee.

| 9th Classis | Clavering and Uttlesford | 2 Ministers |
| | | 3 Elders |

	Clavering Hundred	
	6 parishes	} 10 Ministers
	Uttlesford Hundred	} 23 Elders
	25 parishes	

10th Classis	West Class—	
	Hinckford Hundred	19 Ministers
	22 parishes	31 Elders

11th Classis	East Class—	
	Hinckford Hundred	22 Ministers
	46 parishes	22 Elders

12th Classis	Lexden—	
	Lexden Hundred	22 Ministers
	28 parishes	32 Elders

13th Classis	Tendering—	
	Tendering Hundred	11 Ministers
	33 parishes	22 Elders

14th Classis	Thurstable, Winstree,	
	Witham, Colchester	
	Classis—	

| | Thurstable Hundred | 1 Minister |
| | 10 parishes | 2 Elders |

	Winstre Classis—	
	Winstree Hundred	3 Ministers
	10 parishes	6 Elders

	Witham Classis—	
	Witham Hundred	9 Ministers
	16 parishes	5 Elders

	Colchester Classis	
	Colchester Hundred	3 Ministers
	17 parishes	10 Elders

INDEX

THE END

PRINTED BY
WILLIAM CLOWES AND SONS, LIMITED,
LONDON AND BECCLES.